Consumption, Psychology and Practice Theories

Practice theories of our equipped and situated tacit construction of participatory narrative meaning are evident in multiple disciplines from architectural to communication study, consumer, marketing and media research, organisational, psychological and social insight. Their hermeneutic focus is on customarily little reflected upon, recurrent but required, practices of embodied, habituated knowing *how*—from choosing 'flaw-free' fruit in a market to celebrating Chinese New Year Reunion Dining, caring for patients to social media 'voice'. In ready-to-hand practices, we attend to the purpose and not to the process, to the goal rather than its generating. Yet familiar practices both presume and put in place fundamental understanding. Listening to Asian and Western consumers reflecting—not only subsequent to but also within practices—this book considers activity emplacing core perceptions from a liminal moment in a massive mall to health psychology research. Institutions configure practices-in-practices cohering or conflicting within their material horizons, space accessible to social analysis.

Practices theory construes routine as minimally self-monitored, nonetheless considering it as being embodied narrative. In research output, such generic 'storied' activity is seen as (in)formed, shaped from a shifting hierarchy of 'horizons' or perspectives—from habituated to reflective—rather than a single seamless unfolding. Taking a communication practices route disentangles and avoids conflating tacit and transformative construction of identities in qualitative research. Practices research crosses discipline. Ubiquitous media use by managers and visitors throughout a shopping mall responds to investigating not only with digital tracking expertise but also from an interpretive marketing viewpoint. Visiting a practice perspective's hermeneutic underwriting, spatio-temporal metaphorical concepts become available and appropriate to the analysis of communication as a process across disciplines. In repeated practices, 'horizons of understanding' are solidified. Emphasising our understanding of a material environment as 'equipment', practices theory enables correlation of use and demographic variable in quantitative study extending interpretive behavioural and haptic qualitative research.

Consumption, Psychology and Practice Theories: A Hermeneutic Perspective addresses academics and researchers in Communication Studies, Marketing, Psychology and Social Theory, as well as university methodology courses recognising philosophy guides a discipline's investigative insight.

Tony Wilson is a Visiting Senior Research Fellow at the London School of Economics and Political Science, Department of Media and Communications. He has taught extensively in universities, both for Arts and Social Science Faculties (in Australia, England, Malaysia and Scotland) and Economics and Business Faculties (in Malaysia). The present monograph is his seventh book on hermeneutics.

Routledge Interpretive Marketing Research

Recent years have witnessed an 'interpretative turn' in marketing and consumer research. Methodologists from the humanities are taking their place alongside those drawn from the traditional social sciences.

Qualitative and literary modes of marketing discourse are growing in popularity. Art and aesthetics are increasingly firing the marketing imagination.

This series brings together the most innovative work in the burgeoning interpretative marketing research tradition. It ranges across the methodological spectrum from grounded theory to personal introspection, covers all aspects of the postmodern marketing 'mix', from advertising to product development, and embraces marketing's principal sub-disciplines.

Taste, Consumption, and Markets
An Interdisciplinary Volume
Edited by Zeynep Arsel and Jonathan Bean

Consumption, Psychology and Practice Theories
A Hermeneutic Perspective
Tony Wilson

Also available in Routledge Interpretive Marketing Research Series

Representing Consumers: Voices, Views and Visions
Edited by Barbara B. Stern

Romancing the Market
Edited by Stephen Brown, Anne Marie Doherty and Bill Clarke

Consumer Value: A Framework for Analysis and Research
Edited by Morris B. Holbrook

Marketing and Feminism: Current Issues and Research
Edited by Miriam Catterall, Pauline Maclaran and Lorna Stevens

For more information about this series, please visit: www.routledge.com

Consumption, Psychology and Practice Theories

A Hermeneutic Perspective

Tony Wilson

LONDON AND NEW YORK

First published 2019 by Routledge

2 Park Square, Milton Park, Abingdon, Oxfordshire OX14 4RN
52 Vanderbilt Avenue, New York, NY 10017

Routledge is an imprint of the Taylor & Francis Group, an informa business

First issued in paperback 2020

Library of Congress Cataloging-in-Publication Data
Names: Wilson, Tony, 1947– author.
Title: Consumption, psychology and practice theories : a hermeneutic perspective / Tony Wilson.
Description: New York : Routledge, 2018. | Series: Routledge interpretive marketing research | Includes bibliographical references.
Identifiers: LCCN 2018010280 | ISBN 9781138123939 (hardback) | ISBN 9781315648521 (Ebook)
Subjects: LCSH: Consumption (Economics)—Psychological aspects. | Consumers—Psychology.
Classification: LCC HC79.C6 W55 2018 | DDC 306.301/9—dc23
LC record available at https://lccn.loc.gov/2018010280

ISBN: 978-1-138-12393-9 (hbk)
ISBN: 978-0-367-50095-5 (pbk)

Typeset in Sabon
by Apex CoVantage, LLC

Consumption, Psychology and Practice Theories: A Hermeneutic Perspective is dedicated to my wife Jenny Siow Ai Wei for her perpetual patience and Malaysian people for persuasive practices.

To the Distance Denying Internet

Contents

Preface

In this brief book, planned to offer readers a philosophical purchase on coming to terms with audience and consumer 'voicing out', I discuss *practices*—from choosing apples in a supermarket to the yearly celebrating of Chinese New Year Reunion Dinners. Engaging in everyday practices, we are connecting to an always already meaningful world—a *de facto* challenge to long-standing empiricist claims that such a material relationship operates through passive perception, receiving sensory data or 'impressions' which we then build upon to form ideas of an external reality.

> The basic building block of knowledge on this view is the impression, or sense-datum, a unit of information which is not the deliverance of a judgment, which has by definition no element in it of reading or interpretation, which is a brute datum.
>
> (Taylor, 1971: 7)

Instead of empiricism, placing my perspective within much acknowledged recent discussion and present tensing of ideas, informed by hermeneutic philosophers (Gadamer, Heidegger, Ricoeur) and the practice theorists in sociology (Giddens, Reckwitz, Schatzki), I seek to sustain alternatives distant 'from the baleful influence of the epistemological tradition for which all knowledge has to be reconstructed from the impressions imprinted on the individual subject' (Taylor, 1971: 32). With our 'horizons of understanding' (Gadamer, 1975) online literally and metaphorically shaped through algorithmic tracking and hidden collection of digitally datafied experience, a 'hermeneutic approach to the social becomes all the more important' (Couldry and Hepp, 2017: 175).

This book reflects on audience 'lived practices' (Das, 2017: 1264) of understanding across a range of social roles from consumers of marketing and media to mental health services. At the core of people's everyday discourse or a contribution to focus groups and interviews, as they reflect on parading through shopping malls, perception of marketing media or psychological health issues, are habituated generic practices, visibly *embodied* narratives whereof they can later speak. For we are immersed in accustomed daily practices and familiarities, always already known, thus requiring little consideration or decision from a distracted awareness, unless issues arise or entering a novel world.

Practices implicitly construct enabling material entities as *equipment*—of which it is possible to ask 'what for?' And practices tacitly *emplace* a cultural wherewithal, their affective encircling shared or shareable assumptions, meaningful 'horizons of understanding' (Gadamer), discernible in reflection—whether personal or professional—on the extent and limit of embodied understanding-in-use.

Tacitly recognising surroundings from horizons of understanding, we act appropriately. With our practices, we configure actions, but equally our activity is necessarily generically configured: it is shaped by conformity to social practices. We instantiate a practice while practices form identities, as 'tacit, practical know-how in quotidian cultures' (Moores, 2018: 3).

Employing *Twitter* is generic in its digital use as well as its narrative content and goal directed in purpose. From a hermeneutic perspective, our 'practices of use are integrated within the interpretive practices orientated towards the content itself' (Mathieu and Pavlickova, 2017: 430). Practices thus are always already tacitly emplacing 'horizons of understanding' and cultural perspectives shaping their goal. Activity implicitly incorporates a wider framework of understanding from visiting a *Facebook* page to expecting 'good security from a shopping mall' and selecting an 'apple that looks nicer with no flaws' (female, Chinese visitors to a mall), as we shall later see when emphasising behaviourally grounded hermeneutics. In participant reflection, a previously habitually, hence tacitly, held horizon of understanding emerges to be explored through discussion, realised as cultural position becoming available during interviews evincing often affective 'implicit knowledge' (Klein et al., 2018: 368). Knowing *how* is generic, affective perceiving from embodied cultural horizons of understanding a situation and tacitly responding with appropriate behaviour: 'we, we, we pick the apple that looks nicer with no flaws' (female, Chinese student shopper). Results ensue from our recognising.

Hermeneutic practices (from visiting mall to media use) will be held in the following to be:

1. Pre-reflective or 'ready-to-hand', incorporating an agent's 'practical consciousness' (Giddens);
2. Embodied;
3. Equipped behavioural narratives maintaining/maintained by social structures;
4. Emplacing affective 'horizons of understanding' (Gadamer), politically/ algorithmically shaped;

5. Generic, goal-oriented, incorporating therein a 'hermeneutic circle of understanding' (Gadamer);
6. Tacitly 'prefigured', 'configured', drawn on as 'refigured' (Ricoeur) construction of self-identity;
7. Open to celebratory or critically 'distanciated' (Ricoeur) reflection, simultaneously or subsequently;
8. Consensual 'practices-in-a-practice' or alternative understandings of a 'boundary object' (Star).

Mapping from the shoulders of giants, *Consumption, Psychology and Practice Theories* is a project of integration. Aligned with Anthony Giddens' earlier thinking on 'practical consciousness', articulating further a 'non-media-centric' (David Morley, Shaun Moores) behavioural perspective, the book proceeds through marketing (Craig Thompson), media (Nick Couldry) and psychological research (Jonathan Smith) concerned with our hermeneutic practices—writers more or less formally invoking hermeneutic philosophy from Edmund Husserl to Paul Ricoeur. We consider *practices*:

> The analysis of the images broadcast by television (representation) and of the time spent watching television (behaviour) should be complemented by a study of what the cultural consumer 'makes' or 'does' during this time and with these images. The same goes for the use of urban space, the products purchased in the supermarket, the stories and legends distributed by the newspapers, and so on.
>
> (De Certeau, 1984: xii)

Acknowledgements

I wish to express appreciation of research assistant Michael Tiong Hock Bing's meticulous conducting and transcribing face-to-face and digital interviews in Malaysian Borneo, illustrating a hermeneutics of practices in several chapters. Likewise, visitor narratives at Sunway Pyramid Mall in discussion with Choy Tuck Yun clarified my philosophical understanding of embodied knowing. Considering consumers speaking of their generic response to media branding as a reception practice is illustrated in Chapter 2 by extracts from Michael Tiong Hock Bing's thesis, which I supervised. Dr Sia Bee Chuan's thesis on Chinese New Year family reunion dinners has been a valuable source of hermeneutic practices, exemplifying annually embodied horizons of major cultural assumption.

I am grateful to Professor Shaun Moores at the University of Sunderland who prompted me to return to thinking theoretically about hermeneutic embodiment, not least a 'doubly digital' laptop computer use. Nicholas Davey, Professor of Philosophy at the University of Dundee cleared a path to an understanding of *Lichtung* (or enlightening): his kind illuminating insight is appreciated in this conjoining of philosophy and practice. I was guided in further appreciating the philosopher Charles Taylor's hermeneutic perspective on cultural study by Professor Nick Smith, Macquarie University, Sydney and I am grateful for Professor Nick Couldry's help from the London School of Economics in coming to terms with social theory. Acknowledging diversity of practice theories, I was informed by receiving regular readings from the Beyond Behaviour Change Group based at Royal Melbourne Institute of Technology. A frequent contributing immersion in the Interpretative Phenomenological Analysis online discussion group encouraged my seeking thoughtful clarity.

I acknowledge in gratitude as equipping and informing this project, my supportive Visiting Senior Research Fellow position (2015–2018) in Media and Communication Studies at the London School of Economics and Routledge's agreeing to a similarly lengthy book contract for this volume, enabling wide-ranging treatment of hermeneutic practices in their disciplinary site to be the subject of the following pages. We hear multiple consumer responses in marketing, media and qualitative psychological research, 'voices' both non-Western and Western.

Introduction

Crossing Hermeneutic Horizons of Culture and Discipline

Hermeneutic philosophy informs research across multiple communication fields of focus. In Jensen's *Handbook of Media and Communication Research* (2002), hermeneutic thought and phenomenology are positioned as being two of the four 'main traditions' (15), including rhetoric and semiotics shaping developments within the 'field of media and communication' (ibid.). The

> philosophical stance one assumes in relation to the nature of reality and the nature of knowledge largely determines how the researcher conducts research, what he or she considers as legitimate research evidence.
>
> (Seamon and Gill, 2016: 117)

From this philosophical perspective on human experience, critical of empiricism's narrative of perception as passive (re)presentation of the external world, understanding is primarily practical. Knowing *how*—evident in habitual behaviour—precedes propositionally knowing *that* something is the case, a topic of subsequent reflection. Or to draw on Wittgenstein's later philosophy (1991), people's ubiquitous understanding *how* tacitly (in)forms living, evident in activities—from apple choosing to engaging with the Internet or television, from annual celebration of festivals to a mundane visiting of malls. We leave malls bearing both pre-suppositions-of-practice (or how to 'go about' customary activity) and purchases, routinely, unreflectively (in)forming future activity. More widely, from the practice theory perspective, behaviour is not fundamentally calculative, entertaining reasons for action: the

> research context adopted in a goal-directed perspective forces individuals to adopt an abstract, logical, reflective attitude concerning their experience when, in fact, the actual experience was a form of (routine, unreflective) ready-to-hand engagement.
>
> (Patterson and Williams, 2002: 18)

In writing from a hermeneutic perspective on consumer psychology, marketing and media, I continue an emphasis on the primacy of knowing *how*, arguing that understanding is fundamentally constituted by habituated generic practices—(i) *embodied* or corporeal narratives (ii) unreflectively considering the material world to be more or less enabling *equipment* and (iii) tacitly *emplacing* or putting in place through activity less evident perspectives or incorporated affective cultural 'horizons of understanding' (Gadamer, 1975). Knowing or understanding-in-practice how to choose fruit—a 'simple' example from a research participant which we shall subsequently consider in detail—built a visibly embodied story, later assessed in our focus group as avoiding disabling or 'flawed' apples, a tacit perspective or horizon of understanding the practice presented as gendered. Such horizons will be explored as forming a reflective focus of qualitative research.

In hermeneutic theory, 'the notion of the horizon is explicitly introduced as a metaphor for the way that intellectual understanding mirrors everyday perceptions of visible objects' (Nenon, 2016: 248). But equally 'everyday perceptions' are taken to 'mirror' 'intellectual understanding'. Sighting habituated practices can be read as viewing generic material 'texts', both perspectival and offering a possibility of immersive experience. Configuring experiential meaning is routinely not reflective or reflexive, lacking issues. Sighting/viewing content is informed/shaped by material/cultural location. In this way, marketing's horizons of understanding are written into 'recurrent' (Giddens, 1982) online practices.

We shall pursue this philosophical thesis through discussion of empirical research on consumer and psychological experience in both celebratory and confronting perceptions of a socially situated self. Practices configure identities. As habituated embodied narratives, they can be characterised by momentary 'disequilibria', moments of reflective cheer/concern, before returning to an equilibrium of continued unreflective behaviour. As generic, learning practices is knowledge 'typically acquired *in situ* through models' and by other '"apprenticeship" processes' (Coe and Freedman, 1998).

'Horizons of understanding' could be said to be minimally reflected on or explored generic perspectives from which we discern what is appropriate in adjusting our behaviour. Closer horizons (in)form more specific 'looking'. Expertise expressed in continually goal-directed practices involves more or less consciously adjusting predominantly tacit behaviour to achieve ambition. If attention is paid to 'horizons of understanding' should issues arise or in focus groups, it is deemed 'reflection' on 'our cultural and biographical framework constituting our horizon' (Schlitte, 2017: 41).

Research participant reference to 'needs' (failure or success in satisfaction), 'control' (or its absence) and affective perspective (such as their 'caring') signal these core categories of embodied, equipped and emplaced understanding-in-use. A participant's trial and error in overcoming physical difficulties can be considered by her or him as recovering equilibrium, restoring habituated ready-to-hand practices in getting around at home or at work, as in engaging successfully with media equipment.

In mall research to be considered, evident in one purchaser's selective behaviour was the person's implicit understanding of some fruit as 'flawed', as potentially disenabling users—an interpretation subsequently 'voiced out' in confirming the consumer's gendered competence: '(guys) would say, "It's just the same. Just grab and go"' (female, Chinese). In this account, prioritising a behavioural perspective on the meaning of such habituated activity, understanding *how* (to purchase apples), is emphasised, with narrating this gendered selective practice preceding propositionally her tacit and wider understanding *that* (apples can lack health benefits).

Seeing communication research more extensively from such a behavioural, horizonal 'non-representational' (Moores in Krajina et al., 2014) perspective [or paraphrasing Wittgenstein's (1991) philosophy of 'meaning is use'] offers us a 'paradigm of media research that understands media, not as texts or structures of production, but as practice' (Couldry, 2004: 115). Screen use, corporeal and clearly equipped, emplaces horizons substantiating or subverting engaging with the world, a cultural or ethical and political implicit 'background horizon as framework of interpretation and foundation of cognitive activities' (Kupers, 2015), a place of acquiescent positioning or active protest. Viewing television advertising employing a dubious narrative of Chinese New Year Reunions, for instance, a Chinese consumer (male) vigorously objects: 'a bit offensive; it breaks the (Chinese) tradition'.

In regard to these *a priori* aspects—or in phenomenology's technical terms, 'moments'—of understanding as *embodied*, *equipped*, *emplacing* a wider meaning which underwrites our ubiquitous experience as interpretive, the sceptic's requesting empirical evidence for their continual presence is to misconceive their epistemological status. For, of necessity, they would be caught up in, or evident in making such a mutually intelligible request for 'proof'.

The central argument advanced in these pages is that a hermeneutic perspective on consumer action—as embodied, equipped, tacitly emplacing affective horizons of understanding—initiated and underwrites subsequent practices theorising, not least across the disciplines of marketing, media and qualitative psychological studies. Hence conjoining a hermeneutic perspective and practices theory—which I henceforth refer to as *hermeneutic practices theory*—acknowledges both include concepts in common, ideas which 'focus on the physicality of human doing, the routine aspects of behaviour, the relevance of tacit knowledge, the significance of material artefacts for behaviour and the effects of explicit and implicit rules' (Jonas et al., 2017: xv).

Livingstone argues convincingly that 'one benefit of globalisation is a renewed necessity for researchers to articulate that which is taken for granted' (2015: 439). Reflecting upon behaviourally implicit or tacit meaning (in)forms the hermeneutic practices project (Gadamer, Heidegger, Ricoeur, Giddens, Reckwitz, Schatzki, Warde, et al.). Guided by such a philosophical purchase on everyday circulating of meaning, the following chapters exercise a cross-disciplinary focus: they look from interpretive marketing, media and hermeneutic psychological studies' perspectives, their analytical 'horizons of understanding' (Gadamer), towards audiences and consumer-citizen research.

The pages within contain non-Western as well as Western research participants 'voicing out' with their speech shaping thought about 'struggles over meaning' (ibid.: 443) in familiar habitual global practices—the book's 'de-familiarising the familiar (. . .) in the wider circuit of culture' (ibid.: 444). This volume's 'circuit' extends from Chinese New Year to health narrative and watching television, practicing the 'hermeneutical function of distanciation' (Ricoeur, 1981a).

In pursuing a path of hermeneutic discourse analysis, practices, in short, are here considered to be generic embodied habituated narratives of visibly knowing how, constituting a material world of equipment, emplacing affective horizons of understanding accessible to a later reflection. Action (entering malls, enjoying Chinese New Year) tacitly instantiates—albeit varying—a generic practice, evident in its embodied 'text' (Ricoeur, 1981b) available for discursive disclosure. A practice theory then, viewing human action, 'invites us to regard agents as carriers' of 'bodily movements, of forms of interpreting, knowing how and wanting and of the usage of things' (Reckwitz, 2002a: 259).

'Let's say, a simple one: apples.' Participating in a focus group, a Chinese female contributor to research discussed in this book, refers to her competence in choosing apples 'with no flaws'. She then places her doubtless habitual, even mundane *practice*—selecting health-providing fruit—within a wider gendered tacit conviction unlikely to have been considered when purchasing: 'guys' 'would say, "(the apples are) just the same. Just grab and go"'. Her embodied convinced practice, attending to the fruit rather than to her habituated routine physical movements in selection or to the gendered positioning therein, can be said to be smoothly 'ready-to-hand': only subsequently is it presented for reflection. A practice tacitly (or unreflectively) posits enabling bodies and entities teleologically as 'equipment': the focus of attention where activity occurs without issue is the goal not the process. If suddenly she had been unable to reach for apples lacking 'flaws', this contributor's concerned focus would have been displaced perhaps to an incapacitated arm previously enabling selection. But when successful in choosing fruit sustaining health, her goal becomes achieving appropriate consumption. The perceptual apparatus of tacit projecting from presumptive horizons of understanding the world configures that world (e.g. as containing apples with flaws) within boundaries of concern.

Like this helpful contributor, we engage (bodily) with a world of always already meaningful entities (apples, programmes, woks) from the tacit perspective or horizon of their understanding as being genres (or types) of potential equipment—apples sustaining health—pre-understanding how we would put them to use, practically. Presumptive horizons of practical understanding embodied in an activity, (in)forming our behaviour, can be explored. Here difference in meaning can be expressed metaphorically as instantiating conceptual distance along contours or horizons of comprehension. A philosophical 'horizon of understanding' (Gadamer, 1975) is an embodied cultural perspective from where the world is meaningful (makes sense) or understood *as* generic—apple, 'guy', purchasing—a place of tacit assumption, anticipation and subsequent articulation of a narrative when applicable. Profit-seeking mall management marketing a mall as a place for 'exploration' and visitors enjoying returning as a 'home from home' regard this 'boundary object' (Star, 2010) from distinct horizons. The mall has 'different social significances', from 'diverse viewpoints' (Hawkins et al., 2017: 293). Media consumers can appropriate cultural horizons in aligning or distance themselves in criticism of programmes. By doing so, we can see realised construction of self, 'interplay between the social and personal aspects of identity' (Hood, 2016: 167), from shared or separated perspectives. 'Human beings are self-interpreting animals' (N.H. Smith, 2004: 43) whether apple choosing or audiences.

Positions assumed on a horizon of understanding may invoke ethnicity. Watching television advertising we later discuss, a Chinese consumer voiced his criticism: 'a bit offensive, it breaks the (Chinese) tradition'. We reflect in the following pages on ubiquitous *practices*, embodied, equipped, understanding *how*, emplacing (or putting in place) broader significant shared, often affective, belief, open to discussion during interviews or focus groups. Caring, for instance, emplaces wide concerns. Hermeneutics reflects upon *understanding* as our fundamental mode of being in the world, enabled or elided by our tacit position on the cultural perimeters from which we engage with experience.

Philosophical hermeneutics explores the ubiquitous practice of understanding from attending to advertisements to walking in malls and watching television. Such habituated processes normally receive little reflective attention unless issues arise therein or as the topic of academic investigation.

What are the cultural competences involved? How are they exercised—assisted and constrained—by the 'equipment' or tools (cultural, material, organisation, social) which they implicitly presuppose? For tools are teleological, enabling the achievement of our goals. What are less evident affective or evaluative concerns being tacitly affirmed or established on the horizons of 'understanding how' by such everyday practices? How do these activities anticipate and actualise—or build—behaviourally evident narrative? For practices articulate 'capacities, constraints and power' (Couldry, 2012: 34).

From a hermeneutic perspective, a 'practice can be a way of *not* doing as much as a way of doing' (Dandy, 2016: 1763, emphasis in original) such as routine 'neglect within contemporary UK land-managers experiences of forestry' (ibid.: 1756), configured by avoiding ('neglect' of) potential equipment (cultivation of forestry). Yet this habituated neglect behaviourally affirms or emplaces a hermeneutic 'horizon of understanding'. This is mapped out as 'dominant ways of seeing woodlands and forests as "uneconomic", "unproductive", and, to some extent, as places for wildlife' (ibid.).

Following a studious route through philosophy, social theory, business schools, psychology and media research, this volume seeks to demonstrate that our everyday understanding is *embodied* or behaviourally evident, *equipped* by language, a laptop screen or tooled by television: it *emplaces*, puts in place, affective perspectives (perhaps seeing a shopping mall as 'home from home'), sharing or separating people politically from other consumers. Embodied and equipped, emplacing a wider interpreting of the world, understanding tacitly presumes, projects and produces narrative meaning, (in)forming consumer identity—we 'prefigure', 'configure' and 'refigure' (Ricoeur, 1988) accounts.

Hermeneutics is the ideational reservoir, a source not only of practices but also reception theory—the first associated with a sociological account of experience, the second with our reading narrative. Practices are embodied and equipped, emplacing shared meaning. Reading refigures mediated content. Research participant stories across cultures incorporate these categorical moments in making sense. Themes (from caring to consuming) emerging in talking articulate core aspects of understanding as a bodily incorporated, instrumental generic practice embedding affective horizon or point of view. In short, from a hermeneutic perspective, understanding was habituated, horizonal, knowing *how*—before it was 'foregrounded' in propositions stating an understanding *that* certain situations obtain.

Hermeneutics has informed research in multiple communication disciplines. Literary as well as theological study were early celebrants of this philosophy of understanding. In media research, it is manifest as a behaviourally emphasising 'non-representational' approach to screen consumption while discussing 'epistemology of framing', how narratives construct horizons of understanding. Psychology is shaped by hermeneutics in establishing 'interpretative phenomenological analysis'. Sociology or social theory has seen a hermeneutic perspective adapted as its practice theories. The study of consumers has adopted a research method known as 'hermeneutic interviewing', modified by organisational theory to include interviewees' 'reflection-in-action', as well as subsequent to the habituated behaviour. Likewise, architectural research has called upon this interpretive dimension. Hermeneutics has shaped analyses of media communication to medical consultation (Clark, 2008).

Hermeneutics mobilises 'important resources for cultural studies' (Johnson et al., 2004: 13), while a hermeneutic dimension to intercultural studies is acknowledged in asserting that a disparate language use shapes horizons of understanding: language assembles an 'historical sedimentation' of meanings from which we view the world (Kramsch, 2013). I have mapped out earlier consideration of these hermeneutic interventions (Wilson, 2004, 2009, 2011), complicating across disciplines the dismissive recent claim that 'few researchers apply explicitly the principles of hermeneutics in their research' (Mathieu, 2015: 252). Hermeneutic theorising, indeed, characterises not only a humanities and social sciences purchase on research but also a scientific practice presented as 'solutions of concrete problems that do not call into question the existing horizon of expectations' (Ginev, 2016: 99).

In these pages, we shall consider scholarly engaging with hermeneutics across interpretive horizons, signalling a multi-disciplinary significance of philosophical thinking in its incorporating across the cultural and political study of consuming as meaningful behavioural 'text' (Ricoeur). To clarify the abstract purchase on consumption by such Western theorising, we reflect upon practices within Asian cultures without conceding cultural imperialism, for 'there may be nothing essentially Western in some "Western" theories or traditions (such as phenomenology)' (Ray, 2012: 244). Our hermeneutic emphasis on 'subjectified' (Reckwitz, 2012: 248) behavioural understanding-in-use—from Chinese New Year celebration to consuming in a Malaysian mall—may indeed be more Asian. Wang (2014) draws upon hermeneutics in re-examining cultural differences in academic discourse.

> The shift toward embodied cognition makes a distinct claim about inquiry into such phenomena—that it must be willing to go beyond the disembodied mind of western epistemology and psychological inquiry associated with that tradition.
>
> (Spackman and Yanchar, 2013: 47)

My book makes minor contributions to 'de-westernisation', presenting an albeit slight 'shift in academic knowledge to broaden the analysis by considering experiences, research findings, and theoretical frameworks developed in the rest of the world' (Waisbord and Mellado, 2014: 362). So practices philosophically perused here—instantiating wider perspectives in 'configuring' (Ricoeur) behaviour—range from annual Chinese New Year Reunion Dinners to more mundane apple choice and habituated visits in shopping malls to celebrating the latter on smartphones in social media use, cultivating a 'mass internet access' beyond the global North (Lunt and Livingstone, 2013: 88).

Focus group discussion can bring closer a horizon of consumer understanding embodied in practices. 'A horizon comprises a set of interpretive categories available to the person from a long biography of socialisation and acculturation.' (Jensen, 2002: 23) For hermeneutics, 'the very process of both (viewing) and analysing a text is incremental and creative: (audiences) gradually work out their categories of understanding in order to arrive at a coherent interpretation' (ibid.: 21). Although the habituated practice of arriving at 'coherent interpretations' is generally tacit or little reflected on, nonetheless (as in the consumer amended reception of telecommunications media marketing which I discuss in Chapter 1), 'categories of understanding' can undergo substantial change as a result of audiences engaging with media. 'Understanding serves to reproduce or contest the readers' pre-understanding' (ibid.: 22). Practices can be socially subversive as well as stabilising.

In foregrounding hermeneutic philosophy's emphasis on the fundamentally practical aspect or 'moments' of everyday understanding as hermeneutic practices theory, *Consumption, Psychology and Practice Theories* continues earlier philosophical arguments for *The Unity of Knowledge and Action*, where Frisina (2002) draws critically on the history of Western ideas to underwrite a non-representational theory of knowledge. In the profoundly misleading representational separation of knowing from acting 'impressions (are) made by the world on a purely passive, immaterial mental substance' whereupon thus 'stimulated', the mind 'steps in to work the ideas into coherent thoughts, plans and projects' (23). Rejecting this dualism, from a hermeneutic practices perspective, human perception is always already embodied and engaged in understanding a material world *as* 'equipment', tacitly emplacing wider perspectives or 'horizons of understanding' (Gadamer, 1975), the 'mode of existence definitive of human life' (Grossberg and Christians, 1978: 17) everywhere. Hermeneutics, emphasising the priority of practical understanding, offers a 'non-representational theory' enabling us 'to pay more attention than we've done in the past to matters of embodiment and to related issues of orientation and habitation' (Moores in Krajina et al., 2014: 693). In hermeneutic philosophy, our active, purposeful knowing-in-practices—behavioural cognition—replaces our passively perceiving.

> In dealing with things (*pragmata*) we understand them by way of their 'in-order-to' and 'for-sake-of-which', or the ways in which they are put to work in (our) projects.
>
> (Sturgess, 2016: 28)

Rather than media research being shaped by a correspondence or representative theory of attaining truth as mirroring an external (even ideal) world, with its source in Plato's philosophy, this volume follows

Aristotle's early emphasis on *phronesis* or knowing as practical wisdom (Flyvbjerg, 2001). 'Audience studies are no longer exclusively confided (sic) to specific disciplines', write Zaborowski and Dhaenens (2016: 456), yet studying media audiences has always been shaped more widely by philosophy, with consumer psychology also fundamentally formed by philosophy (Creswell, 2013). In short, I accede to Freeman and Vagle's (2013) imperative, 'placing philosophical questions about the meaning of being at the centre of qualitative inquiry' (726), hermeneutically.

Hermeneutic Philosophy Prefiguring Practice Theories

> Custom, then, is the great guide of human life. It is that principle alone which renders our experience useful to us, and makes us expect, for the future, a similar train of events with those which have appeared in the past.
>
> (Hume, 1748)

The Scottish philosopher Hume argued (1748) for 'custom' or our habitual experience as the basis of expectation or anticipation inductively established. Our conviction that entities will behave generally according to their generic type is the 'great guide of human life'. So presuming and hence projecting the future, we equally reconcile expectation with event where necessary and produce our behavioural narratives or *practices*, from choosing an apple to watching television. Here Hume has introduced a hermeneutics of understanding time and its tacit incorporation in habituated behaviour as we unreflectively maintain our embodied 'home understanding' (Taylor, 1995a: 150).

More recently (2001), McLeod, writing about human psychology, argued that the 'roots of all qualitative research lie' in philosophical hermeneutics and phenomenology (56). Espousing similar aligning with the horizon of ubiquitous understanding delineated by hermeneutics, Giddens argued, 'the collapse of positivistic philosophies over the past decade or so, however, has led to a strong interest in hermeneutics, its traditional rival' (1981a: 771). Empiricist philosophies wherein our knowing accrues in passive acquisition of external 'sense-data'—constituting or caused by external objects—are challenged by a hermeneutics of fundamental knowing (how) as habituated behaviour and our being in the world successfully engaging with entities tacitly considered as 'equipment'. Hence acknowledge Halpin and Monnin (online, 2016) the 'overwhelming importance of the practical task in defining the very world we live in', even for their thinking theoretically about the Internet. Here we address understanding consumers of marketing, media and psychological services in listening to accounts of practices—recognising our research to have entered a 'post-positivist era' (Reed, 2010).

In these pages, I follow hermeneutics—arguing that understanding is primarily or primordially practical as well as perspectival—across conceptual horizons of multiple disciplines from marketing to media, psychological to sociological studies. My book offers an accumulated account of practice theories which have become pervasive from business to sociology's research. In doing so, it locates this thinking as closely shaped by hermeneutic philosophy. Early chapters consider instances of our communication, consumer and cultural behaviour viewed in terms of hermeneutic practices theory.

Practice instantiates philosophy. The analytical narrative of pre-reflective routine (set out as eight 'axioms') presented in the first chapter draws on hermeneutic concepts, discussing contributions from Gadamer and Ricoeur, establishing a philosophical platform from which to view our habitual behaviour and establishing its latent understanding of the world made manifest through our subsequent reflective awareness, albeit in focus group discussion of choice. 'Let's say, a simple one: apples.' In focusing on selecting fruit without 'flaws', reflection on its functioning to equip health is marginal if not entirely absent. Visible and vision-employing consumer choice is 'reversibly perceptible and perceiving' (Sobchack, 2004: 312) here, later placed within a horizon of gendered understanding as being a female competence. The practice of apple choosing is 'refigured' (Ricoeur) in this political discourse which could be equally a statement about 'commodification' and constituting consumers' time between/within the practices of manufacturing and purchasing 'equipment' for living.

Practice theories of our equipped and situated construction of a participatory meaning (as in media and marketing consumption) are frequently characterised as lacking common ground or core principles. This book explores whether by travelling to their conceptual grounding in philosophy, a shared territory shaping research (especially on audience and consumer narrative) can be located as hermeneutic practices theory. 'Most authors seem to agree that practices should be seen as recurrent processes governed by specifiable schemata of preferences and prescriptions' (Cetina, 2001: 185).

Moreover, through returning to hermeneutic first principles, the book shows that a series of spatio-temporal metaphors become available—appropriate to analysing communication as a process across disciplines in which it is considered. For a 'hermeneutical theory of metaphor' can enhance the 'productive dimension of imagination' (Geniusas, 2015: 231). Exploring such ideas as 'horizon of understanding' and the 'hermeneutic circle of understanding' (Gadamer) as metaphors, 'having escaped the confines of reality, productive imagination can also offer its re-description' (ibid.: 233). Migrants cross behaviourally emplaced cultural as well as material horizons in their understanding national practices. Visiting a mall with expectations of security is to enter from an affective horizon of understanding, structuring tacit anticipating of internal as opposed to external urban space. Focus groups and interviews for qualitative research trace out thematic 'horizons of meaning' (Callahan, 2011: 319) from whence their participants have pre-reflectively accorded significance to events. So, looked at from a gendered horizon of meaning construction, choosing fresh apples without 'flaws' embodies a feminine competence distinct from the guys who 'just grab and go' (Chinese consumer). Here hermeneutic reflection is haptic, rejecting this masculine mode of touching, grasping apples, foregrounding rather a horizon of understanding emplaced in habitual embodied practical selecting. Practices are '*situated*' (Shotter, 2015, emphasis in original). We tacitly—or unreflectively—engage with entities 'primordially' as equipment from an identity assigning horizon of understanding from whence we always already see a meaningful world in 'cultural categories' (McCracken, 1986: 72). Our embodied horizon of understanding maps out our 'intentional arc' (Merleau-Ponty, 1962).

A hermeneutic practices perspective offers a set of spatio-temporal metaphors with which to reflectively engage people's processes of using social media across space and time, both in so far as they produce content embedded within 'horizons of understanding' and through their behaviourally constructing contexts of consumption. In Chapter 5, we consider how this content and context are equally shaped by implementing a ubiquitous generic 'fore-understanding' (Heidegger, 1962). Since

> mobile media are spatial in nature (i.e., we take them with us on our everyday journeys and use them to give meaning to these spaces), the sites at which we engage social media on mobile devices are just as important as the content being exchanged.
>
> (Farman, 2015: 1)

Discussing Ricoeur, Grondin writes appropriately of the 'linguistic innovation brought about by what happens in the audacity of a metaphor which broadens our view of the world' (2015: 152). So one can consider, for instance, the conceptual implications of asserting that media users engage (enter) digital text from diverse 'horizons of expectation', with a productively enlarging 'fusion' in 'horizons of understanding', thereby 'projecting' a new narrative, integrated in a 'hermeneutic circle' of meaning production. Here 'horizonal' presumption tacitly incorporated within social media or shopping mall practice (e.g. of gendered difference in purchasing fruit) is not only metaphorically spatially displaced from attention as foundational but also temporally precedes, shaping behaviour. Both wide-ranging cultural preference and specific competence are inscribed in the practice. When instituting deeper or wider analysis of discourse in research, 'horizons provide perspective by being the implicit and explicit beliefs that furnish the context for understanding' (Vessey, 2009: 537).

'Horizons of understanding' are generic, enabling recognition of a particular instance (from shopping mall to social media). One can change, cultivate, inhabit, disregard, narrow or move away from a cultural horizon of understanding. Such discursively recoverable tacit framing of experience is distinct from the competency with which it is negotiated in particular contexts of recognising its instantiation, enabling and eliding production of meaning, creating texts of action, signifying sense.

People can occupy differing locations on a 'horizon of understanding' from which they articulate habituated intelligible activity without reflection, subsequently justified as rational action. Practices relate through horizons of understanding (e.g. management maintaining the shopping mall as a site of security, enabling the visitor's embodied anticipation in shopping and walking). Or there can be 'gaps in horizons between consumers' (Ringma and Brown, 1991: 70) and prevailing authority.

Disclosed in a focus group or an interview, implicit participant themes denote *processes* of active attainment—their caring as intervention or learning as (successfully) reflecting upon routine. Imbricated in habituated activity, our 'lived' cultural horizons of understanding can be constraining or enabling, forming 'our background understandings of practices' (Brinkmann, 2008: 405–406). A metaphorical horizon of meaning (as with its material counterpart) is public, shareable and resists change, a place of 'common understanding' (ibid.) enabling a perspectival vision of the world. We take up position on a perhaps elliptically defined horizon of understanding, assuming its viewpoint. 'Let's say, a simple one: apples. Maybe the apples look the same to the guys (laughter). No offence. But, we, we, we pick the apple that looks nicer with no flaws.' (female, Chinese student mall visitor) This embodied practice—'picking apples'—in its 'experiential understanding' (Brook, 2010: 409) is tacitly shared within a circle of understanding extending to some, albeit excluding others, an area of common agreement available to be reflectively marked out, drawn and defined. Behaviour perhaps ironically regarded as ritual—such as regular supermarket purchasing of apples—invokes 'everyday practices of categorisation' (Couldry, 2003: 8), emplacing horizons of gendered and hierarchical understanding. Our mall visitor refers to a 'background of distinctions of worth' (Taylor, 1985: 11), defining herself.

Following Ricoeur (1981a), the politics of communication studies can foreground a horizon of cultural understanding—thereby enabling critical 'distancing'—in Foucault's words (1981/1988) by 'pointing out on what kinds of assumptions, what kinds of familiar, unchallenged, unconsidered modes of thought the practices that we accept rest'. A marketing narrative's consumers both tacitly and reflectively occupy particular places on a horizon of understanding and response, as aligned or alienated. Media users pass over borders of changing, revised perspectives, immersively active in a narrative. Horizons of comprehending one's experience can be psychologically emancipating or be defended to 'buttress a fragile sense of stability in psychic space' (Midgley, 2006: 217), shareable or contested. We both see *from* positioned horizons and see *further* horizons delineating some potential achievement as 'coherent frames' (Russell and Babrow, 2011: 240) and frameworks for establishing coherency. A shared horizon or an 'experience of common ground' (Weissmann, 2013: 142) enables communication between otherwise silent interlocutors. 'Distanciation' enables possible critique, 'an indefinite range of readers and readings within different sociocultural contexts' (Ricoeur, 1975: 18). Horizons of understanding circumscribe political-social positioning, assumed/entered/ occupied at particular points of embodied perception, from where a discursive analysis and direct action arise.

Practices research can now not only be discerned in multiple disciplines but also equally crosses disciplines. The ubiquitous practice of media use in *YouTube* and other visual vehicles by managers and visitors to a shopping mall—the mediatization of malls into 'forms or formats suitable for media representation' (Couldry, 2008a: 377)—responds to investigating not only with media user expertise but also from an interpretive marketing perspective. Has the branded identity of the place been changed? This question demonstrates how mediation of 'brand culture forms part of a larger call for inclusion of cultural issues within the management and marketing research canon' (Schroeder, 2009: 124).

Emphasising our generic understanding of entities in a material environment as 'equipment', practices theory enables quantitative correlation of perception and demographic variable as a '*Zeug* Score', given that culturally (in)formed understanding is 'intrinsic to awareness' (Sikh and Spence, 2016: 1). Thus different (e.g. gendered) groups while experientially enabled by the same equipment may conceive of the artefact in varying ways, modes of awareness generated by their positioning on separate horizons of understanding. Varying thematic perception of function is quantifiable. Hence there is no pressure for 'paradigm wars' (Given, 2017) between qualitative and quantitative thought. Access to datafied acknowledged 'liking' can be further explored through interpretive interview.

Human behaviour is fundamentally habitual—shaped by its tacit assumptions—occasionally interrupted by reflection. Practices theory acknowledges such action to be minimally monitored yet nonetheless considers it as projecting understanding. Presented in research, 'storied' behaviour can be seen to be (in)formed from a shifting hierarchy of 'horizons' or of perspectives—from habituated to reflected on—rather than a single seamless narrative. In the hermeneutic health psychology which we discuss in Chapter 4, pursuing 'caring' maps out participants' horizon of understanding more focussed generic practices. This communication practices perspective avoids conflating tacit (taken for granted), transformative and theoretical understanding in research, stressing the 'importance of uncovering and interrogating presuppositions' (Bevan, 2014: 137). Practices embody subjectivity.

In short, a historically grounded and unifying statement of contemporary practices theory enhances its potential as a tool in communication, consumer and cultural research for landscaping interpretive horizons of human behaviour. It explores culturally formed narrative, equipping and incorporated (reflectively, unreflectively) in people's everyday lives—or meaning in the mundane. Meaning is 'spatially and temporally embodied, lived' (Sobchack, 2004: 2) and values affectively. Looking at consumers immersed in malls to movies, we consider genres of tacit understanding-in-use, the 'interdependence of skill and presupposition', as 'embodied knowledge' (Turner, 1994: 14). Our everyday equipped practices are implicitly experienced as 'ready-to-hand' (Heidegger, 1962), yet paradoxically they also exercise or put into place a wide set of tacit presuppositions, a horizon of understanding which marketing, media or psychological research explores in qualitative research, presenting participant experience as 'illuminated quotidian' (LeMahieu, 2015: 471). Our 'reflective, deliberative agency emerges from pre-reflective activity' (Martin and Sugarman, 2001: 105).

Intercultural Hermeneutic Interdisciplinarity

In this brief book, I ask a question: 'Is a hermeneutic perspective on practices present across disciplines from business schools to psychology, sociology and studying our watching television?' My answer in Chapter 2 and thereafter is a hermeneutic social theory of practices considered as behavioural genres manifested (albeit tacitly) through an individual's activity: to 'submit production to genres (is) to produce an individual' (Ricoeur, 1981a: 136). How can a person's referring during a focus group to her or his behaviour (e.g. when present in a mall) as a 'specific instance' be considered a 'foundation for identifying deeper, more generalisable patterns, structures and meanings' (Seamon, 2000: 160) or type of tool-using? 'Why not we just take one of those pictures?' (Malay mall visitor). Distinct from quantifying genre occurrence, hermeneutic qualitative research sees a genre of picture taking, understanding-as-use within this informal 'community of practice' (Wenger et al., 2002). In its demonstrable capability as generic, practical understanding presumes, projects and produces action. Hermeneutic 'interpretation seeks to elucidate meaning that is implicit' (Willig, 2017: 278).

Chapter 1 draws on the philosophers Husserl, Heidegger, Gadamer and Ricoeur to outline a hermeneutics of practices as embodied and equipped, tacitly assuming and anticipating while also articulating activity with public criteria of achieving. We are always already generically immersed in practices—in 'custom' (Hume). A second chapter discusses the proximity and distance between a hermeneutics and social theories of practice (Giddens, Reckwitz, Schatzki), with its wider ambition of integration to form an 'epistemology of practice' (Cook and Brown, 1999: 383).

Later chapters pursue this idea across disciplines of marketing and media study, psychology and more widely, seeking in synthesis an augmented reception theory of our consumer practice as *praxis*, a generic narrative, visually evident as understanding-in-use, equipped, socially emplaced—embodying an affective perspectival horizon of alignment or provoking distancing, a perception of 'fractured horizons' (Taylor, 1989) in branded or personal narrative. Viewing media marketing can prompt identifying or taking up a position of alienated distrust. The *praxis* of consumption is tacitly shaped and informed in being a 'continuous act that is renewed at every instant' (Schmidt, 2016: 69).

In presenting human activity as interpretive and therein goal directed, tacitly teleological, I am distancing myself here from the causalist stimuli accounts of behaviour discussed in earlier volumes (Wilson, 2009, 2011, 2015). Yet positivist models responsible for such statements continue to appear in consumer or marketing journals. 'Communication stimuli trigger a positive effect in the customer as recipient.' (Schivinski and Dabrowski, 2015: 36) Rather than our perceiving sense-data and being pushed by 'stimuli', we are 'ineluctably hermeneutical'—or purposive in ubiquitous user-generated understanding of an entity's meaningful 'signifying dimensions' (Wajcman and Jones, 2012: 683). 'The thinking, rational subject can exist only as embodied agent, as a being in the world, not as some transcendental entity free of any context or medium.' (Redhead, 2002: 152) Distinct from positivism's atomistic separation of cognition and culture, the mental and physical, we are always already positioned on horizons of understanding, tacitly (in)forming embodied practices.

> We do not meet things by taking on board dumb sense data; we always encounter things *as* something or other, where, in traditional language, the 'as-what' and the 'how' point to the meaningful presence (*Anwesen*) of the thing. . . . Our *a priori* engagement with intelligibility—as our only way to be—entails that we are ineluctably hermeneutical. We necessarily make some sense of everything we meet (even if only interrogative sense), and if we cannot make any sense at all of something, we simply cannot meet it.
>
> (Sheehan, 2014: 255–256)

1 Mind the Gap?

Bridging Philosophical Hermeneutics and Practice Theories

Project

In this first chapter, I begin to explore co-incidence or distance between practice theories and philosophical hermeneutics. Both argue for understanding-in-practices—or practical habituated unreflected upon understanding *how*—evident in our everyday 'coping' behaviour as fundamental. Propositional understanding *that* something is the case—or reflection—is secondary. I trace a threefold narrative of 'moments' characterising practical understanding, following its theorising through hermeneutics (Husserl to Heidegger, Gadamer to Ricoeur), seeing it finally flourish as generically configured action, embodied and equipped, embedded within habituated horizons of understanding. Tacit horizons of focussed behaviour or practical understanding (such as concern for human dignity in caring) are often distant cognitive frameworks of involvement, far from the attention of an actor. As such, they are an eminently suitable subject for research from health psychology to marketing. In this chapter, I commence constructing a hermeneutic perspective on social practices from 'making' meaning while watching television to our purchasing everyday products in the local supermarket.

Considered from a hermeneutic perspective, our human understanding is fundamentally or 'primordially' exemplified by using equipment, in the philosopher Heidegger's example, a hammer. We can be said to 'understand' its usage. Visibly incorporated in habituated, hence 'ready-to-hand', behaviour as an embodied narrative belonging to an accustomed generic goal-directed practice, our understanding implicitly or tacitly anticipates and actualises an activity subject to a public standard of achievement. In practices, attention is upon aim or goal rather than embodiment or equipment.

> Our engagement with entities ready-to-hand does not involve explicit awareness of their properties; instead, we 'see through' them to the

task we are engaged in. When we are smoothly driving in nails with a hammer, our focus is on the thing we are building not the size or shape or colour of the hammer.

(Dotov et al., 2010)

Such habitual, little reflected on, 'skilled coping' (ibid.) in material circumstances involves our knowing or understanding *how* to act appropriately. This embodied perception of surroundings precedes secondary reflective propositional knowing *that*. 'Performative' knowing is distinct from 'declarative' asserting (Brown and Duguid, 2001: 199). So, for instance, a female Chinese frequent mall visitor told us in a research focus group: 'Basically, I expect good security from the mall'. Her statement can be interpreted hermeneutically as referring to material/metaphorical 'horizons of understanding' (Gadamer, 1975) from which she enters this shopping mall, supporting her forward 'projecting' (ibid.) there of 'good security' from an enabling equipped 'social tool' (Burchell, 2017). Her embodied understanding of the mall as secure is evident not in concurrent propositional assertion but rather as projected by her habitual mode of walking, thus visible in her behaviour (e.g. how she carries valuables, displaying a tacit view of the place as equipped to deter 'snatch thieves'). 'Whatever they are called—practical understanding, habitus, tacit knowledge, skills, competences—capabilities are embodied through practices.' (Wallenborn and Wilhite, 2014: 60) Visual evidence of affective intentionality (understanding) (e.g. finding a mall secure) can be constituted behaviourally. Embodying assumptions formed through repetition, a horizon of understanding informs action—or as Bourdieu, similarly, writes, 'embodiment is the creation of a memory by repetition' (1977: 59).

Importantly, truth conditions for this embodied public narrative of projecting and producing participatory activity need not include (indeed may be taken to exclude) her thinking about security when in the mall. Rather, the evidence is 'embodiment in publicly accessible activity' (Rouse, 2006: 504). While not reflected upon during this practice, a subsequent occasion of research allows her to speak about her expectation, integrated with mall events in a 'hermeneutic circle' (Gadamer, 1975) of her behavioural 'assemblage' (Canniford and Shankar, 2013), conjoining meaning and material. Albeit mundanely instantiated here in a mall, understanding 'constitutes the basic being-in-motion (*Bewegtheit*, movedness) of the existing human being (*Dasein*)' (Gadamer, 2006: 39).

As Davey writes, unpacking the qualities of 'unquiet understanding', 'the notion of practice is central to how we understand ourselves as hermeneutic subjects' (2006: 55)—not least in a focus group. Here Heidegger's hermeneutics moves our understanding of 'understanding' from replicating subjectivity (Dilthey) to projecting and producing public meaning in a behavioural narrative. What then is the 'primordial' structure of 'being there' in everyday living as understanding-in-practices? How do our wider 'value-laden horizons of (generic) expectations' (Livingstone, 2012: 189) (such as 'good security' in a mall) (in)form or shape more specifically occupied 'orientations' (Morley, 1992: 50) in understanding particular practices (e.g. purchasing products) we appropriate—or are alienated from—in daily living? How is their embodied ideational relationship evident?

Understanding-in-Practices: Presuming, Projecting and Producing Behavioural Narrative

Practices produce narrative incorporated in behaviour. From supermarket apple selection to seriously watching sports, we actualise a meaningful story. Bodies display a purpose. We are always already immersed in projecting understanding of our circumstances—implicitly future orientated. I see a suitcase—not (empiricist) sense-data. Albeit distracted by more immediate items—at the 'back of our minds' we visibly co-ordinate our conduct during repeated visits to a shopping mall or social media site, thus constituting meaning from a 'horizon of understanding' (Gadamer, 1975) the world that can subsequently be 'voiced out'. Behaving thereby tacitly aims at intelligibility, shaping 'life-narratives' (Gaviria and Bluemelhuber, 2010: 127). A sequence of action belongs to a cultural 'form of life' (Wittgenstein, 1991), referenced in subsequent reflecting. 'Forms of life' are visibly evident behaviourally, conceptualisation woven into an activity, ideationally imbricated in the landscapes of our everyday doing, supporting our realised tacit expectation shaped within background boundaries, the 'horizons of understanding' mapped in hermeneutic philosophy of practices.

Cultural memory is incorporated in behavioural movement. On a horizon of understanding, the 'sediment of past experiences' is 'converted' into 'dispositions for future actions' (Wallenborn and Wilhite, 2014: 58). Our making sense (viewing or visiting) involves our presuming, projecting and producing a story in our intelligible behaviour, aligning and alienating us from others, or simply generating apathy. Thus understanding (in)forms life. Behaviour projects narrative meaning from an interpretation of one's situation evident in activity where entity as equipment is perceived not as object but rather as enabling (or disabling). So in short, 'everything (people) touch and do is infused with the underlying order that gives them their expectations of the world (. . .) characteristic of their particular society' (Miller, 2008: 287). Generic expectation accommodates/is amended by event.

> By means of the lived body human agents possess knowledge about how to cope with what is at hand that neither presupposes conscious representation nor a representation in propositional terms but is 'knowledge in the hands' (Merleau-Ponty, 1962: 144).
>
> (Gartner, 2013: 342)

Hermeneutics asserts our fundamental understanding of entities as 'equipment' answering to our immediate interpretive interests (fruit with 'no flaws') from wider reflective concerns (health)—the 'meaningful presence of something to someone in terms of that person's concerns and interests':

> thus 'we alone have the ability to make sense of things, and we do so by connecting a possibility of something we encounter with a possibility or need of ourselves: we take what we meet in terms of its relation to our everyday concerns and goals'.
>
> (Sheehan, 2014: 256–257)

Understanding is then the tacit teleological way we manage practices, forming habituated activity aiming at implicit goals, locatable as a 'level of competence or performance prior to (. . .) verbal articulation' (Rouse, 2006: 515). 'Interpreting', on the other hand, as during a research focus group, takes for its theme such pre-reflective understanding, now presented reflectively as informed by 'horizons of understanding' (Gadamer, 1975) shaping practice. 'Basically, I expect good security from the mall', as our participant interpreted shopping site, understanding seen behaviourally. Here her thought is 'a *derivative* aspect of the overall intentionality that we exhibit as we actively engage with the world around us' (Larkin et al., 2006: 106 emphasis in original), a future-oriented concern.

People's habituated 'capacity to encounter objects as ready-to-hand involves grasping them in relation to (their) own possibilities-for-being' (Mulhall, 2005: 77). Such tacit 'projection' is the

> core of what Heidegger means by 'understanding'. But any such projection both presupposes and constitutes a comprehending grasp of the world within which the projection must take place (ibid.: 81). (Halting understanding when issues arise or in research discussion) we engage in what Heidegger characterises as 'interpretation', and the structures of our everyday comprehending engagement with these objects thereby become our explicit concern (ibid.: 84).

Hermeneutic theory of practices—initiated by Heidegger (following Husserl), then shaped socio-politically by Gadamer and Ricoeur—provides accounts of ubiquitous human understanding incorporated in everyday activity. Heidegger's thesis of understanding's temporal dimension, with its consecutive 'moments' of 'fore-having' resources, 'fore-seeing' possibility and actualising 'fore-conceptions' links the first phenomenologist with later hermeneutic writers. All rejected empiricist theorising of perception as immediately seeing (unmediated) 'sense-data'. While Heidegger can be considered to have replaced the Cartesian dualism (separation of mind and body) which he attacked with a subsequent dualism (between ready-to-hand habituated behaviour and reflection), historically his inclusion as initiating a history of hermeneutic ideas reinvoked as practice theory is inescapable. His narrative of embodied human understanding as ubiquitous holds despite recent evidence of his unacceptable political turn to fascism and anti-Semitism in Hitler's Germany (Hadjioannou, 2017).

> For Heidegger, interpretive or hermeneutical understanding was not the province of specialised human disciplines (nor of a transcendentally construed phenomenology) but rather a constitutive feature of every human being inserted both in the world and in the movement of temporality.
>
> (Dallmayr, 2009: 26)

So how should we consider, consent to or criticise as well as position theoretically mundane practices of always already making meaning, embodied/embedded/emplaced/evident in watching television, using the Internet or walking around our shopping mall but rarely reflected upon while we engage in such activity? More exotically, we can philosophically reflect how, 'in conceptualising high-speed motorcycling as a practice, we are concerned with the interconnections between material technologies, ways of understanding, forms of bodily action and meanings' (Murphy, 2015: 3).

How are our dispersed horizons of understanding not only vocally, but visibly incorporated in behaviour shaped politically or structured by a distant 'power and domination' (Grossberg, 1984: 399)? What can consumer researchers learn about practices as habituated modes of understanding (and identity construction) when presented by a participant in marketing or media, psychology and sociology focus groups? 'Mature social agency is habitual through and through' (Crossley, 2001: 95). How does ready-to-hand unreflective behaviour reproduce challengeable assumptions?

> Let's say, a simple one: apples. Maybe the apples look the same to the guys (laughter). No offence. But, we, we, we pick the apple that looks nicer with no flaws . . . . Like this apple looks fresher. Something like this. Normally, they would say, 'it's just the same. Just grab and go.'
>
> (Female, Chinese student mall visitor addressing a focus group)

Here a research participant reflects upon a past purchase. Uncertainty over a precise account ('something like this') suggests she is making explicit a practice lacking concurrent reflection—her immersing in implicitly anticipatory custom, generic behaviour involving habituated, ready-to-hand bodily movement, to which there is normally no need to attend, let alone reflect on wider horizonal considerations. (In Chapter 4 on psychology, we hear from a research participant lamenting pain as signalling a failure of bodily 'equipment'.)

Hearing this account, we learn of a tacit *fore-structured* understanding-in-practice, assuming, anticipating and actualising a shared narrative. So assuming 'we' will *(fore-)have* apples from which to choose, this participant presumes without reflecting or *fore-sees* typical characteristics requiring attention. The fruit will not all 'look the same': there will be some that 'look nicer with no flaws' or 'fresher', so indicating enhanced ability to function as a nutritional tool (*Zeug*). Visibly exercising a choice shaped by this *concerned fore-conception*, its behavioural inclusion means she will not 'just grab and go' but rather act, emplacing (albeit unreflectively) a horizon of affective caring.

Moreover, this *fore-understanding*, partially constituting the *horizon of understanding* from which she enters the shopping mall, is emphasised as gendered. 'Maybe the apples look the same to the guys.' Embedded in her behavioural *being-with-others*, this speculative purchase on a shareable positioning informs her selective behaviour as a way of looking at entities—her perspective legible as attending to presenting 'fresher' apples for selection, but only reflected upon in the focus group. Exercising a habituated expertise, her attention will be on the apples, not on her bodily activity. Her practice is distinct from (say) the accomplished pianist who attends to their finger movements with the aim of expressive playing where 'the playing is continually responsive to (their) thought about the piece, (their) decisions to speed up or slow down, and the like' (Annas, 2012). Here, the piano playing is clearly embodied and instrumentally enabled, 'finger-focussed' generic activity with its specific qualities emerging (in)formed by an affective positioned understanding of the 'piece'.

Many of our mall visitor's other regular activities (such as her slipping on shoes) are likely to be *ready-to-hand*, requiring lesser attention, if also incorporating assumptions about equipment or environment. Similarly among the 'guys' for whom selectively picking fruit seems unnecessary when their differing expectations are confirmed by experience, 'it's just the same. Just grab and go'. Only if apples were found to be indubitably 'fresh', 'with no flaws' or unavoidably visibly 'flawed' would habituated and tacit anticipation require attention, revising—or expectation be *presented-at-hand*. Here there is an account of perceiving as a cultural practice far from seeing empiricist 'sense-data', embodied narrative emplacing a horizon of gendered alignment: 'we' are apart from 'guys'. Our Chinese shopper positions her apple purchasing as a 'gendered practice' (Martin, 2003).

Italicised terms are taken from the early Heidegger's *Being and Time* (1962), an initiating if problematic treatise on philosophical hermeneutics. They show how an everyday, habitual activity or a practice embodies 'constitutive elements', 'materials, meanings and competences' (Shove et al., 2012: 13, 15). Engaging with hermeneutics as a philosophical analysis of activity, so articulating a perspective on practices as assembling meaning, the following pages consider behavioural narrative from audiences watching television and mall visitors to participants in health psychology research.

> A *Dasein* (being-in-the-world) is defined by its intentionality and the various practical projects that it engages in, from hammering a nail to posting a photo online, and these activities transform the entities into equipment (*Zeug*).
>
> (Halpin and Monnin, 2016)

Heidegger positioned generic 'understanding' as embodied and primarily practical. This account is directed at Descartes' dualism, the separating of mental and physical activity or positing a human 'ghost in the machine' (Ryle, 1949) as a 'basic misconception' (Ricoeur, 1974: 223) in philosophy.

> Heidegger had to struggle against this (conceptual) picture to recover an understanding of the agent as engaged, as embedded in a culture, a form of life, a 'world' of involvements, ultimately to understand the agent as embodied.
>
> (Taylor, 1993: 318)

However, it can be argued that Heidegger's own fundamental distinction between a *habitual* unreflective use of 'ready-to-hand' equipment and *reflective* attending to (or a 'presenting-at-hand') tools with troubles is itself a dualist opposition, which ironically excludes, for instance, a habituated reflective awareness of issues evident in professional philosophical conduct itself (Crossley, 2001). Equipment is itself, of course, also the product of reflected-upon practices, a 'human intentionality embedded within the objects that is released as the user interacts with them' (Dant, 2008: 13).

More widely, our habitual action is diverse: it ranges across behaviour definitively excluding attention (walking presuming security in the shopping mall) to activity requiring extended attention (such as picking apples). 'A thorough-going phenomenological account of habit has to acknowledge the different roles played by habit at the individual and the collective levels.' (Moran, 2011: 56) Yet when immersed in habituated generic practices, attention to their embodiment is customarily absent.

Whether as researchers or the researched, people can find it difficult to present their implicit 'knowing how to get around' (Moores, 2012: 95) in achieving understanding places or programmes—embodied memory instantiating 'fundamental ability (. . .) to get around in the world' (Polt, 1999: 65). Nonetheless, practices are positioned within discoverable horizons of formative understanding. Hence, writes Finlay, 'our goal is to move beyond what the participant (or text) says of experience to what is implicitly revealed about the pre-reflective experiential realm in the telling' (2014: 125).

The Structure of Sense-Making (McLeod, 2001): A Hermeneutic Perspective on Habituated Practices

Drawing critically on Heidegger's (1962) philosophical account of our always already being engaged in making our surroundings intelligible (our 'primordial' mode of *Dasein* or 'being there'), the hermeneutic approach to practices holds that we fundamentally understand entities in habitually using them with embodied expectation *as* equipment (*Zeug*) rather than as mere objects. Practices involve the 'establishment of corporeal routines and specialised devices': so they 'provide the basic intelligibility of the world'. 'Actions presuppose practices and not vice versa' (Thrift, 2008: 8), or as Watson writes, defending the analytical primacy of 'practices' for theory, 'practices are constituted and reproduced by the flow of human action and in turn they shape that flow' (2014: 13).

Practices are generic, enabled by equipment, encircled by horizons of understanding from where the material world is disclosed as teleological order, as items employed 'in order to' attain goals. Our awareness of entity as thing with qualities is secondary, in our diagnosing dysfunctional issues subverting 'our everyday coping practices' (Dreyfus, 2001: 162). In thereby asserting the primacy of the practical 'intertwinings of the human and the nonhuman' (Pickering, 2001: 176), Heidegger rejects empiricist-positivist theorising wherein we as subjects fundamentally perceive objects (or 'sense-data'). For hermeneutics, the latter is a secondary mode of perception. Instead, it is philosophically necessary that 'we start out from a description of ourselves as we are in the midst of our day-to-day practical affairs' 'caught up in the midst of a practical world' (Guignon, 1993: 6). 'Heidegger regards our practical involvement with the things of everyday life as ontologically prior to the theoretical attitude that determines the formation of concepts and propositions' (Bruns, 2004: 31) in the reflective pursuit of a 'logical relation highlighted by the propositional attitude' (ibid.).

'*Dasein*'s primary way of looking at things is not detached observation but rather dealing with the world.' (Lahtinen, 2014) Exploring such primacy, I resist Heidegger's hammer below, taking a domestic rather than a workshop example. One 'fore-has' (Heidegger, 1962) or brings to bear on a situation multiple implicit assumptions regarding enabling entities. I am always already engaging with the world from horizons of (its) understanding, arriving from a cultural-material background. Instantiating generic 'fore-conceptions' or our knowing about familiar types of entities, practices tacitly incorporate pre-conception—future-oriented 'fore-seeing' (ibid.) carried forward in action. Touching is temporal, presuming, projecting, producing meaning. 'In touching the world we are constantly prefiguring, refiguring, and configuring our experience.' (Kearney, 2015: 21)

With scant attention in the busy kitchen, I have assumed I am picking up a heavy pint glass but mistakenly grasp a light plastic beaker: then I suddenly realise that the embodied anticipating of weight incorporated in my movement (my bodily knowing or informed understanding-in-practice) is mistaken. My experience at this point clashes with tacit, 'non-deliberative' (Polkinghorne, 2000: 457) expectation of equipment. An apparently 'ready-to-hand' (Heidegger, 1962) course of action—usually requiring minimal thought (picking up a glass)—prompts on this unusual occasion, focussed awareness of diminished weight in presenting the beaker 'at hand' (ibid.).

> If knowing is to be possible as a way of determining the nature of the present-at-hand by observing it, then there must first be a deficiency in our having-to-do with the world concernfully. (. . .) (In) holding-oneself-back from any manipulation or utilisation, the perception of the present-at-hand is consummated.
>
> (Heidegger, 1962: 88–89)

My implicitly anticipating ['projecting' (ibid.)] articulating/ producing a generic experience (heaviness) is initiated by my 'having-to-do with' an entity I tacitly understand as a type of tool. Yet this simple story, embedded in my engaging with equipment, appears 'deficient' (ibid.). My specific 'fore-conception' of the tool is erroneous—the tool presents itself as an issue. Momentarily holding myself back 'from any utilisation', I reflect on the beaker in terms of its weight, rather than readily making use of it as item of equipment. Practice precedes theorising. It is then culturally emplaced '*praxis* of human beings that makes available to them entities susceptible of becoming objects of theoretical concerns' (Vandevelde, 2016: 436).

From such horizons of understanding entities in practice as instantiating instrumental types (glass, mall, media), we tacitly project—anticipate and commonly actualise appropriate event (such as drinking from the glass). We thus produce subsequent participatory embodied narrative through integrating, in activity, anticipating ['fore-understanding' (Heidegger, 1962)] with later occurrence. This ubiquitous process is implicitly incorporated in everyday behaviour (e.g. using media), evident visually, but also later made explicit in speech (e.g. in focus groups). Shaping a habituated activity, consumer assumptions—their 'pre-reflective' (ibid.) cultural horizons of understanding a genre or a mode of being equipped—can be explored philosophically or politically. Thus researchers may find that a vast mall is nonetheless regarded by returning visitors as 'home from home', cultivating habit, far from its marketing as a purchasing 'adventure'. 'Habits are aligned with the domestic.' (Coyne, 2010: 77) Embodied in their returning, consumer horizons of understanding mark a 'wider context of ideological competition and resistance from below' (Curran, 1990: 144).

Here a 'horizon' is a sense-making 'locus of meaningful action on which individuals may come to reflect' (Burkitt, 2002: 225). Their understanding a shopping mall as second home is likely to be visible in their mundane 'practical comportment' (Moran, 2000: 231), 'unformulated' (Taylor, 1995b: 179) during visits, yet available to be 'voiced out'. In a rather different mode, the conceptual geography of a religious 'horizon' can be characterised as politically a place of cultural manoeuvring, contestation or even powerful consensus (Izberk-Bilgin, 2012).

To briefly take a further example of understanding-in-practice from an undergraduate project on consumer reception of media marketing, or exploring 'receiving horizons of a spectator' (Davey, 2013: 12). Viewing a story on screen he is informed is advertising, and seeing a 'middle-aged man showing his car key to his wife (it's like flaunting his new car to his wife)', a male Chinese research participant reports that he initially projected a narrative of probable 'car-sale' marketing. A generic pre-existing knowledge is thereby drawn upon and directive. Hence watching its subsequent story of 'people conversing through mobile phones', he found this narrative 'really surprising'. His fore-seeing an account of vehicular merit clashed with his viewing experience. Reflecting on this issue, with the goal of configuring a coherent screen narrative, he turned back in a hermeneutic circle of understanding retracing his epistemic path, 'bracketing' an initial identification (or fore-conception) of the text to posit telecommunications marketing. Here habituated viewing has been removed from its status as easily ready-to-hand consumption: a generic projection is revised. Following Carbaugh et al. (2011) one can claim that so employing 'theoretical reflexivity' involves 'conceptualising the scene as one involving fundamentally different genres of communication' (4). In hermeneutic terms, this research participant reviewed his initial textual configuring to realise a coherent refiguration—or 'reconfiguration' (Borisenkova, 2010: 92) of his projecting and production of narrative. Whether a narrative is televisual or behaviourally constituted in walking through a mall, 'fore-projections are constantly revised as new meanings emerge from the (cultural or concretised) text, constituting the (viewer or visitor's) movement of understanding and interpretation' (Turner, 2003: 6).

This theorising has been developed in specific disciplinary contexts, notably as practices and reception theory. From such a perspective, the authoring audiences of social media and consumers visiting shopping malls, for instance, can be considered behaviourally analogous: they articulate in what they do and say, visually and verbally, narratives of being-with-others. Audiences/consumers everywhere exhibit such a tacit immersive understanding, evident in mundane behaviour, and subsequently available to be 'voiced out' as a practice in focus group discussion with a researcher. Thus *Dasein* 'always operates within some particular understanding of its own being' (Mulhall, 2005: 18), within 'culturally sedimented human self-understandings' (ibid. 38).

Following Ricoeur, to consider an 'action-event' or behaviour as a practice is to recognise it as generically meaningful—perhaps habitually, hence unreflectively, visiting shopping malls or social media. A 'dialectic' operates between the action's 'temporal status as an appearing and disappearing event, and its logical status as having such-and-such (incorporated) identifiable meaning or "sense-content"' as 'text' (1981b: 205). The 'sense-content' of everyday action is generated mostly without a concurrent monitoring consciousness, tacitly anticipated and articulated, taking shape as a type of structured, participatory projection and producing of narrative. *Dasein* 'dwells' (Heidegger) 'within a set of sense-making practices and structures with which it is familiar' (Wheeler, 2011).

> Understanding, which always occurs from out of a particular place and particular time, is the way and manner humans are in the world.
>
> (Nelson, 2001: 150)

Heidegger, then, argues (*Being and Time*) that people necessarily understand their material environment in habitual practices as equipment. Our mode of using tools generates their meaning. 'Encountering objects as ready-to-hand (and so as referred to a particular possibility of *Dasein*'s being) is the fundamental ground of *Dasein*'s being-in-the-world.' (Mulhall, 2005: 52) Using a pen is possible by virtue of our 'fore-having' a 'horizon of understanding' from which we can without reflecting 'fore-see' generic possibilities, a 'schemata of action' (De Certeau, 1984: xi). Writing, we articulate behaviourally (and tacitly unless issues arise) this 'fore-conception' with particular events, producing individual action, a narrative 'device' (Gonzalez-Polledo and Tarr, 2016: 1457) equipped by paper and pen—emplacing wider perspectives in our achievement.

> We conceive of (an entity) in some particular way or other (our fore-conception), a way which is itself grounded in a broader perception of the particular domain within which we encounter it (our fore-sight), which is in turn ultimately embedded in a particular totality of involvements (our fore-having).
>
> (Mulhall, 2005: 85)

The intelligibility so 'projected' on entities as employed equipment is thereby actualised in accordance with our generic, albeit not reflected on 'fore-sight', that is our preceding 'fore-conception' of the items or 'fore-understanding' (Heidegger, 1962). The meaning of a 'mall' is materialised in the event of use, realising our expectations. Meaningfulness is thus 'fore-structured' (ibid.) by public concept: 'The world is always the one that I share with others' (ibid.). We so use hammers with an already acquired practical understanding in modes of (directly or indirectly) 'being-with-others'. Knowing is thereby 'ontologically founded on being-in-the-world' (Moran, 2000: 228). Hermeneutics here is not only an account of interpreting the world—epistemology—but also of our core constitutive nature as existing in that world or an 'ontological hermeneutics' (Chang and Horrocks, 2008) of practices. In this way, understanding is the primordial 'mode of being' in the world (Koch, 1995: 831).

Our instantiated generic awareness (experiencing entities as types of equipment) underwrites subsequent actions as our realising their possibility, our behaviour being 'grounded in *something we grasp in advance—in a fore-conception*' (Heidegger, 1962: emphasis in original). The fore-conceiving of entities is synthesised with events—customarily without reflection—to produce a specific narrative, the 'definite character' (ibid.) which focuses fore-understanding. Behaviour narrows a perspective embodied in particular activity. The body is seen as 'a purposeful activity engaging the world in its projects' (Polkinghorne, 1994: 139). Yet should routine expectation clash with eventual experience, requiring resolution, we experience 'facticity' (ibid.). In summary of this hermeneutic thinking,

> our understanding is *interpretive* from the very start and that interpretive involvement with things need not be at a level of intellection or cognition, but more usually comes in concernful, practical dealings.
>
> (Moran, 2000: 231; emphasis in original)

Philosophers following in such a hermeneutic tradition of regarding intelligibility as being fundamentally practical (notably but not only Gadamer and Ricoeur) emphasise their metaphorical spatio-temporal model of understanding as (in)formed by 'horizons' of cultural interpretation, with which we may align—or from which audiences, consumers and readers can distance themselves in critical 'alienation'. So, for instance, writing on a 'hermeneutics from the margins', Kumar (2017) holds that the 'task' is to 'describe the alienating traces that the coloniser's conceptual imposition has left on her present concepts' (19). 'Horizons' are conceptually a familiar, if little considered or reflected-upon 'frame of reference' (Bruun, 2010: 727). Horizons of understanding, the line which we take, is our perspective on experience. We can arrive from horizons of understanding, be located on horizons of understanding or turn our backs. Horizons can be intruded on, enforced.

Positioning as well as being positioned by the person, mentally and materially, 'horizons of understanding' are not only cultural boundaries framing and informing our speech. For they can be seen as embodied and behaviourally evident as in a visitor whose style of confidently walking declares, 'basically, I expect good security from the mall.' Cultural-material 'horizons' are our distant points of reference for rendering 'fields' of engaging with the world (such as malls) intelligible: they form positions from which consumers engage in habitual activity. Horizons mark out 'habitus' (Bourdieu, 1990), shaping our being circumscribed or 'predisposed' (Burkitt, 2002: 225) to respond in modes unreflectively held as appropriate to places, through habituated action not consciously calculated for a reason. Socially (in)formed affective horizons of understanding or personal habitus have 'instilled generic dispositions' (Maciel and Wallendorf, 2016) to anticipate and act accordingly, behaviourally incorporating normally little attended to cognition and competence. Habitual practices, writes Susen, tracing out a political dimension for habitus, are 'situated within a background horizon' of shared belief providing 'symbolic and material resources': thereby embodied and culturally underwritten, 'an ideology permeates people's quotidian practices', so 'structuring embodied actions' (2014: 105, 91). Horizons of understanding can be challenged, or analytically explored, becoming reflectively disputed territory as 'schemes of perception and appreciation deposited, in their incorporated state, in every member of the group, i.e. the dispositions of the habitus' (Bourdieu, 1977: 17). From this hermeneutic perspective, my 'lived body can be the carrier of my personal past' (Koster, 2017: 171).

The little regarded habitus or embodied horizon of understanding from which we proceed in the world shapes our disposition to behave appropriately (as we would claim on reflection).

> The habitus—embodied history, internalised as a second nature and so forgotten as history—is the active presence of the whole past of which it is the product. As such, it is what gives practices their relative autonomy with respect to external determinations of the immediate present.
>
> (Bourdieu, 1977: 56)

A 'habitus', argues Crossley (2001), 'consists in dispositions, schemas, forms of know-how and competence' (83), clearly linking Bourdieu's concept with Heidegger's preceding formulae of generic understanding-in-practices shaped by cultural horizons (see the following section). However, he concludes, reluctantly, 'the concept of the habitus hints at the possibility for a hermeneutic dimension to social analysis but sadly does no more than hint' (ibid.: 98). Below, this 'hint' is hermeneutically pursued.

Understanding-in-Practices: Reflecting on Consumer Culturally Situated Behaviour

> Just as the objects with which we deal must be understood primarily in relation to purposes and possibilities-of-being embedded in cultural practices, so we must understand ourselves primarily as practitioners—as followers of the norms definitive of proper practice in any given field of endeavour.
>
> (Mulhall, 2005: 72)

In this summative paragraph, concluding a discussion of Heidegger's hermeneutics, the philosopher is clearly foregrounded as practice theorist, arguably the first. My later chapters will consider the extent to which subsequent scholars in business and media studies, psychology and sociology can also be regarded as hermeneutically inclined practice theorists of consumption.

Here it is useful to set out a statement of hermeneutic practices theory, to which reference can be made in deciding whether a disciplinary contribution is hermeneutic, a practices theory or invokes both perspectives on empirical research as does Bourdieu, who is clearly aware of scholarly horizons shaping investigative material, meaning and competence. If Heidegger warns of analyses inflected by the 'obvious undiscussed assumption of the person who does the interpreting' (1962: 192), Bourdieu writes of an observer who 'interpreting practices, is inclined to introduce into the object the principles of his (sic) relation to the object' (1977: 2). Likewise, recommending caution in constructing textual meaning, Gadamer emphasises, 'the important thing is to be aware of one's own bias, so that the text can present itself in all its otherness and thus assert its own truth against one's own fore-meanings' (1975: 269). Allocating content to categories is not merely an exercise in the recent or remote history of ideas (important as that can be): future oriented, such a positioning process also supports perspectives on advancing disciplinary research, even the very questions that it suggests one asks of research participant 'voices' on a page of transcription. 'Meaning-making is at the core of human experience' (Shaw, 2010: 235) drawing upon memory to shape coherency.

'Understanding', then, for Heidegger, is fundamentally understanding-in-practice. 'Such an understanding is contained in our knowing-how-to cope in various domains rather than in a set of beliefs that such and such is the case.' (Dreyfus, 1991: 18) Our tacit practical understanding can be later interpreted, yielding the essentially temporal 'fore-structure' (below) of eight 'moments'. As Polt puts it, 'Heidegger is proposing that being has to be grasped *in terms of time*: our sense of what it is to be must depend on temporality' (1999: 25) (emphasis in original).

Hermeneutics distinguishes between the subjectively experienced or internal 'differentiated time or a qualified duration which in turn is constituted of repetitions, ruptures, and surprises' and the 'time of the clock and the metronome' a 'homogenous and quantitative parameter' (Lefebvre et al., 1999: 9). 'Repetitions' and 'ruptures' are an aspect or characteristic moment of anticipated and habituated experience, disrupted by unexpected events challenging the activity's goal-directed tacit hermeneutic circle of integrated completion. Measured clock time is 'homogeneous'. As Urry wrote on touristic travel, 'there are multiple kinds of time involved in the process of travel and not just the measured clock-time that people seek to minimise in getting from A to B' (2006: 358).

A hermeneutic perspective on the audience or consumer habituated practices of constructing communal meaning can be briefly stated, instantiated by mall visitors. Practices are implicitly typical: exemplified by engaging fore-structured anticipation with enabled action, they generate meaning from their 'shared background of shared specific anticipations' (Shotter, 2015: 75). Following earlier philosophical communication research seeking to establish a 'set of core themes centring on human action' (Dahlgren, 1988b: 189–190), practices, I argue, articulate a triple 'thematic infrastructure' as embodied, equipped, embedding or emplacing wider perspectives in behavioural circumstances. As statement of a structure, these themes are 'somewhat timeless and universal in character' (ibid.).

In habituated practices, embodied generic understanding is without reflection instantiated by particular behaviour as in earlier examples of rejecting 'flawed' apples or walking securely through the mall—involving more or less attention. Their unpacked narrative can constitute a philosophical rejection of empiricism's 'unmediated' seeing—for 'understanding already presupposes in its fore-structures what interpretation is to provide' (Bilimoria, 1998). So transcending Heidegger's (1962) dualist opposition between unreflective habituated behaviour and subsequent reflection in the face of issues, *practices* in their visibly—and probably vocally—constructing publicly available meaning:

i. are tacitly 'fore-structured' (ibid.)—presupposed by their analytical 'interpretation' (ibid.): such structuring is indicated (ii to viii) and disclosed in reflection during discussion in focus group/ interview;
ii. assume 'fore-having' (ibid.) available *resources*, that is their 'involvements' (ibid.) with cultural/ material equipment (e.g. visitors to malls where research was conducted often carried a cell phone with camera, used routinely);
iii. anticipate or 'fore-see' (ibid.) *meaning* built from shared *generic* 'horizons of understanding'—namely, from a point of view 'pressing towards' (Dreyfus, 1991) instantiating a type of activity (thus, one of the mall visitors suggested to a friend, 'why not we just take one of those pictures?');
iv. articulate *competently* (Shove et al., 2012) a behavioural narrative, tacitly negotiated through their implicit 'hermeneutic circle of

understanding' (Gadamer, 1975) between such embodied habituated generic understanding or 'fore-conception' (Heidegger, 1962) and equipment at hand (taking that picture);

v. actualise participatory 'being-with-others' (ibid.), through immediate and related behavioural narrative (the mall visitor appearing above exclaimed, 'when we meet, that time you know, it was like, like after letting out everything': the photograph 'was a closing of our meeting').

Generic understanding (iii) informs our anticipatory fore-conception (iv) so materialised in production. Participating can shape (vi) alignment and hence (vii) 'application' (Gadamer, 1975) or alternatively (viii) 'alienation'—a distanciating practical criticism (Ricoeur, 1981a) with formation of audience 'self'. A mall visitor decried, as 'younger generation', 'sometimes when we go into certain shops they look at us as if we don't have money to buy . . . I think that is just the negative side'.

Where anticipation parts company with fact, fresh horizons of understanding and habits can be discovered. 'As active elements of a practice, perception and memory yield to adjustments and accommodations between bodily gestures and a material arrangement.' (Bourdieu, 1977: 59) Thus a horizon of expectation can be explored philosophically and practically.

Such an account of mall visitor responses advances beyond an opposition between the 'pre-reflective' consumer understanding embodied in a practice tacitly integrating fore-conception with fact and their reflecting on an 'object of thought' (Crossley, 2001: 90) when issues arise (Heidegger, 1962). Horizons of understanding may easily accommodate experience, but can be challenged. As noted earlier, our focussed reflection can itself become habituated as an 'ongoing, embodied process of reflection' (Couldry, 2009a: 580). Moreover, liminal consumer celebratory reflection may occur in the midst of habituated practice, for a monitoring 'moment' suspending a pre-reflective process.

> It was a happy . . . happiness but is something more because I remember at this moment when we took the picture it was something that you want it to last.

In summary, I have set out initially my perception of 'practices', variously referenced from business to societal studies. Although its source is Heidegger, he has in his turn appropriated theory from Husserl (such as the latter's temporal ideas of 'protention' and 'retention' or anticipation and remembering). Moreover, while attacking Descartes' dualism, Heidegger's fundamental distinction between pre-reflective and reflected-upon behaviour is itself dualistic. 'Horizon' as a philosophical concept is earlier seen at the heart of Husserl's phenomenology, and it is more thoroughly given its historical and sociological significance by the later Gadamer. Nonetheless, Heidegger prompted the hermeneutic turn from the subjective and can be regarded as an initiating source of practice theory. In a fore-structured understanding pervading everyday practices, people project intelligibility upon the world from cultural horizons as 'principles of vision and division' (Bourdieu, 1998: 8). Arguing that 'we have preconceived sets of expectations which we carry in our heads' (Marotta, 2009: 280), Heidegger anticipates Ricoeur's thesis that narrative practices are generically 'prefigured' (1988).

> Throughout the various experiences sedimented in personal history, a generalised experiential horizon is gradually shaped and reshaped in a dynamic process that sediments to inherent anticipatory features of *how things appear to me* (. . .) it is generally a process that takes place pre-reflectively.
>
> (Koster, 2017: 181; emphasis in original)

Gadamer: Hermeneutic Practices as Reading: Understanding's Applicative Aspect ('Moment')

Gadamer's *Truth and Method* (1975), while focussed on the practice of textual understanding rather than our making sense of behaviour more widely, places Heidegger's account of knowing in a context of historical and social thought. As Thompson writes, this 'fundamental historicity of being unveiled in Heidegger's analytic of *Dasein* forms a central theme in the work of Gadamer'. Time is theorised as locating in tradition: 'projection of meaning which governs understanding is not the act of an isolated subjectivity, but stems from the tradition to which one belongs' (1981a: 40–41). Here Gadamer's (ironically entitled) *Truth and Method* focusses on projection of textual meaning:

> Whereas Heidegger is primarily concerned with the anticipation of existence that is involved in every understanding and that his hermeneutics of existence is interrogating, Gadamer seems to concentrate more on the certainly more limited problem of text interpretation in the human sciences.
>
> (Grondin, 2002: 48)

Yet audience and consumer literacy—their constructive understanding of texts—is central to the 'critical analysis of people's engagement with media' (Livingstone, 2008: 53) with which we are concerned. Gadamer continues Heidegger's emphasis on understanding as process and practice, on applicative knowing *how* as preceding knowing *that* a state of affairs obtains. 'To understand is thus to apply, Gadamer strongly argues, following Heideggerian premises.' (Grondin, 2002: 38)

Our understanding as habituated consumers in/of malls and media, engaging with their use, tacitly presumes their being ready to hand in equipping us. Through this 'anticipatory movement of our pre-understanding' (Pickering, 1999: 181), we apply or project a generic knowing *how*, producing behavioural narrative. For Gadamer, continuing the Aristotelian emphasis on practice, the 'idea of application is inherent in hermeneutics' (Tharakan, 2014: 227) or as Roy and Oludaja (2009: 261) more explicitly assert, 'Gadamer sees philosophical hermeneutics as situated in practice' with its embodied, equipped and (broadly) ethical goal attaining or teleological commitment intact. Thus understanding a text is a particular instance of practical understanding: 'To understand a text can also mean that one knows one way around the text' (Grondin, 2002: 40).

As 'hermeneutic subjects', rather than assembling empiricism's 'sense-data' to constitute our environment of material entity, 'we do not respond to the world with an untuned sensibility' (Davey, 2006: 51) but rather from culturally inflected horizons of understanding. While our perspective may be limiting, occluding difference, rendering the curious 'incapable of framing certain questions, and entertaining certain possibilities' (Taylor, 2002: 130), a point of view can be augmented and broadened. The practice of understanding is culturally (in)formed: thus 'all understanding proceeds from what precedes it—this is the *Vorstruktur des Verstehens*, its prestructure' (Roberge, 2011: 7). So engaging with the world from a horizon of understanding we experience its worldly content *as* chairs, tables, yellow suitcases, not as sensory 'data' which we then (instantly?) assemble into objects. Seeing a chair, we tacitly assume ['project' (Gadamer, 1975)] that this generic 'equipment' on our examining would be perceived as possessing further features. We experience entities from a horizon of actual and possible perceptions constituting knowledge of their identity, placing them within a horizon or framework of temporal belief (some of which may be specific to the equipment) as well as spatially. Practical use of equipment emplaces (and is equally emplaced within) a horizon of assumption—practices 'make contact with the world' (Cahill, 2016: 515) through meaningful, unreflective action.

Here Gadamer employs his core spatio-temporal metaphor of 'horizons' in obtaining a wide conceptual purchase on the practice of understanding. 'Understanding is always the fusion of these horizons supposedly existing by themselves' (1975: 306). Making sense of a media programme, we extend our horizons of understanding to include (albeit not necessarily align ourselves with) perspectives on screen. As Vessey writes in commentary on the concept of 'horizon', 'horizons might function as a limit at a particular time, but they are always also gateways to something beyond' (2009: 533). Equally, in entering a shopping mall from a horizon of understanding its space as secure, this perspective on place is integrated with its material horizon incorporating such supportive arrangements (e.g. with 'built in' closed-circuit television). Corporeal and concretised horizons of understanding merge. In commenting on 'servicescapes' like shopping malls, Johnstone remarks that such places have been 'viewed in terms of (their) temporal, spatial, natural, and social dimensions' (2012: 1399), thereby pointing to a practices analysis as here appropriate in terms of considering these locations as being engaged by visitors entering from spatio-temporally shared horizons of understanding.

'Horizons change for a person who is moving' (Gadamer, 1975: 304). While understanding pursues integration of meaning (accommodating content within a horizon of understanding), it can also be dialogically challenged by subjective experience (Warren, 2005: 19), reflected on and revised with a new perspective adopted. Grondin holds that a 'basic hermeneutic experience (in the strong sense of *Erfahrung*)' is for Gadamer 'experience that our anticipations of understanding have been shattered' (2002: 44). Davey makes the point in a more restrained mode: 'reflective reappropriation' of 'overlooked fore-understandings' occurs (2006: 11) as potential horizons of understanding. 'We cannot think beyond our horizons, we can only expand' (Trede et al., 2009) their perspectival view, by our epistemologically moving to 'boundaries where different communities of practice interpret the same object in different ways' (Powell, 2015: 379).

Importantly, Gadamer is decisively not a constructivist arguing that our 'conceptual grids are differently constructed': looking at life-worlds from such a philosophical perspective, 'how will we ever be able to convince each other, even understand each other?' (Taylor, 2002: 136). He is instead a 'conversationalist'. 'Understanding emerges in the fusion of these horizons as the two are brought together in dialogue' (Gimbel, 2016: 79). Through discussion our far from shuttered or sequestered perspectives can be extended, our horizons of understanding 'fused' or indeed revisited and revised. Understanding as a process 'requires and perpetuates a mode of differentiation' (Davey, 2006: 5). From distinct horizons of understanding, an object can appear differently or on the boundary of interpreting, a conversational 'bridge' between varying dialogical cultural perspectives:

> Boundary objects are defined by their capacity to serve as bridges between intersecting social and cultural worlds. Anchored in, and thus meaningful across, these worlds, they create the conditions for collaboration whilst, by way of their interpretive flexibility, not requiring 'deep sharing'.
>
> (Nicolini et al., 2012: 614)

In Gadamer's philosophical hermeneutics, then, the idea of behaviour deploying a culturally and historically located 'horizon of understanding' becomes both central and clearly articulated, not least in his analyses of a perspectivally extending 'fusion of horizons'. To anticipate and actualise a narrative is to bring it within the horizon of its generic understanding. Our fundamental anticipation—particularly in operating the integrative hermeneutic circle—is of an intelligible or coherent world. Yet we can see limits to our horizons of understanding, curtailment of perspectives. Here we reflect upon 'narratives in which we find ourselves': 'insofar as we are "thrown" (therein), their languages and trajectories necessarily provide the contours for our understanding' (Warnke, 2002: 80).

> Hermeneutic reflection merely uncovers the conditions under which understanding *always already* and in each case operates—as our 'pre-understanding' (. . .) philosophical hermeneutics concludes that understanding is in fact only possible when one brings one's own presuppositions into play! (emphasis in original).
>
> (Gadamer, 2006: 45)

The literary theorist Iser subsequently draws on and develops a Gadamerian hermeneutics, materialising his account of manufacturing meaning, asserting that where content is 'indeterminate' an informed audience fills out a textual narrative. So presuming possibility of understanding a text, habituated media users project a generically shaped fore-conception of content, without reflection producing (in a hermeneutic circle relating expectation to event) specific narrative (cf. Das, 2016). Consistent with practices theory, texts can become refiguring equipment to 'interpret, negotiate and make sense of real, lived relationships and reality' (Das, 2016: 352).

Establishing his reception theory of a reader's practices underwritten by earlier hermeneutic phenomenology, Iser asserts that a 'reader's mind' works on the 'raw material of the text' ('sentences, statements, information') producing narrative 'connections'. This cumulative process of 'anticipation and retrospection' does not 'develop in a smooth flow': instead, it is said to involve an uneven 'sort of kaleidoscope of perspectives, preintentions, recollections' (1974: 279). Nonetheless, on an occasion where the 'flow is interrupted' by the unexpected, readers have a particular opportunity to synthesise a story. Thus 'while expectations may be continually modified' and 'images continually expanded' the 'reader will still strive, even if unconsciously, to fit everything together in a consistent pattern' (ibid: 283). In short, Iser argues, summarising this reception 'process (which) is virtually hermeneutic':

> The text provokes certain expectations which in turn we project onto the text in such a way that we reduce the polysemantic possibilities to a single interpretation in keeping with the expectations aroused, thus extracting an individual, configurative meaning.
>
> (285)

Iser and Jauss develop an account of reception practices (Holub, 1984: 83). As noted, Iser argues that a reader's projection of narrative meaning overcomes 'indeterminacies' in the text—so coherent stories are constructed. In this context, the essentially hermeneutic thesis that consumers' awareness of aesthetic form and genre establishes an interpersonal framework or a 'horizon of what is expected' (Jauss, 1982a: 17) is a useful conceptual tool. It allows reception studies to analyse our awareness of books as a knowledge of past narrative pattern so supporting the psychological play of anticipation and connecting in the reader's textual understanding, in their presuming, projecting and producing meaning. Consumed always already within a tradition shaping sense-making,

> the new text evokes for the reader (listener) the horizon of expectations and rules familiar from earlier texts, which are then varied, corrected, altered, or even just reproduced.
>
> (Jauss, 1982b: 23)

A text makes 'offers of identification' (Jauss, 1982a: 93), allowing consumers and characters to agree in achieving intelligible narrative. Positioned similarly in establishing sense, those reading and those read may also identify ideologically. Politics and meaning can be mediated. As subjects-in-play, we are embodied stories (in)formed by developing narrative projects. Play has a central role in the 'determination of the meaning of hermeneutic universality' (O'Connor, 2016: 267). Thus Vilhauer writes emphatically that the idea of '"play" elucidates the very structure of understanding in general—that understanding which stretches through all of our hermeneutic experience' (2009: 359)—to be appropriated in renewed self-perception, 'absorption in new meaning and return to self' (ibid.: 362). The centrality of ludic activity fulfilling anticipation in the everyday practice of our understanding, completing a hermeneutic circle integrating intelligible generic narrative, supports our 'taking play seriously' (Kücklich, 2004: 4) in understanding tacit consumer response to mall and media. Play is implicit in tacit unreflected upon negotiation between fore-understanding and fact, with occasional 'collision of fore-understanding and material not fitting' (Smith, 2007: 10).

> The play-process of understanding can occur both verbally (as when one reads a text, or has a conversation) and non-verbally (as in dance, silent rituals, or a multitude of basic practical tasks involved in our 'being in the world') (Vilhauer, 2015: 1), an embodied achievement of narrative, tacitly yet teleologically building intelligibility.

Ricoeur: Practices as Generically Configured Behaviour

We have seen that for Ricoeur actions have 'temporal status' as events and 'logical status' as texts for he does not consider 'all texts are linguistic entities' (Piercey, 2016: 413). Whether they are engaging with actions or texts through habitual practice, consumers are understood to unreflectively presume, project and produce 'sense-content' (Ricoeur, 1981b: 205), a behavioural narrative.

> Heidegger rightly says, in his analysis of *Verstehen* in *Being and Time*, that what we understand first in a discourse is not another person, but a 'pro-ject', that is, the outline of a new way of being in the world.
>
> (Ricoeur, 1976: 37)

The meaning of a text, like actions, is tacitly prefigured: it is 'projected in accordance with an anticipatory schema' (Thompson, 1981b: 16) or 'preunderstandings' (Wilson, R.E., 2015: 888). In the process of its realisation, content is configured generically, able to be recast or refigured locally in being appropriated by a 'reader'. 'Without the reader who accompanies it, there is no configuring act at work in the text: and without a reader to appropriate it, there is no world unfolded before the text.' (Ricoeur, 1988: 164) Appropriation or an application to the reader's world presumes generic placing of action or text: 'if a work is produced according to generic (and genetic) rules, it is also produced as a singular being' (Ricoeur, 1976: 77).

Explicitly connecting (a tacit) generic prefigurative understanding to configuring a practice, Ricoeur establishes for discursive meaning a thesis equally applicable to action. To 'impose a form'

> 'upon material, to submit production to genres, to produce an individual: these are so many ways of treating language as a material to be worked upon and formed. Discourse thereby becomes the object of a *praxis* and a *techne*' (1981a: 136), an individual text or action tacitly produced as cultural and technical accomplishment.

Submitting 'production to genres' or perceiving instance as conforming to 'custom', fundamentally underwrites understanding. Whether practices produce action or text, a 'genre is implemented in the production of a singular work' (Thompson, 1981a: 52) and recoverable in reflecting. Hermeneutics is thus 'concerned with the textual treatment of social settings' (Harvey and Myers, 1995: 20).

As a much travelled quilter in Hui's (2013) research on the phenomenon asserts, 'I saw this piece of work and it was very similar to what we'd been doing' (7). Despite her crossing cultural and geographical horizons of understanding, perspectives from which her production is (in)formed differently, she recognises the details of a sighted 'work' as 'very similar' to generic past practice.

Likewise in regard to audience reception practice, a 'configurational act' that 'com-prehends (sic), that "grasps together" details of action' within 'recognising the formal rule, the genre, or the type exemplified by the narrated story' (Ricoeur, 1983: 76). Configuring itself involves the complex behavioural genre of viewers tacitly producing an 'individual' narrative meaning 'worked upon and formed' (Ricoeur, 1981a: 136) through a prefigured response to media content. Genre traverses both the 'world of the text' and 'its complement, the life-world of the reader' (Ricoeur, 1985: 160).

In television audience research, Hamzah and Syed (2013) discuss the generic 'exercise' by Malay women in producing meaningful narratives for foreign soap operas of 'cultural resources' or 'competencies for negotiating the depiction of modernity in soap operas while retaining their values and expectations' (2013: 148), so maintaining their cultural horizon of understanding. Such skilled managing 'to make meanings' from cultural resources is evident in tacitly exercised cultural *praxis* or 'second nature' 'watching competencies'. Thus 'there is no precise or set framework demanding application, more an inbred sense of what is the right and fitting response in the circumstances' of watching 'foreign soaps' (Syed and Runnel, 2014: 6–7), enabling appropriate modes of being-with-others beyond the generic practice of producing meaning on screen. Paradoxically, the continuous serial from overseas equips these women in 'placing primacy on the Malay cultural order' (ibid.). Their watching competencies extend beyond tacitly conjoining narrative segments to form a story—as tacit knowing how to make/see meaning appropriately from cultural horizons of understanding.

In summary, the horizons of understanding from which we enter practices—remembering or initiating action—are generic: we engage not with entities *simpliciter* but with instantiated types of 'work'. From walking securely in the mall to watching television, generic knowing (albeit mostly tacit) constitutes 'generative' competence enabling particular implementation of a practice—a work.

> To master a genre is to master a 'competence' which offers practical guidelines for 'performing' an individual work. We should have to add that the same competence in the reader helps him (sic) to perform the corresponding operations of interpretation according to the rules prescribed by the 'genre' for both *sending* and *receiving* a certain type of message: a 'genre has a *genetic* function rather than a *taxonomic* function': 'it belongs to the function of "genres" to be directed toward the production of those individuals which we call works'.
>
> (Ricoeur, 1973: 135–136, 137; emphasis in original)

While Ricoeur shares Gadamer's account of appropriating meaning, one's distance from the text, particularly temporal, offers a space or a disjunctive separating of horizons, in which alienated critique becomes possible: thus within such 'productive distanciation', 'the predicament of cultural distance would be transformed into an epistemological instrument' (Ricoeur, 1976: 89). Necessarily to be overcome in the productive understanding of narrative, nonetheless cultural distance between Malaysian female audiences and foreign soap opera (Syed and Runnel, 2014) facilitates criticism:

> I know that Korean and Filipino soaps show many habits of urbanised western lifestyle such as drinking, clubbing and pre-marital sexual relationships. I guess all of these things that we consider unacceptable are part of their lifestyle.
>
> (Female, city dweller)

Critique of ideology here 'rests on the moment of *distanciation*' (original emphasis) (Ricoeur, 1991a: 35). Ideological distortion can be held to inflect the 'interpretation that a social group offers of itself by means of collective representations' (Ricoeur, 1981c: 38) or the shared horizons of self-understanding from which practices are entered and engaged. A critical hermeneutics directs itself at cultural 'emancipation (which) would be quite empty and abstract if it were not situated on the same plane as the historical-hermeneutic sciences (. . .) communicative action' (Ricoeur, 1991b: 303). Via such a route, ideological critique of media representations can be 'reinvigorated' (Phelan, 2016).

'Cultural estrangement' (Ricoeur, 1976: 43) may be exercised by consumers from marketing media whose generic narrative meaning they have configured. 'Voicing out', for instance, viewers can distance themselves from an advertisement because of concern appropriate to ethnic citizenship. Responding to cell phone network branding on television showing a Chinese family reunion dinner where all are using the global company's routes to call *elsewhere*—rather than chat with physically nearer and so presumably dearer relatives—my Chinese research participants occupied a 'horizon of suspicion', distinctively distant from embodied horizons of understanding within the text. 'It seems like the relationship between the family is not very close' (female, Chinese).

> Just '(when) the whole family is taking the dinner, you're supposed . . . don't answer the phone': 'a bit offensive, it breaks the (Chinese) tradition . . . . You really have to focus on the dinner, not on the phone' (laughter) (male, Chinese): it is 'out of your culture' (male, Eurasian): 'you better go out to talk with your friends, lah!' (female, Chinese).

Understanding again is application, shown to be finding one's way around text and life. 'From the Ricoeurian standpoint any interpretive activity is intimately related to self-understanding' (Dorairaj, 2000: 407). Advertising is here (inadvertently) challenging the prefigured practice of Chinese New Year Reunion, prompting reflection on the horizons of understanding from whence it is conducted. Appropriating meaning or alienated, the 'reader' (or the viewer) is the 'ultimate mediator between configuration and refiguration'. This reading is 'no longer that which the text prescribes; it is that which brings the structure of the text to light through interpretation' (Ricoeur, 1988: 160, 165). Organising 'events into a narrative unity' prescribed in life or text, refiguring 'emplotment', is open to the reader's interpretation:

> 'This process of emplotment, which moves from prefiguration through configuration to the refiguration of experience, offers practical proposals for living, prescriptions *for* identity (. . .) through the refiguring reconnection of the world of the text to the world of the reader'—so transforming ' "seeing as" into "being as" '.
>
> (Venema, 2000: 240, 242)

Summary so far: To initiate a practice is to engage in generically configured habituated hence tacit behaviour (Ricoeur). A practice's embodied and equipped action (Heidegger) or narrative presumes, projects and produces shared horizons of understanding (Gadamer). One can join practices (align), be alienated (Ricoeur)—or be apathetic towards an instance of these behavioural genres. Practices are (re)integrated with reality, materialising a hermeneutic circle of understanding (Gadamer).

'Heidegger holds that these non-deliberative coping skills are the most fundamental way humans make sense of things' (Polkinghorne, 2000: 458), so 'primordially' understanding entities as equipment employed in embodied 'knowing-in-action' (Willems, 2018: 24). These incorporated, instrumental and implicit aspects (or 'moments') of understanding thereby define the 'essential or universal structures of our experience as worldly or bodily situated subjects' (Olivier, 2017: 9).

In this chapter, we have now considered practice theories' roots—or should one say routes?—within hermeneutic phenomenology and the latter as the source of appropriate analytical concept. Hermeneutics from the outset emphasised the teleological 'primordial' (Heidegger, 1962) practical moment of understanding as equipped, as a tacit negotiation between generic 'prefigured' assuming and actuality, or one's 'configuring' (Ricoeur, 1988) behaviour. Configured action can be 'appropriated' (Gadamer, 1975) or 'refigured' (Ricoeur, 1988) in reflection, both celebratory and critical (Langdridge, 2008).

Hermeneutic spatio-temporal metaphor, moreover, (such as 'circle of understanding', 'fore-understanding', 'distanciation', 'fusion', 'horizons', 'projection') supports exploring quite discrete as well as socially shared 'understanding', so appearing analytically apposite to discussing spatially significant behaviour as with travelling [e.g. from our 'horizons of expectation' (Jauss (1982a)]. The theorising of 'action' as 'text' (Ricoeur, 1981b) is a further core metaphor, enabling specific action to be considered as tacitly instantiating genre, or a pattern implicit in practice.

Literary and media theory have long acknowledged genres to be more or less encompassing, as with behavioural types.

Horizons of understanding can be said to circumscribe political-social positioning, assumed/entered/occupied at particular points of embodied perception—enabling anticipatory projection of narrative. Hermeneutic meaning-making practices underwrite ubiquitous media production as well as reception, implicitly instantiated by mundane walking in malls as well as watching people go by. Practices can be specific (buying apples) or more extended (enjoying security). The conceptual—or logical relationship—between supportive generic narrower and wider horizons of understanding in communicating is worthy of study, not least when crossing cultural borders. What is the dispositional connection between expecting security in a mall and expressing 'bonding' in cell phone photos?

People are always already engaged in generic practices, tacitly recognising and responding to entities (apples, narrative) in producing their meaning as equipment from collective horizons of understanding. Echoing such philosophy, albeit considering more socially encompassing practices, Schatzki argued in his early defining practice theory (2001a) that the 'social is a field of embodied, materially interwoven practices centrally organised around shared practical understandings' (12). A practice's 'constitutive elements' are, summarily, 'meanings, competences, materials' (Shove, 2014a: 419). Practices (from choosing apples to viewing television programme without 'flaws') can involve a tacit implicit 'tactics of consumption, the ingenious ways in which the weak make use of the strong, thus lend(ing) a political dimension' (De Certeau, 1984: xvii) to consuming.

Embodying horizons or 'parameters' (Morley, 1992: 52) of understanding, *praxis* produces our appropriate achievement or right living. '*Praxis* involves ethical know-how' (Roy and Oludaja, 2009: 260). Recognising the Aristotelian 'philosophical precursors of the practice industry' (Rouse, 2001: 198), the next chapter pursues integrating earlier hermeneutic philosophy with practice social theories to constitute practices as hermeneutically oriented, implicitly constructing meaning. Habitually embodied 'horizons of understanding', from where entities are experienced as being equipment, are politically and socially constituted, shared or distancing (as is a mall marketed as 'adventure').

Heidegger's philosophy (1962) and practice theories (Reckwitz, 2002a) concur in viewpoint.

> That aspect of the world that is closest to us is the structure of equipment, of things ready for use, that immediately surrounds us, and this structure is one that is essentially ordered in terms of what such things are *for*—it is ordered teleologically.
>
> (Malpas, 2006: 83; emphasis in original)

2 Hermeneutic Social Theory of Practices

Conjoining Philosophy and Sociology

Project

In this second chapter, drawing on hermeneutic philosophy, we shall consider further the thesis that practices are generic (Ricoeur)—hence little reflected on—purposive patterns of socially emplaced and embodied, equipped, habituated (Heidegger) activity. Our practices are instantiated by behaviour presuming, projecting and producing shared horizons of understanding (Gadamer), from celebrating 'bonding' photographically to our walking evincing faith in a facilitated security. We live within an ideational horizon from which we always already experience a meaningful world, projecting within our practices identities for its entities as equipment or tools for our purposeful use.

To what degree do the accounts of practice theories by Giddens, Reckwitz and Schatzki revisit—converging with or differing from—this earlier thesis? Can present conjoining of philosophical and sociological narratives underwrite a hermeneutic social theory of practices, enabling more analytical insight into socially located consumers talking about generic habituated behaviour?

Giddens: The Hermeneutics of Practical Consciousness

In writing he acknowledges as shaped by preceding philosophical hermeneutics ['under the influence of Heidegger' (Joas, 1987: 16)], Giddens anticipates subsequent practices theory, with its fundamental distinguishing between tacit or unreflective pursuit of equipped goal-oriented routines and enlarging, contextualising awareness discursively reflecting on horizons of this understanding-in-use ('ready-to-hand' and 'presented-at-hand' activity—to use Heidegger's distinction):

> The theory of the subject I outline involves what I call a 'stratification model' of personality, organised in terms of three sets of relations: the unconscious, practical consciousness, and discursive consciousness.
>
> (Giddens, 1979: 2)

> At the heart of this distinction are the 'differences between practical consciousness, as tacit stocks of knowledge which actors draw upon in the constitution of social activity, and what I shall call "discursive consciousness", involving knowledge which actors are able to express on the level of discourse'.
>
> (ibid.: 5)

Giddens and practice theories 'emphasise tacit knowledge, social routines, context, social practices, materiality, frames and agency' (Haslett, 2012) in relating a social structure to human activity. Tacit knowing-in-action or 'practical consciousness' is a 'largely implicit everyday orientation that may, however, be retrieved and reflected upon' (Jensen, 2005: 9).

Giddens wrote more than thirty years ago (1982) that both subject (human agent) and object (society) are 'constituted in and through recurrent practices' (8). Explicating the constitutive process further, following a hermeneutic route in presenting pre-reflective behaviour, Giddens later defines 'practical consciousness' as being 'all the things which actors know tacitly about how to "go on" in the contexts of social life without being able to give them direct discursive expression' (1984: xxiii).

Cultural conventions embodied in generic and generally habituated activity (from purchasing apples to using social media) tacitly inform or impede as a complex social structure referenced in research participant reflective narrative or 'discursive consciousness' (ibid.). Practices in their turn, when not amended or constrained, reiterate social conventions. Earlier (1979) Giddens argued:

> Structures are not external to action, but are only reproduced through the concrete activities of daily life, and must be analysed as historical formations, subject to modification—as structures constituted through action, as much as action is constituted structurally.
>
> (Morley, 1992: 18)

'Structure derives above all from regularised practices', Giddens writes in his *New Rules of Sociological Method* (1993: 7). Writing on 'Structuration Theory: Past, Present and Future' (1991a), he summarises his analytical thesis: 'in structuration theory, the core concern of the social sciences is with recurrent social practices and their transformations' (203).

'Discursive consciousness', 'pre-reflective understanding' (or 'practical consciousness') and 'reflection-in-action' are formulations shaping a discourse hermeneutics of participant contributions to focus groups or interviews. Discursive awareness is what we hear in discussion, making explicit (in so far as possible) a person's earlier, embodied, little reflected-upon understanding. However, a dualism between reflection during discussion and previous unreflected on behaviour is disturbed by occasional reflection-in-action. So, for instance, we later discuss a Malay cell phone photographer in her shopping mall referring to habituated, routine, little reflected-upon behaviour—taking 'selfies'. But she makes the point that in this sustained activity, there also occurred a 'moment' of reflection-in-action: for 'it was something that you want it to last', expanding intimate temporality. Here she brings to our attention the moral horizons of her hermeneutic practice: *praxis* 'carries a moral dimension', competence emplacing a '"concern" for other beings' (Roy and Starosta, 2001: 7).

As we shall see articulated in action (not least during Chinese New Year Reunion Dinners), social (even extended familial) convention in practices can powerfully configure ethnic as well as gendered identity. Here structure is 'present only in its instantiation' (Giddens, 1979: 54) through 'regularised acts' or in 'situated practices'—with the latter concept being recognised by Giddens as 'expressing a major mode of connection between action theory and structural analysis' (ibid.: 56), embedding structural 'rules and resources' (ibid.: 64). His thesis that practices within 'our horizon of day-to-day life' (Giddens, 1991b: 4) provide continuing interactive support for individual action and social structure is reiterated by Schatzki's arguing more recently in similarly hermeneutic mode that 'all social phenomena transpire in the plenum of linked practices and arrangements' (2015: 6). Holism and individualism as accounts of the nature of society or its ontology are here reconciled, albeit with the powerfully productive 'plenum' necessarily a further focus of political reckoning.

Likewise, Taylor regards human agency and consequently identity as (in)formed, as enabled but elided by our positioning on a structuring horizon of understanding: so he 'puts great weight on the human capacity to articulate the frameworks, horizons, and social imaginaries that constitute our identities' (Brinkmann, 2008: 406). Perspectival horizons shape inquiry and answer reflecting upon a practice as a cultural 'form of life' (Wittgenstein, 1991) underwriting action.

> The human agent 'exists in a space of questions. And these are questions to which our framework-definitions are answers, providing the horizon within which we know where we stand, and what meanings things have for us': 'doing without frameworks is utterly impossible for us'.
>
> (Taylor, 1989: 29, 27)

Cultural horizons are 'points of orientation, the reference points provided by frameworks of qualitative contrast' (N. H. Smith, 2002: 97). They are shareable, public, structural and resistant to change—like beliefs about 'guys' as consumers or shopping mall 'security'—albeit that individuals can occupy distinct positions along those epistemological horizons and so act accordingly.

Reckwitz: The Philosophical Genesis of Practice Theory

> One could point out the philosophical background of practice theory, above all Ludwig Wittgenstein's late works (. . .) and Martin Heidegger's early philosophy (. . .) and their radical attempts to reverse common philosophical and everyday vocabularies—and in fact, we find everything that is original in practice theory already in the work of these authors.
>
> (Reckwitz, 2002a: 250)

In this chapter, we follow further the philosophical underwriting of—or identification with—sociology's practice theories. We now explore the distance or proximity between phenomenology's hermeneutics and such theorising by considering a more all-embracing version of Reckwitz' thesis—that 'everything that is original in practice theory (is) already in the work' of Heidegger, Gadamer and Ricoeur as principal proponents of this European philosophy. Resourced within Heideggerian thought is a basic rejecting of *passive* perception as a privileged source of sense-data representing an external world. Instead, *active* understanding-in-practices, modes of knowing *how* constitute the fundamental engaging with the world. 'We use our everyday coping skills or tools without mental representation' (Conroy, 2003: 38). We engage with a material world of purpose-serving equipment as embodied human beings, always already having established its identity within historical horizons of understanding (Gadamer), albeit open to critical distance-taking revision (Ricoeur).

> If we really want to develop a natural conception of ourselves and the world, Heidegger thought, we should reject the representational theory of perception and we should also reject the idea that at the deepest level of analysis the subject is related to the world primarily by perception.
>
> (Philipse, 2009: 32)

As we have now seen, hermeneutics maps out multiple spatio-temporally formed concepts appropriate to interpreting the 'practices' with which this philosophy argues we primordially encounter entities. Practices theory further elaborates.

In his definitive paper 'Toward a Theory of Social Practices' (2002a), Reckwitz argues for seven epistemological characteristics of such a theory related to how 'knowledge', 'body', 'mind' and 'things' are presented as contributing to an underlying recurrent 'structure/process' integrating 'agent/individual' and 'discourse/language' (pp. 251–256). Practices are patterned: they 'necessarily imply certain routinised ways of understanding the world, of desiring something, of knowing how to do something' (ibid.: 251). These 'ways of understanding' are—or can be—shared.

Regarding practices as embodying equipped 'know-how', emplacing an affective 'way of understanding' or 'interpretative perspective', Reckwitz considers 'single agents' entering a practice.

> Single agents in their single mind/ bodies then—independent of one another—'take over' the practice, and thus also its interpretative perspective. Yet, the knowledge that is a constitutive element of a practice is not only a way of understanding; it is—in connection with that—also a know-how and a certain way of wanting and feeling.
> (2002a: 254)

As in the generic, mundanely routine activity of visiting a shopping mall ('basically I expect good security from the mall'), such a practice tacitly 'embraces (collective) ways of understanding, knowing how, ways of wanting and of feeling that are linked to each other within a practice' (253). 'Things' are understood as 'equipment': 'carrying out a practice very often means using particular things in a certain way' (252). Thus meanings are ascribed teleologically (e.g. to security cameras) 'in order to (enable one to) do something' (255). Practices are a fundamental molecular constituent of society: so 'the social world is first and foremost populated by diverse social practices which are carried (out) by agents' (256). People engage with enabling, albeit limiting social structures (e.g. the regulated provision of security). Challenged routines in 'crises' 'break' but can alter, 'shift' with the 'inadequacy of knowledge with which the agent, carrying out a practice, is confronted in the face of a "situation"' (255). As in seeking security in the shopping mall, actions are 'held together' as being a practice, viewed as presuming, projecting and producing a goal from a horizon of understanding.

> This way of understanding is largely implicit and largely historically-culturally specific—it is this form of interpretation that holds together already for the agent herself (the carrier of the practice) the single acts of her own behaviour, so that they form parts of a practice.
> (253)

In a second paper, reminiscent of Heidegger's much earlier positioning of knowing as being practical, Reckwitz emphasises the functional status of 'things' as more than the 'content of cultural "representations"' (2002b: 209). In a practice, entities are equipment. Hammers are 'handled'.

> The central issue then is that certain things or artefacts provide more than just objects of knowledge, but necessary, irreplaceable components of certain social practices, that their social significance does not only consist in their being 'interpreted' in certain ways, but also in

their being 'handled' in certain ways and in being constitutive, effective elements of social practices.

(Ibid.: 210)

Reflecting a decade later (2012), Reckwitz emphasises the epistemologically embedded, embodied and equipped characteristics of 'practices' as core: 'theories of social practice proceed from two interconnected assumptions: one claims that practices are based on tacit knowledge; the other anchors these practices materially in both human bodies and non-human artefacts' (248). Here the generic assumptions or a horizon of understanding which tacitly shapes the conduct of practices earlier referred to as '"type" of behaving and understanding' (Reckwitz, 2002a: 250) are summarised as the 'cultural schemes that pre-consciously execute the work of classification, thus enabling and constraining possible activities' (2012: 248). Tacit prefiguring (in)forms action. In classifying, affects ensue, as when a shopping mall is seen as a site of security: 'affects only form when a space is practically appropriated by its users, which always activates these users' implicit cultural schemes and routines', 'tacit knowledge and schemes of interpretation' (ibid.: 255, 252).

The 'notion of routine' (Schäfer, 2017: 37), embodying little reflected upon, albeit challengeable, knowledge of 'generally and automatically applicable' 'generative schemes' 'always functioning in the implicit state' (Bourdieu, 1977: 16), is central to understanding the mundane maintaining of practices. These tacit competences emerge explicitly in the focus group and research interviewing, encircled by wider horizons of understanding: 'maybe the apples look the same to the guys . . . But, we, we, we pick the apple that looks nicer with no flaws' (female, Chinese). As Papacharissi writes (2015), accessing such '*situated knowledge(s)*' is to 'emphasise the importance of the subject and the context in perceiving, generating, and reproducing knowledge' (1097, emphasis in original).

Schatzki: Practices as Fundamental Social Phenomena

> Social practices 'are nexuses of human activity, open-ended sets of doings and sayings organised by understandings, rules, and teleoaffectivities. These organised activities are inevitably, and often inextricably, bound up with material entities'.
>
> (Schatzki, 2015: 2)

For Schatzki also, practices are (in)formed by participant horizons of understanding. Using terms reminiscent of Wittgenstein's cultural 'forms of life' (1991) inscribed in action, practices are 'collective, social arenas of action that are pervaded by a space of meaning in whose terms people live, interact, and coexist intelligibly' (2005: 470). Purpose, procedures and principles are equally established within this 'space of meaning' (e.g. cell phone photographing in a mall)—'maintaining fields of intelligibility in whose terms they themselves proceed' (Schatzki, 2003a: 190). Earlier, in discussing Giddens' work, he writes 'practice theorists are united by the proposition that practical understanding and intelligibility are articulated in practices.' (Schatzki, 1997: 284)

In Schatzki's systematic narrative of practices, 'purpose' within the 'space of meaning' is denoted as the practice's 'teleoaffective structure' (ibid.) or their 'end-project-action combinations (teleological orderings)' with 'maybe emotions' (2006: 1864). Procedures are 'complexes of know-hows', and their principles or 'rules' are 'explicit directives, admonishments, or instructions' (ibid.). 'We pick the apple that looks nicer with no flaws', asserts our research participant, referencing the 'teleological-affective structuring' (ibid.) behaviourally evident in her rule-governed 'know-how'. 'By teleoaffectivity, I mean orientations toward ends and how things matter' (Schatzki, 1997: 302). For Schatzki, akin to Reckwitz, practices tacitly project (and so produce) their share(able) meaning, centred around socially emplaced, 'corporeally constituted perception' (Kupers, 2015) or embodied competent 'knowing how' (from apple picking to our watching television). Purpose is embodied in practices (McConnell-Henry et al., 2009) as an implicit 'teleological orientation' (Zhok, 2009: 192) circumscribed by wider perspectives. Apples with no flaws cultivate health.

'Practices are both the most basic social phenomenon and the site where intelligibility is articulated' (1996: 13), wrote Schatzki, claiming a Wittgensteinian approach to human activity. The concept of 'practice' can accommodate both experience of constraint from social structure and the latter enabling creative agency: 'social order and individuality (. . .) result from practices' (ibid.).

Considered from a perspective of undertaking sociological research, then, practices, albeit 'action-centred' (Tresch, 2001: 320), are ontologically the fundamental source of insight. Practices are generic, tacitly rule-governed, bodily enunciating horizons of understanding 'acceptable' action.

> An action belongs to a given practice, then, when it expresses understandings, observes rules, and/or expresses one of the range of right and acceptable orders of life conditions that organise the practice.
> (Schatzki, 1997: 304)

'Practice theory holds that social life is made up of, or takes place in or as part of, a plenum, or more neutrally, a big bunch of practices' (Schatzki, 2014: 10). Here practices are foundational molecules (with their purposive procedures and principles as atoms) from which 'social orders are established' (Schatzki, 2002: 23). 'Carried', or composed and continued in a social practice, are 'understandings' or meanings 'expressed in the doings and sayings that compose practices' (ibid.: 58). Hence 'the meanings of the entities amid and through which humans coexistently live derive from activity' (ibid.: 56). Meaning is consequent upon referring to an object's use, suggesting the 'lines of relevance' (Schatzki, 2010: 28) or horizons of intelligibility in what can be said. 'We pick the apple that looks nicer with no flaws' because as fruit, healthy apples provide us with nutrition. 'We *show* or *express* or *manifest* our understandings (of surroundings) in our actions' (Shotter, 2015: 61, emphasis in original), exhibiting our identity-constituting comprehension of 'equipment'.

Practices construct embodied meaning. 'Basically I expect good security from the mall', the research participant informed her focus group, a horizon of expectation from which she enters the mall, articulated and evident in how she carries bag and items bought. These 'mental matters' are 'expressed by bodily doings', the 'manners in which doings are carried out' (Schatzki, 1996: 22).

The meaning of 'manners' is practice-dependent, encircled by shareable horizons of understanding. Similar behaviour (such as a relaxed mode of maintaining personal security, inattention) in distinct practices can express disparate 'mental matters'—carefree shoppers in a familiar mall and careless tourists in unfamiliar street. Behaviour appropriate to particular practices is learned over time from 'reactions, attributions, teachings, and corrections of others' (ibid.: 88).

Discussing organisational practices, Schatzki holds them to be 'organised by practical rules, understandings, teleoaffective structures, and general understandings' (2012: 15). They are clearly socially embedded and as generic maintain 'teleoaffective structures' just as for instance, the genre of cinematic melodrama circulates and celebrates in screen narrative the structure of family life. In this way, inhabiting generic practices of everyday life 'pre-structures' (Schatzki, 2003b: 314) action.

Somewhat tautologically, Schatzki more recently (2016) summarises—dismissing, for instance, an account of society as fundamentally composed of individuals—his view that all 'practice theories are joined in the belief that social phenomena should be analysed by reference to practices, actions, and the organisations of and relations among practices' (29). In turn, Schatzki asserts that practices can collectively constitute 'bundles', or alternatively relate together as 'constellations': a 'bundle' is 'a relatively tight, densely knit agglomeration of practices and arrangements', while a 'constellation' is a 'looser, more thinly interwoven set of such agglomerations' (2015: 5). In malls, perhaps able to be characterised as 'bundles', 'diverse sets of practices anchored in extraordinarily disparate material arrangements converge around an increasingly standardised form' (Shove, 2014b: 31).

Reckwitz and Schatzki provide a closely articulated, philosophically resourced account of a social practice with its 'space of meaning' centred on action, open to being conceptually synthesised with hermeneutic narrative of generic meaning created and instantiated by particular acts. *Practices* from a resulting hermeneutic social theory perspective can be considered to invoke a generic pattern of equipped (requiring know-how), embodied and socially emplaced (hence rule-governed) activity—presuming, projecting and producing goals (or 'teleological-affective structuring')—engaged from a tacit horizon of wider cultural or 'general understanding' (Schatzki, 2006: 1864) of behaviour. As noted earlier, Shove's summative statement that a practice's 'constitutive elements' are 'meanings, competences, materials' (Shove, 2014a: 419) provides a suitable conclusion to exploring a synthesis of theory.

Before viewing accounts of visiting malls and media from a hermeneutic social theory perspective on practices as understanding-in-use, we discuss the 'practice turn in contemporary theory'. For 'understandings are carried in the practices in which the actor participates' (Schatzki, 2000: 100).

Unfortunately, Schatzki's work does not explore locations where horizons of understanding emerge from political struggle or submission to political strength. For 'each of us comes to act in a pre-existing world that is the result of a history of struggles over shared resources, resources which include the power to solidify interpretations into categories' informing action (Couldry, 2012: 64).

The Practice Turn in Contemporary Theory

Introducing a defining collection of essays *The Practice Turn in Contemporary Theory* as one of its editors, Schatzki writes of many social theorists regarding 'practices' as being a 'primary generic social thing' (2001a: 10). Following Ricoeur's hermeneutics, we have discussed the generic status of 'practices' as equipped narrative types of understanding-in-use, 'teleoaffective structures' instantiated by socially emplaced (or rule-governed) goal-directed activity embodying horizons of intelligibility. Here 'actors share a practice if their actions are appropriately regarded as answerable to norms of correct or incorrect practice' (Rouse, 2001: 199).

Thus 'we pick the apple that looks nicer with no flaws . . . . Like this apple looks fresher', reports our mall visitor, gendering as female this (apple) equipped generic social practice aimed at consuming fresh fruit, a selectivity clearly embodying a wider perspective on health making sense. Such tacit 'tactics of consumption' 'make use of the strong' (De Certeau, 1984: xvii) supermarket.

> Here 'the persistence and transformation of social life, rests centrally on the successful inculcation of shared embodied know-how (. . .) the skilled body commands attention in practice theory as the common meeting point of mind and activity and of individual activity and society'.
>
> (Schatzki, 2001a: 12)

In a first contribution to this set of essays, Barnes follows Schatzki by according to practices a teleoaffective structure, writing of their 'goal-directed enactment' (2001: 29). As with a consumer genre of mall or media visiting, practices are habitual or routine; consequently, they involve merely tacit adjustment of means to an end (e.g. viewers 'suturing' edited fragments on screen to form a film narrative). 'Mastery is purpose-relative' (Turner, 2001: 139). 'Genre' is here a 'family resemblance' concept (Wittgenstein, 1991). Shopping malls, for instance, are expected by their visitors to possess some but not all of a given set of characteristics. Yet events or excellence not anticipated arise (e.g. no 'health food' shop) requiring prompt reflective purposive interpretation of content, perhaps from philosophical horizons of (re)vision rather than simply understanding-in-use directed at achieving.

Barnes takes 'vegetarianism' to be an 'exemplary' instance of a practice (2001: 26). Viewed from the present perspective of hermeneutic practices theory, being a vegetarian involves a generic narrative of understanding-in-use (cooking, eating), being equipped (*prima facie* by vegetables), as well as being socially emplaced (governed by a variety of rules, not least of which is avoiding meat).

Generically constituted by its teleoaffective structure, the practice of vegetarianism aims at sustaining a philosophy of valued life, a shared horizon for its understanding embodied as well as extended in the daily activities of culinary consuming, whether solitary or in a social group. Should the latter be challenged or encounter issues, practitioners can reflectively consider this perspective. In their doing so, they maintain their 'praxis-relevant identities' (Coulter, 2001: 44).

Schatzki (2001b), in his own essay in the volume, makes it clear that although practices are characterised by a teleoaffective structure or are generically (in)formed by internally defined goals, habitually or routinely tacitly achieved, they 'cannot be identified with regularity *qua* repetition of the same' (50). Mundane immersion in cinematic melodrama or shopping mall on one occasion will not involve identical generic embodied understanding-in-use bearing expectation a second time. A practice genre can be instantiated differently without issue for its horizons of anticipation are wide, whether tacitly assembling media narrative or progress through known malls: 'skilled performances manifest a (. . .) directedness toward a goal through varying means' (Rouse, 2006: 514).

Practices social theory 'brings into view activities which are situated, corporeal, and shaped by habits without reflection' (Thévenot, 2001: 64). As familiar responses, they are tacitly flexible, albeit (in)formed by horizons of understanding, 'actors' preoccupation with the good' (ibid.: 67), whether 'bonding', buying fresh fruit, security in the shopping mall or being vegetarian. Practices, in short, 'enact schemas' and so 'may be read for the *transposable* schemas they contain' (Swidler, 2001: 88, emphasis in original), instantiating teleologically driven genres of understanding-in-use, interactive yet tacit rule-following participation in the 'priority of practice' (Bloor, 2001). Citing the work of Garfinkel, Lynch writes, the 'praxiological orientation' concerns 'situated accomplishments by the parties whose local practices "assemble" the recurrent scenes of action' (2001: 140).

We noted earlier when discussing Schatzki's founding contribution to practice theories that reminiscent of Wittgenstein's cultural 'forms of life' (1991) inscribed in action, he argues practices are to be understood as 'collective, social arenas of action that are pervaded by a space of meaning in whose terms people live, interact, and coexist intelligibly' (2005: 470). Practices can be said to be circumscribed by characteristically tacit horizons of understanding, the subject of reflective thought in moments of celebration, crisis or contribution to focus groups. 'Basically, I expect good security from the mall'. In discussing a 'forms of life approach' (2001: 118) to our tacit assumption, Collins writes that from this perspective, 'what we take to be certain has more to do with the social groups in which we are embedded than to do with the reasons we provide' (ibid.: 118–119). As habituated generic narratives of regular understanding-in-use, practices share an embodied perspective. With reflection upon action, 'practices tend toward their own elaboration' (Spinosa, 2001: 210). In such reflecting during focus group or interviews in consumer research, interaction occurs between 'two worlds, perceptions or stances' (Vandermause and Fleming, 2011: 370). Here participant 'general understanding' is 'reflectively and actively re-cognised in consciousness' (Sobchack, 2004: 290).

Researchers gain access to another's embodied 'stance', a 'storied event' (Vandermause and Fleming, 2011: 372) putting in place a different horizon of understanding, initiating a conversation constituting intersubjective extension or fusion of horizons, perspectives on experience. For always 'by the fact of our being-in-the-world, we are already seeing the world *as* something' (McCaffrey et al., 2012: 218, emphasis in original), oriented, positioned upon a culturally (in)formed horizon.

A Hermeneutic Perspective on Practices as Generic Production of Narrative

> Why not we just take one of those pictures?
>
> (Female, Malay mall visitor)

> Social practices are embodied, and the bodily skills through which they are realised are intimately responsive to the affordances and resistances of their surroundings.
>
> (Rouse, 2006: 536)

Writing on matters of securing and sustaining public health, Maller proceeds from a social practices perspective (2015). After reviewing a similar range of practice theorists to those we have (or will) discuss, she arrives at her own statement, evoking Ricoeur's generic analysis of *praxis*:

> I define a practice as being constituted by meanings about how and why to do things (cultural conventions, expectations and socially shared meanings), materials (objects, tools and infrastructures), and competences both tacit and explicit (knowledge and embodied skills).
>
> (58)

Here practices are generic narratives (hence shaped by 'conventions' and 'expectations') of equipped understanding-in-use, 'competences' with 'tools', not least of which is a tacit knowledge (Cook and Brown, 1999: 388). Behaviour embodies horizons of understanding as 'socially shared meanings' (Maller, 2015). A helpful example is 'eating breakfast' (ibid.), with albeit varying cultural convention, competence using culinary equipment and social presumption of significant consuming. Embodied generic narratives, we have seen, are 'teleoaffective' (Schatzki) or explicitly/ implicitly goal-seeking, pursuit of ends unusually (e.g. while 'eating breakfast') disturbed by 'disequilibria' or 'indeterminacy' (Iser). Rarely is attention required to the process (e.g. moving an arm), for 'habitual practices require a minimum of reflection or deliberation' (Hunt, 2010: 70).

Practices we here consider to be generic behaviour, tacitly producing a typical narrative of response to/with equipment—embodying a horizon of understanding in aligning or alienating other persons. Realising use of equipment in its reception can be seen as socially embedded in memories. 'Maybe the apples look the same to the guys (laughter). No offence. But, we, we, we pick the apple that looks nicer with no flaws', remembers the mall visitor, aligning generic activity and gender. As Dreyfus writes, the 'being or intelligibility of entities depends on our practices' (2001: 161). Here, a tacit horizon of gendered understanding encircles her behaviourally established identity.

Always already fore-understanding familiar life-world, in recognition, embodied expectation is met by event, setting into play assumption, anticipation and achievement. While 'practitioners' of a genre may have 'only tacit knowledge of the form itself', such a behavioural type 'exists because it works, in some sense or other, as a response to the situation' (Coe and Freedman, 1998), thereby facilitating a hermeneutic circle of practical understanding through integrating expectation with event. Practices are habituated (typical) responses rather than a hermeneutically distinct reception (Dhoest, 2015)—embodying a horizon of understanding circumstances (seeing the shopping mall as being 'secure'), predisposing individuals to a type of behaviour tacitly regarded as appropriate. These 'habituated predispositions' are thereby 'integrated into the practices' (Arsel and Thompson, 2011: 804).

Responses are contextualised by broader perspectives. Their genres are spatio-temporal both literally and metaphorically: within a genre of social action or practice, participants share a horizon of understanding, perhaps concealed or distant from immediate awareness, but becoming apparent in reflecting. Entering a practice from a horizon is to 'assume the forms of a genre, is to step into a specific social world with its vastly ramified values, practices and obligations' (Kress, 2003: 101).

Illustrating this thesis, one can turn to a Chinese (male) reflecting in a colleague's research (Sia, 2012) on the annual practice of the New Year Reunion Dinner. Extended families, recognising the old year ending, return home to re-unite, securing a past as well as 'horizon-setting' (Bordwell, 1991: 28), establishing shared future perspectives on the world. Here they engage materially with a generic 'repertory of schemata and routines' (ibid.: 132) in this practice of reunion 'once in a year'. Drawing on Couldry's defining 'media rituals' (2003: 29), we see that a Chinese New Year Reunion Dinner is ritually defined by participants' 'formalised actions organised around key (. . .) categories ("once in a year") and boundaries ("hard work"), whose performance frames ("shares"), or suggests a connection with, wider ("family members") values'.

> You know, once in a year we have our dinner together, and just to usher in the new year the next day. But the most important, the significant part of it, is because you see after a year's of (sic) hard work that we come together, and we have dinner and then we can share all the things among ourselves, family members especially.

In this generic social practice, tacitly instantiated by 'family members', participants in 'our (CNY) dinner together' 'come together', sharing an embodied horizon of understanding shaped by their year of 'hard work'—a communal perspective presumed, projected and produced in 'shar(ing) all the things among ourselves'. Here, 'things' equip an extended family reunion 'together'.

> My brother-in-law is a Muslim. Therefore they cook a separate, they use a separate wok to cook for him. No pork . . . and everything that they cook for him is halal. So my sister will sit on a separate table which is still together (with the family) and we will have the Reunion Dinner together but they will have the Muslim food.
>
> (Male)

This family's regular (if annual) practice of integrating their male Muslim relative within a Chinese Reunion Dinner has established a 'sub-genre' (Chandler, 2014) of behavioural response to culinary religious requirement. As the narrative informs us, equipped activity (using the 'separate wok' and 'separate table') enables an embodied horizon of understanding family unity as valuable to be secured: so 'my sister will sit on a separate table which is still together (with the family) and we will have the Reunion Dinner together'. The extended family remains materially 'together'. As Postill reminds us, 'practice theory is a body of work about the work of the body' (2010: 11).

Arguing for a 'normative conception of practices', Rouse (2007) asserts that a 'performance belongs to a practice if it is appropriate to hold it accountable as a correct or incorrect performance of that practice' (48). 'Sitting at a separate table', 'still together', confirms their 'Reunion Dinner'. As Rouse continues, 'these patterns of interaction constitute something at issue and at stake in their outcome' (2007: 50), informing an understanding of appropriate performance. 'The most important, the significant part' of the annual family reunion dinner is that 'we come together' (Chinese male).

Here it is appropriate to remember 'genre' is a 'family resemblance' concept (Wittgenstein, 1991). Not all instantiations of a practice genre, for instance, will employ identical equipment: a Chinese New Year family reunion, while nonetheless celebrating its social emplacing, may lack a shared table. Nor will all members share an identical belief regarding the reunion's significance—see the occasion similarly positioned on a horizon of understanding. As a practice, reunion occurs within a horizon of variably directed viewpoints focussed on differing aspects of 'family': 'people who constitute "a situation" together, know different things and speak with different interests and experience' (Linehan and McCarthy, 2000: 438) from a shared cultural framing of the practice.

Generic responses incorporate 'sets of expectations' (Culler, 1975: 150). Socially embedded, embodied, equipped practices as little reflected on behavioural genres occur in the context of—and conform to—characteristically tacit horizons of expectation, so enabling 'entirely automatic' (Kress, 2012: 24) interpretive responses or deployment of conventions. Watching news television becomes 'seemingly "natural"' (Das, 2011a: 78), naturalising 'interpretive competence' (Culler, 1975: 110). As Sobchack writes of practices more widely, 'we are primarily intending toward the world and our projects and not toward our modes and processes of perception and expression' (2004: 5).

Practices from viewing screen media to visiting shopping malls embed genres of behaviour or repeated responses to a 'recurrent situation' (Miller, 1984: 151), 'continually useful for mastering states of affairs' (ibid.: 157). Constituent acts signal an initiating of easily recognised intelligibility, a source of justification or 'cultural rationality' (ibid.: 165). Like 'media frames', the 'key function' of a generic practice more widely exercised is to 'reduce the complexity of the world, and thereby render it comprehensible and meaningful' (Geise and Baden, 2015: 46). Little revised habituated behaviour confirming established horizons of expectation generates minimal hermeneutic demands.

A practice is, in short, a generic response to mall, media or, more widely, articulating social emplacement with equipment, embedding a tacit horizon of understanding. Practices are embodied narratives of equipped understanding-in-use. Discussing Orlikowski's (2000) 'practice lens' on the understanding of entity as equipment, Leonardi argues from this view of 'sociomateriality', 'people formed interpretations, in the practice of their work, about how the technology's features would help them accomplish tasks and social interaction with others' (2013: 64). 'Sociomaterial entanglements' (Mutch, 2013: 32) are diverse in practice and consequently theorising (Scott and Orlikowski, 2013). Regarding understanding screen content as materially and visibly embodied in equipped practice is 'particularly appropriate where the interactive pleasures on offer are primarily kinaesthetic' (Lister et al., 2009: 24), as in the case of interactively enjoyed computer games.

Cell phone photography of close friends, choosing apples, securely shopping is enabled and constrained by personal competence and structural regulation, along with a wider affective vision of 'bonding', buying and safety. As with viewers responding to television programme type, generating content, social practices are immersively underscored by a 'complex repertoire of generic forms and cultural competences in play in the social formation' (Morley, 1992: 118).

Consumers view advertising from their 'current horizon of visual expectation' (Scott, 1994a: 270). Assumption and 'actuality', however, can occasionally clash, not least where engaging with a normally 'transparent' screen media, producing 'complex' issues prompting user reflection on 'how to understand' content or 'capture' a meaning escaping from the accustomed practice of viewing. A generic response 'enabling schemata' to be employed (Bordwell, 1991: 148) making sense may falter in the face of complexity:

> 'For me, the reality of investing in HSBC is as complex as how to understand the image', or to 'capture' meaning [female, Malay respondent asked by a Chinese focus group facilitator: 'Do you feel you can relate to the (branding) video?']

The generic familiarity of habituated practice—its being ready-to-hand—is synonymous with its being an unlikely topic for reflection. Familiarity enables tacit immersion in generic narrative of understanding-in-use, from cell phone photography to choosing apples. 'For the most part', Dreyfus writes for the *Practice Turn in Contemporary Theory*, 'we encounter people, equipment, and even natural things as both perceptually and instrumentally familiar and inextricably bound up with our everyday practices' (2001: 167). Yet reflecting can emerge in celebration or criticism of a practice, attending to horizons of understanding embedded in everyday life. Continual confirming of these assumptions affords unchallenged familiarity to our wider life-world, thereby affirming a 'holistic perspective on being human' (Todres et al., 2007: 53). Exploring horizons of understanding enacts 'hermeneutic philosophy as research in practice' (McCaffrey and Moules, 2016).

Horizons of understanding extend for varying lengths, incorporating assumptions of varying dimensions. The mundane practice of visiting a mall, parading and purchasing products embodying presumption of security, enfolds more specific practices, (in)forming their mode of accomplishing. Purchasing apples can be assured. 'Not all practices are equal. Some practices are deeper and more enduring and shape other practices' (Phipps and Ozanne, 2017: 363).

Generic Practices in Using Screen Media: Mapping Horizons of Understanding

Tacitly submitting 'production (of behaviour) to genres' (Ricoeur, 1981a: 136), recognising from a horizon of expectations a 'bonding' moment in a mall as typically a time for taking pictures and responding accordingly, prompts visitor suggestion of a practice—'why not we just take one of those pictures?' Her idea is temporal, integrating past, present, and future (in)forming anticipation: it is a reference to generating generic 'routinised bodily movements' (Everts et al., 2011: 325).

Discussing the wider use of cell phones or smartphones by students as information-gathering equipment, Chan et al. (2015) consider two broad genres: 'types of learning practices emerge from the participants' lived experiences; *serendipitous and purposive learning*' (101) (original emphasis). The former is a 'spontaneous' employment of equipment, while the latter involves searching. Both genres of behaviour are socially emplaced in 'formal and informal learning contexts' (ibid.).

Embodied in generic practices of smartphone use are participant horizons of understanding, perspectives (prominent or tacit) aligning or alienating them from other 'carriers' of the practice:

> Because the Internet is still not fully trustable, people can tell lies, you know people can turn the stories here and there, like politics and stuff like that.
>
> (Andy; ibid.)

Smartphone users' behavioural screen responses involve absorbed, articulated production of narrative, an extended hermeneutic circle of constructing meaning: 'I don't do (reading) all at once but it accumulates' (Stevie). Online narratives present selves: '*Twitter* is who you really are' (ibid.). Implicitly generic, these practices are purposive, rule-governed and open to aesthetic evaluation or are 'organised by understandings, rules, and teleoaffectivities' (Schatzki, 2015: 2). So friends 'just explain to you. Umm . . . you could also take (a shot) from this angle and you could have a beautiful picture' [Deeptzer in Chan et al. (2015)]. Practices, as noted, are socially emplaced, here constituted by 'everyday smartphone practices and learning life-worlds of a group of youths' (ibid.: 98). In our regarding practices, 'critical reflexivity' becomes equally a 'social practice' (Mao et al., 2016: 1).

Practices from viewing screen media to visiting shopping malls embody narrative seeking to resolve disequilibria, from comprehending 'complex' image to consumers avoiding 'flaws' in fruit. Habituated practices as responses to genres (e.g. bank branding narratives) themselves conform to socially shared genres, with people 'caught up' in an immersive narrative assembling process. In the following discussion, we consider a practices genre wherein our consumers bring to bear their social emplacing on articulating meaning for equipment—media branding motorcycles—and in subsequent research display wider horizons of understanding these artefacts—a 'teleoaffective' subjectivity. The generic practice of media use whether in recognition and response to motorcycle marketing or mall is structurally no different from ubiquitous generic production of narrative enabled by equipment. *Praxis* as understanding-in-use is socially emplaced, embodying shared horizons of intelligibility: practices 'engender common understandings and sources of difference' (Livingstone, 2012: 187).

Media Branding: Generic Practices of Producing Narrative

Discussing consumers speaking of their generic responses to media branding or a reception practice, we draw from a graduate thesis (Tiong, 2013) on marketing supervised at a public university in Sarawak by this author. Here audience 'fore-conceptions' (Heidegger) guide anticipating and articulation of a branded meaning: behavioural narratives *in* consumer meaning construction produce narrative of behaviour *on* screen. Unlike psychological studies conducted with the individual participants we consider later in Chapter 4, the marketing research was undertaken in focus groups 'allowing multiple voices to be heard at one sitting' (Palmer et al., 2010: 100), both materially and virtually instituted. Here 'experiential claims' (ibid.) related to hermeneutic 'moments' in textual reception such as fulfilling anticipation.

This research assembled and analysed from a hermeneutic practices perspective responses to Malaysian media marketing—often aesthetically attractive accounts which respect consumers and raise interesting issues of ethnicity, gender and generational identity. Small focus groups were both face-to-face and conducted online. Discussion after watching enabled viewers to reflect in detail on how, bearing past (genre-related) assumptions, they had pre-reflectively recognised (or were unable to recognise) screen content and hence project and produce narrative—how their understanding-in-use generated accounts with an accompanying affective (moral and political) evaluation. Reception instantiated themes related to audience articulation, alignment or alienation from branding narrative. Here, indeed, research exemplified a 'hermeneutics of branding' (Hatch and Rubin, 2006).

Within their 'readings' of motorcycle branding on screen, we can distinguish at least two sub-genres of response—where informed consumer expectation is realised or wholly fails to be attained. Associated with these audience behavioural narratives are their (dis)equilibria, success or failure in completing (the hermeneutic circle of) understanding, producing integrated sense in their reception of the brand mediated action. (Sub-)genres are varyingly 'teleoaffective' not only in achieving their purpose (producing screen stories) but in aligning with/being alienated from perceived narrative—so displaying a 'sense of oughtness and acceptability' (Everts et al., 2011: 326). Below we consider two sub-genres (I) and (II) of success and failure in producing brand narrative.

(I) Generic Consumer Expectation Meets Anticipated Content. Here our audiences tacitly produce a 'transparent' narrative (with no reference to its editing or textual composition; subsequent accounts, as noted next, contain terms such as 'clear'). A reflective interpretation follows the practice of reception (e.g. in focus group), not least audiences considering a perspectival horizon of viewing from which media content has been understood without issue 'as' asserting typical identity, instantiating patterns [motorbikes as '*gaya* (stylish) and *lincah* (agile)'].

So, for instance, responding in an online focus group to a screen narrative marketing a brand of motorcycles as offering the freedom of a bird, a female Indian consumer commented, 'it met my expectations . . . freedom and a bird on the sky . . . I am very clear about the message'. Here content can be accommodated without issue within the audience's horizon of generic media expectation.

Likewise, a female Chinese focus group member responded to media marketing a different brand as possessing the agility of a skateboard: 'it met my expectations. That video is clear . . . fits the theme . . . is fast enough . . . a symbol of motorcycles . . . fast, cool, agile and stylish.' Indeed, this creative comparison while conforming to her anticipation of advertising motorcycles as being 'fast', was absorbing: 'comparing a motorcycle with a skateboard, I've never thought of that'. She shared the marketing's 'preferred reading' of the brand's motorcycle product: '(I) identify. To me, it brings out the message that the motorcycle is *gaya* (stylish) and *lincah* (agile).' Consumption, marketing and practice analyses concur with a fundamental concern in media studies, audience reception of a text's preferred readings in narrative construction.

(II) Generic Consumer Expectation is Not Fulfilled by Branding Content. Without this recognition, no immersion in tacit productive understanding of narrative occurs, but rather a reflective thinking within the practice of reception. (Subsequent accounts, as noted next, contain terms such as 'chaos' and 'messy'). Consumer horizons of understanding are distanced from constructions of product identity, 'people's cognitive and emotive frameworks' (Couldry, 2008b: 104) of interpretation are affirmed.

Despite creative comparison of motorcycle and skateboard as fast and agile being without issue for one female Chinese viewer, for another, it lay beyond her horizons of clear comprehension: for 'it did not grab my attention and it's messy'. 'It is quite a chaos. I only know that it is about the motorcycle being as easy and flexible as the skating . . . skateboard, something like that.' The first female Chinese consumer responded similarly to branding a different make of motorcycle where its narrative led beyond her horizon of understanding: 'I cannot really get the story.' 'I'll distance from the advertisement because I didn't understand the message and it did not meet my expectation.' Here her understanding-in-use—generic embodied anticipation—engaged unsuccessfully with the 'message'.

Mall Media: Reflecting On/In Generic Practices of Producing Narrative

'Why not we just take one of those pictures?', a Malay mall visitor asks. Her instantiating a generic practice, through taking 'one of those pictures', produces a behavioural narrative (practical understanding) in response to a mall, articulating emplacement with 'embodied expertise' (Wenger et al., 2002: 9). Shooting the 'selfie' along with her close friend marks out, if momentarily, a shared horizon of embodied reflective interpretation from which such picture taking is seen as perpetuating a broader social practice of 'bonding': 'it was something that you want it to last'. 'Selfies' define 'embodied identities': people 'reconfigure the meaning of their bodies' (Kelly et al., 2017).

There are multiple genres of practical intelligence evident in a mall, behaviour incorporating horizons of understanding, from bowling to skating. Drawing on the author's collaborative research, we shall consider two instances where visitor-generic practices in responding to a mall (its reception practices) are (I) followed by consumer reflective interpretation during focus group discussion and (II) suspended momentarily by a mall visitor's self-prompted celebratory reflective interpretation.

(I) Reflective Interpretation *On* Generic Reception. The habituated practice of immersion in their shopping mall, enabling tacit production of behavioural narrative, is a topic for reflection by many contributors to interviews. This is delayed reflection on generic understanding-in-practice, referring often to its 'teleoaffective structure' (Schatzki, 2006) during a discussion with researchers (we 'just come here, see, look and then just enjoy the crowd'). A Chinese female visitor for whom the hugely distinctive 'Egyptian look' of this suburban mall is 'very unique, *lah* . . . I mean you don't find it in other place(s) in Malaysia, right?' acknowledges that a generic presence in the place enables her to 'catch up with old friends' (laughing) 'like reunion'. 'Decoration' signals celebratory difference:

> You come here you can sense the mood actually. Because one thing is because of the decoration. Another thing is because of the crowd . . . (At this mall) there is always . . . big crowd of people . . . so sometimes we don't come here for shopping, we also just come here, see, look and then just enjoy the crowd . . . the atmosphere, *lah*.

In other regularities of returning to this massive mall, a male Chinese celebrated the 'health option', 'bowling, exercise or the gym' as providing 'for you to enjoy your healthy living styles'. He reflects on socially emplaced generic participatory narrative with enabling equipment. Potential and actual activity could both be enjoyed. Revisiting his desire, this visitor confessed, 'firstly I don't know how to play ice skating but I saw people playing with their friends with joy and fun'.

Reflecting upon her repeated visit, a female Chinese lecturer invests in stereotype to express excitement. 'This place never fails to make me feel excited about shopping. It brings out the Asian in me.' She looks to her cultural horizon of self-understanding as 'Asian' tacitly incorporated in this mall equipped and embodied practice of 'shopping' in mapping out a personal identity to 'frame the meaning of and give order to opinions and experiences of the world' (Törrönen, 2013: 94). Here a subject position (Asian female) is related to 'structure of viewpoint and focalisation' (ibid.) through a generic ('Asian') narrative of actualising anticipation, producing her projected being 'excited'.

An older female Chinese teacher clearly visits this mall from a horizon of ludic expectation focussed on equipment ['I always come to (the mall) actually', 'oh, *ya*, (its) mega lane'], producing in Seamon's terms a 'place ballet' (1979) of vivid consumption ('every Thursday we have our bowling lesson here'). She is celebrating strength in overcoming chronic illness, especially when this mall's Chinese New Year decorations promote positive anticipation if not utopia (Murtola, 2010):

> We are having a team called Pink Power. I'm a cancer survivor actually so we Pink Power are the cancer survivors team.

In all these instances of visitors 'voicing out', reflective interpretation occurs in discussion, subsequent to people visiting a mall, engaging with circulating crowds and sometimes serious play.

(II) Reflective Interpretation *In* Generic Reception. Research participants presented their narratives of why they visited the mall, constituting its vast spaces as a place familiar from frequent visiting. Mall practices were viewed from their articulately mapped shared horizons of understanding such 'habitats' (Bloch et al., 1994), evident in collective behaviour. Perceiving this extended urban space from adjacent points on these metaphorical horizons of anticipation, it was understood ('projected') as enabling visitors configuring modes of generic being (such as 'bonding' and 'hanging out'), or a participatory involvement in 'being-with-others' (Heidegger, 1962), friends.

During an interview, one participant talks about her photograph taken after meeting a friend: 'when we meet, that time you know, it was like, like after letting out everything',

> this photograph 'was a closing of our meeting'. 'It was a happy . . . happiness but is something more because I remember at this moment when we took the picture it was something that you want it to last.'
>
> (Female, Malay)

Surprised by 'something more' than simply 'happiness', in this brief introspective narrative (Caru and Cova, 2008), she switches for a 'moment' from habituated ready-to-hand experience of mall visiting to reflecting within the practice, regretting its transitory quality, wanting 'it to last'. In this temporary but transformative longing, she crosses the liminal borders between tacit immersion and thoughtful, if passing, inspection. From a hermeneutic perspective, both are modes of ludic (play-like) projecting and producing participatory intelligibility—so immersively integrating an existential narrative (Gaviria and Bluemelhuber, 2010). The mall is thus momentarily experienced differently, 'reframed' (Schön, 1983) from briefly changing horizons of understanding, regarded not as a place of passing consumption but of more prolonged pleasure through using this 'singularised object', a cell phone camera (Epp and Price, 2010). In taking a photograph, tacit pre-reflective consumption (i) has been transformed by a moment of reflection-in-practice on a horizon of understanding (ii). She presences a renewed sense of her 'self-understanding' (Arnold and Fischer, 1994: 55), thus celebrating 'communitas' (Turner, 1967)—an embodied empathy within this vast shopping mall.

Here we have closely observed memory, a presencing in/of a tacitly configured practice or generic habitual behaviour ('ok, why not we just take one of those pictures?') by a consumer who considers this mall as enabling a 'bonding session'. Her narrative vividly accompanies concurrent celebration, refiguring its reception: 'it was something that you want it to last'. Pictures record that 'something', 'place ballet' (Seamon, 1979)—a transcending display of her embodied cultural capital.

At this 'moment' (both hermeneutic as well as human) of reunion, rekindling and relief, one photograph shows behind the close friends a women's lingerie shop as a mall *mise-en-scene* which serves to underwrite the occasion's 'sense-content' (Ricoeur, 1981b) of intimacy, warmth, comfort and solidarity in bonding. Such reflective images are a suitable focus for media advertising.

Participating in the mall from a shared horizon of understanding it as a 'superb hanging out place' (female, Chinese), this Malay woman produces (behaviourally or implicitly in her action and explicitly in later talk) an account integrating expectation with later event. A celebratory moment is marked by closing equilibrium: it was 'a relief after finishing', in their re-affirming close friendship. Here, indeed, 'materiality and human relationships are inextricably intertwined' (Price, 2013: 304), albeit that identity has been enhanced not through consumer purchase but confirming friendship. In terms of Ricoeur's (1988) analytical concepts enabling reflection upon configured action, a generic, hence anticipated 'prefigured' practice (taking cell phone photos in the shopping mall) is 'refigured' as narrative pursuing selfhood: 'when we took the picture it was something that you want it to last'.

Reflectively presenting her celebratory moment (characterised as being 'something more' than happiness, 'something that you want it to last') as challenging the habituated—or ritualistic—practice of smartphone camera use ('ok, why not we just take one of those pictures?') was as Peters and Allan write (2016: 9) indeed an instance of 'users affectively and self-consciously deploying the technology to try to arrest the ephemerality of daily life, however fleetingly'. However, while they regard the practice as *generically* 'related to positive emotions', an activity which 'evinced strong social bonds and encompassed a future-oriented perspective' (ibid.: 8), here the widespread custom of taking 'one of those pictures' in the mall appears to be dismissed by this visitor as routine, albeit to use a Heideggerian phrase in Coyne's architectural analyses, an affective 'tuning of place' (2010).

Celebratory reflecting-in-practices can be momentary enlightening amidst a forest of habit. But it may also be behaviourally evident as in a visitor taking photographs. The mall's aquatic and historical displays offered empowerment and peace to an older male Indian: 'the water, to a large extent has a kind of soothing effect on the soul'. He reflects *in* taking his distinctive photograph on the detailed decoration ['the stuff that (they) put there'] as equipping 'different' activity, as mapping out alternative horizons of understanding embedded in behaviour other than 'just the norm'.

His action belongs to the genre of evaluative comment rather than photography epitomising visual representation. In subsequent reflection, he attributes the 'force of agency' (Epp and Price, 2010) to the subject seen, understood in his narrative to manifest a preferred reading as a 'challenge'—and a construct also, we suggest, suitably addressing an adventurous consumer in advertising. Inspiration has been achieved across ethnic groups, respecting both Chinese and Indian history: consumer culture is enabling individuals to escape from, to transcend, little reflected-upon habituated consumption.

> A display 'has quite lot of history background to the early days when they use the sail boats and the journeys that the Chinese did during that era . . . . I think it, it kind of challenge(s) us to do something different other than just the norm'.
>
> (Male, Indian)

This chapter has endeavoured to display continuity of thought concerning human behaviour between philosophical hermeneutics (Heidegger, Gadamer, Ricoeur) and practice theory (Reckwitz, Schatzki, contributors to the *Practice Turn in Contemporary Theory*). Practices are constituted by a generic embodied, equipped production of meaning—which can be itself generic (as in media use). Practices are hermeneutic, sense-making. Writing about organisational practices, Weick argues that sense-making involves a 'placement of items into frameworks, comprehending, redressing surprise, constructing meaning, interacting in pursuit of mutual understanding, and patterning' (1995: 6). In these initial two chapters of this brief book, we have seen appearing in research participant accounts instances of these multiple phenomena, from comprehending to designations of 'chaos'. 'Struggles with identity', of person or product, 'appear to involve the root act of sense making' (ibid.: 77). Our referring to participant cell phone photography enabled, as has been achieved elsewhere in research, a 'greater insight into participants' embodied experiences' (Burles and Thomas, 2014: 193). Where we have included an extended family Chinese New Year Reunion Dinner as a valuable instantiation of practices, we have sought to be 'sensitive to cultural meanings' (Goh and Göransson, 2011: 269) as their embodied horizon of understanding displayed materially around a home. More mundanely, 'frames of interpretation and orientation' are 'grounded in daily practices' (Schröer, 2009).

In the second half of this chapter, we reflected on equipped generic practices exemplified in using screen media, both in response to branding and being in a shopping mall. A further discussion of media practices will be postponed to a fifth chapter on viewing screens. There we shall consider 'habitus-capital' (Meyen et al., 2010: 875), consumers' embodied perspectives on web content (e.g. product choice) sponsored by underlying corporate calculation. Internet user practices, for instance, negotiate within *TripAdvisor* algorithmic delineation of travellers' horizons of understanding hotels, with consumers sharing or separating themselves from marketing—aligned, alienated or apathetic. *Amazon*'s 'frequently bought together' signals a shaping horizon of expectation. Digitally exploring websites, audiences inhabit both close and critical terrain of consumer use.

Reflecting on Research Practices: Positioning Hermeneutic Phenomenology

Proposing a hermeneutic practices analysis of communication—from marketing to media and psychology in the following pages—is clearly to advocate a particular route through research. Mortari argues for four 'main philosophical approaches to reflection' (2015: 3): 'pragmatistic' (sic), critical, hermeneutic and phenomenological. Emphasising participant embodied activity and when identifying participant 'horizons of understanding' (a phrase initiated in Husserl's phenomenology) open to distanced assessment of their power to shape consumer perceiving, a hermeneutic practices approach to research integrates this fourfold philosophical underwriting of investigative reflection.

Embodied narrative, as in mundane walking through a mall or manifest in habituated viewer behaviour when watching television is practical consciousness in use, focussed on a product, goal directed, rather than the process, on the purchase or programme meaning. Identities are constructed through this continuing 'knowledge-in-practice' (Moen, 2006: 65), established for an (un)successful consumer or the screen content. Research reflection invoking participants' discursive consciousness presents the process of achieving, thereby bringing 'practice up close' (ibid.) within wider horizons of cultural or political understanding, perceiving values: '(guys) would say, "just grab and go"'. To sight social norms is to see their constructing or constraining, facilitating or repressing practices. 'A critical hermeneutic approach affords a space for repressed voices to speak out' (Kinsella, 2006).

Summary so far: In this chapter, drawing upon hermeneutic phenomenology (Heidegger, Gadamer, Ricoeur) and practice theorists (Reckwitz, Schatzki, Shove) we arrived at an account of consumer practice as *praxis*, as our generic understanding-in-use, equipped, socially emplaced, embodying shared horizons of intelligibility. This narrative of habituated, customarily tacit human behaviour is exemplified by consumers viewing cinema, watching television, visiting malls when/where generic expectation is met by event. Our building film narrative from its edited segments usually receives attention only in media analysis. We walk in the mall without reflecting on rule-following. Where comprehension of content is an issue or in our celebratory moments, however, reflection is evident, seeking cogency in this 'messy' narrative media or discerning an enduring insight.

Practice genres, as we noted, are informed by 'norms of correct or incorrect practice' (Rouse, 2001: 199). As modes of embodied reception, they are to be distinguished from the entities to which they constitute a response, the material equipment genres of branding, malls, television—and so on. As genres, consumer practices (with activities by which they are constituted) can be characterised as 'sharing the common reference point of certain ends, projects and beliefs' (Couldry, 2010: 41).

The first two chapters in this book have endeavoured to underwrite an account of the practices perspective, drawing less on social theory (despite multiple references to the pioneering work of Schatzki) but rather more substantially on philosophy, notably contributions by Heidegger, Gadamer and Ricoeur. Thereby travelling from North America to Europe and across disciplinary foundations, we anticipate the view of progressive marketing theory (the topic of the next chapter) which is articulated by Firat and Tadajewski (2009) in their paper 'Critical Marketing—Marketing in Critical Condition': 'much of this interest (in critical marketing theory) in the English-speaking world comes from the UK and Europe (. . .) not led by North American scholars' (128). In the following chapter, we consider the major contribution to marketing theory by Craig Thompson, much cited as the initiating source of hermeneutically informed research on consumer practice. Drawing on the hermeneutic discussion of practices as grounded in routine generic narratives of understanding-in-use, embodying horizons of understanding here established earlier, we can critically assess hermeneutic marketing research. For 'meaning in everyday life is anchored in the routine and the repetitive' (Dahlgren, 1988b: 198).

3 Hermeneutic Practices in the Business School

Reflection On/In Habituated Consumption

Project

With a hermeneutic social theory of practices assembled in earlier chapters, the present chapter considers marketing and organisation studies of human behaviour from this viewpoint. If consumer behaviour involves fundamentally habituated generic understanding-in-use, occasioning second-order reflective attention only when prompted by malfunction, moments of celebration or research, what does this imply for interpretive marketing analysis discussing interviewee reports? Here, in the context of evaluating marketing and organisation theory's engaging hermeneutics, we view consumers' reflective interpretation of everyday practices in a mall. Understanding-in-use is equipped, evades attention (with momentary reflection-in-practice) and, epistemologically generic, incorporates roles (e.g. gendered) with associated rules and horizons of evaluative understanding. Articulated in practices, consumer agency is thereby both enabled and encircled by social structure: 'We are carried by the meanings of the past before we find ourselves in a position to judge them' (Kearney, 1991: 60), whether materially or mentally embedded to advance critically and creatively. In this chapter, we address the 'need for an interpretive perspective in consumer research' (Holbrook and O'Shaughnessy, 1988: 400) with a discussion of consumer hermeneutic practices, asking how does consumer research accommodate accumulated mundane meaning in behaviour—the 'always-already givenness of the world at hand' (Seamon, 2013: 144)?

Distanciating Familiarity: What Is the Role of Reflecting in Consumers Responding to Equipment?

Research announced as structured by hermeneutics—or its intellectual genesis of practices theory—occupies a significant role in marketing studies as elsewhere in the business school [e.g. analysis of globally mobile knowledge worker practices (Jarrahi and Thomson, 2017)]. This chapter presumes both to focus and further that role by (re)turning to core concepts in hermeneutic practices theory, so augmenting analysis of consumer practices, their self-reporting of narrative from visiting malls to viewing television. We draw as exemplar on consumer responses in shops or simply being mundanely in a mall, 'embodied meaning-making' (Wetherell, 2012: 4). In doing so, more widely, we distance ourselves from empiricism or positivism, discarded views of perception as passive, a philosophical shaping of marketing research as deriving law-like generalisations from data. Thus, 'in terms of how it has been read into consumer research',

> logical empiricism generally refers to a research strategy that is ontologically realist, epistemologically positivist and seeks law-like generalisations. Generally this type of research aims to produce managerially useful insights that aim to predict consumer behaviour in order to better control it.
>
> (Tadajewski et al., 2014: 1749)

Guided by its project of reviewing reflection in marketing theory (notably pioneering work by Craig Thompson), the chapter advances spatio-temporal concepts, previously discussed, of tacit generic practice, shaped by—or embodying—participant horizons of understanding. ['My boyfriend is always by my side', 'I know some men will not want to accompany their girlfriends (shopping).'] As in a previous chapter where the embodied, equipped practice of purchasing apples incorporated a wider penumbra of female self-understanding as gendered, so here we consider 'what constitutes our core cultural constructs in consumer behaviour' (Giesler and Thompson, 2016: 497).

Consistent with theorising in organisational studies, we draw on hermeneutic philosophy to further a practice perspective view of human behaviour as at its foundation being a routine process of constructing participatory meaning—regarded as presuming, projecting and producing narrative, where entities consumed are 'primordially' implied to be (dis)enabling 'equipment' (Heidegger). In this precise way, a practice is 'an activity entangling matter with meaning' (Gherardi, 2015: 14). So laptop understanding-in-use 'entangles' materially significant equipment with virtual meaning. Thus practices are tacit, tooled and customarily 'ready-to-hand'. 'Things matter, and some things matter a lot': possessions are 'tools for magical thinking', 'props for continuing bonds' and 'pitfalls' (Turley and O'Donohoe, 2012: 1332, 1338), a topic of sometimes subsequent reflection.

Having mapped this perspective in the context of marketing and organisational studies, it is used in the chapter as a template to consider consumers reflectively transcending in discussion their habituated, product enabled activity. We return to visiting the small project in a large suburban mall, our focus in the previous chapter when distinguishing between research participants *Reflecting On/In Generic Practices of Producing Narrative*. 'Active meaning management' enables consumers to 'emerge as the true sources for the symbolic and cultural values' of artefacts and brand [Cova et al., 2011: 7–8, summarising audience creativity as maintained by 'Understanding Value Co-Creation in a Co-Consuming Brand Community' (Pongsakornrungsilp and Schroeder, 2011)]. Generic experience is expected, engaged, extended—anticipating, advancing and assembling narrative, in the 'taken-for-grantedness of everyday social practices' (Thompson and Haytko, 1997: 16).

We commence as in the foregoing chapters from the philosopher Heidegger's (and Hume's) concern with foregrounding 'familiarity' of 'being-in' the material world as underwriting the very possibility of understanding everyday life. In lacking such an enabling recognition—experiencing 'surroundings' as fundamentally a hermeneutic 'homeland'—we could not actualise being in the world as already meaningful modes of consuming, enjoying 'a contrast between space, as tied to measurable extension, and space as tied to place, to that in which one dwells' (Malpas, 2006: 78).

'(I) came back to the homeland, feeling so warm and so comfortable and glad to be back to the surroundings where I was grown up', a female, Chinese mall visitor confides in a focus group, celebrating her 'ontological security' (Giddens, 1991b). A female respondent in Penman and Omar's research (2011) carried this theme forward in likewise talking about achieving a 'sense of security' through eating food from 'home', thereby configuring an embodied narrative of consumption, here refigured as achieving a sense of identity, 'as it has always been' (345). Philosophically, Heidegger emphasised identifying of 'being' with familiarity so that 'in our first phenomenal indication of the fundamental constitution of *Dasein*, and the clarification of the existential meaning of being-in' it 'was defined as dwelling with . . . , being familiar with' (Heidegger, 1962: 176).

From a hermeneutic perspective, we have seen, familiar, habituated activities, undertaken in the absence of reflective consideration, but nonetheless producing embodied narrative, are *practices*—or 'ready-to-hand' (Heidegger, 1962) equipped action enabling 'being-with-others' (ibid). Using a hammer can produce—eventually!—a house. *Hermeneutics* considers how such narratives are built, with tacit anticipating resting on assumptions about the world (or in Heidegger's terms 'projection' from a 'horizon of understanding') and our integrating expectation with events. Practices can range from the very activity of consumer and marketing researchers [and regarded reflexively through a 'perspectival' lens (Bettany and Woodruffe-Burton, 2009: 671–672)] to such a commonplace genre of behaviour as we consider, taking photographs in a seasonally decorated suburban shopping mall. In shopping or 'snapping', increasingly instantiating territory as generic, as easily and unreflectively categorised, our habitual activity 'makes a place out of space' (Tosoni, 2015: 149).

This chapter explores 'being familiar with' the habitual in practices (such as our shopping). For mundane activities can nonetheless—as in our snapshot here of visiting a shopping mall—enable consumers' celebratory moments of reflective insight. Taking pictures (as did research participants) involves a tacit set of intersubjective assumptions as a practice, a 'mode of social relation, of mutual action' (Taylor, 1971: 27). Neither this action (swiftly 'taking snaps') nor its assumptions are likely to be explicitly reflected upon—unless impeding issues or illuminating insight arise.

Within thinking about marketing, it is important that consumers' (i) tacit understanding of practices (in which little self-monitoring occurs) is not conflated with (ii) a transformative (albeit transitory) celebratory and critical considering. Both modes of their understanding need in turn to be distinguished from (iii) narrative contribution as participants to research focus group/interview where reflection surfaces and (iv) theoretical interpreting as 'secondary derivative' (Alvesson and Skoldberg, 2009: 95). In short, acknowledging that a hermeneutic perspective includes our habitual behaviour, rather than a seamless presenting of participants' narratives, this chapter proposes such biographies of consuming contain a conjunction of tacit and transformative meaning making. Our narratives in everyday life are 'both *lived and told*' where the latter reflectively presents an 'implicit background horizon of orientation' (emphasis in original) (Laitinen, 2002: 57, 61).

Appropriate orientation in embodied perspective needs no reflection in familiar contexts.

> In a football game 'both the strategic and the "traditional" orientations of the player's action are achieved without reflection. The player does not think about the game. There is no time. They must act spontaneously and pre-reflectively, seeing and acting in accordance with the logic of the game, but without thinking that or about how they are doing so.'
>
> (Crossley, 2001: 89)

Orientation to the mall is not the result of reasoned calculation: it is the result of entering the mall from a habituated, tacitly crossed horizon of understanding such familiar places of consuming. In arriving at a known place, anticipation, absorption and appropriate action emerge from recognition.

In what follows, we reassemble a hermeneutic practice perspective and relate this viewpoint evaluatively to hermeneutic marketing theory as 'conceptual lens' (O'Shaughnessy, 2013: 78). The second part of the chapter returns to our brief study of media use in the mall, exploring implications for such consumer theorising. Here the philosophical 'language-game' of hermeneutic concern with understanding everyday life is advanced, employing in Wittgensteinian mode empirical experiment by talking to visitors enabled (or equipped) in contribution by celebratory artefacts prompting their thoughtful reflection through photographing a large suburban shopping mall.

In this exploratory experiment with photography as popular activity by mall consumers, we recognise that such devices shape practice in the market (Pantzar and Ruckenstein, 2015). Holding familiar cell phone cameras (branded for smooth simplicity in use), consumers snap ready-to-hand shots—with attention focussed on potential outcome (the picture), not easily managed equipment. A practice is tool-using, tacit in presupposition yet encircled by horizon of understanding, implicitly thought-laden. Emphasising the visible, Orlikowski writes that 'capacities for action are seen to be enacted in practice, and the focus is on constitutive entanglements (e.g. configurations, networks, associations, mangles, assemblages, etc.) of humans and technologies' (2009).

A Hermeneutic Practices Perspective (HPP): Consumer Habituated Behavioural Narrative

Drawing on Heidegger's *Being and Time* (1962), consumers can be regarded as continually (explicitly/implicitly) engaged in understanding material surrounding as equipment, thereby tacitly anticipating events: such expectation is narratively reconciled with actual occurrence by invariably participating in activity with others present. It can be that this habituated process—little reflected upon—is evident only behaviourally, although subsequently conveyed in accounts to researchers. 'Practices consist of both doings and sayings', wrote Warde (2005: 134) in which an understanding is developed and deployed. Via this embodied epistemological route, consumers make their intelligible way around being in shopping malls or social media—exhibiting generic understanding-in-use.

Our routine, little monitored, comprehension of material circumstances involves knowing or understanding *how* to act appropriately. Embodied generic practical recognising and responding to our surroundings precedes (and is distinct from) subsequent reflective propositional knowing *that:* from a hermeneutic practices perspective, 'representational thinking' is 'decentred' (Mei, 2009).

For instance, we noted a female mall 'regular' consumer informed her research focus group that 'basically, I expect good security from the mall'. Entering this space from such a 'horizon of expectation' (Jauss), her tacit understanding of the mall is manifest in behaviour, with her presence of mind being focussed on shopping not 'snatch thieves'. Her assumption is left for statement in the focus group, albeit 'written into' her mode of earlier walking in the mall. Interpreted as reference to her practice in this place, the veracity of her focus group contribution is publicly verifiable.

How, we ask, are such mundane consumer practices involving our assuming and activated skills projected and produced in participation with others? How is pre-propositional understanding-in-practice with 'habituated norms' (Coskuner-Balli and Thompson, 2013: 27), our very 'habituated behavioural tendencies' (Thompson and Ustuner, 2015: 239), related to reflection in the course of consumption or considered subsequently? As Halkier and Jensen ask in discussing 'methodological challenges', how is habituated consuming incorporating shared 'tacit and embodied knowledges and procedures' (2011: 110) *done*? And how is it related to celebratory and critical reflection?

In a hermeneutic account of human consumption, ontology and epistemology coincide. That is, our being is defined by reference to our knowing or understanding. In *Being and Time* (Part I), Heidegger argues that fundamentally ('primordially') we are always already recognising entities in our material circumstances (e.g. as chairs and tables) and that their meaning is realised in practices. In his much cited instance of understanding-in-practice, we can be said to understand a hammer if we know how to use this tool. Familiar equipment becomes 'ready-to-hand' where its employment requires minimal attention: we focus on product (e.g. words on a page) rather than process (typing).

With little regard for the process, *Dasein* (being present) we actualise our knowing how in familiar, habitual circumstances as understanding incorporated in activity: distracted from our doing so, with attention elsewhere, we take our seats. Our embodied behaviour (with its implicit expectation of our equipment), with minimal self-monitoring is put into play, acted as appropriate from tacit horizons of recognising surroundings as generic, instantiating type (of office, study). Entering a known mall, visitors are 'epistemologically' equipped to walk around with little conscious self-direction, unless major reconstruction prompts a pause for thought on route, to present it 'at hand' (Heidegger, 1962). Otherwise, consumers attend to companions or purchasing. Knowing how to get about their familiar malls is relegated to the background of living (albeit evident in action) at least until we ask visitors to share their practical understanding in research as narrative—propositional knowing *that*.

This philosophical psychology can be restated using the heuristic spatio-temporal metaphor available in hermeneutics. Heidegger's concepts of (a) 'fore-understanding' ('projecting' narrative from a 'horizon of understanding') and consumer productive reconciling of expected content with eventuality through (b) a 'hermeneutic circle of understanding' offer a theoretical prism, enabling reflection on participatory equipped practice. How does little reflected on assumption accommodate actuality and in so doing allow intelligible everyday habitual consumer behaviour?

Research from a hermeneutic practices perspective, as these terms are presently used, concerns consumers embodied habituated (a) *projecting* meaning from (b) a *presumptive* horizon of understanding entities as equipment, so (c) *producing* behavioural narrative as a genre or a mode of 'being-with-others' (Heidegger, 1962). Heidegger, Gadamer and Ricoeur each offer accounts of the varying relationship holding between 'horizons'—here seen as consensual, contested and critical points of view. So describing the hermeneutic practices perspective draws upon a philosophically oriented literature discussing the habituated construction of meaning—unreflectively or in 'ready-to-hand' (Heidegger, 1962) action. This is ubiquitous, from visiting shopping malls to frequent use of social media.

Walking in malls or, more widely, behaviour tells a story in which we are always already 'projecting' (Heidegger, 1962) a narrative of understanding-in-practices—*meaning*—enabled and engaged in our embodied activity of comprehending, producing sense for situations—addressed in marketing. 'Conventions of "doing walking" are produced and reproduced by the members of the community involved and are consequently sensitive to culture and situation' (Shove and Pantzar, 2005: 47). Visiting a restaurant anticipates and actualises a story, thereby negotiating behaviourally between expectation and event in a 'hermeneutic circle of understanding' (Gadamer, 1975). So to consider an 'action-event' or behaviour as a practice is recognising the productive dialectic between its being 'appearing and disappearing event' and its generic status as meaningful embodied narrative (Ricoeur, 1981b: 205), surrounded by a sometimes disclosed horizon of understanding.

Our actualising ready-to-hand knowledge has been reception theory's concern considering media audiences who far from reflectively construct apparently transparent access to (for instance) television content. Access is 'unpacked' during theory classes, challenged in non-realist cinema. As Peters wrote (long ago) 'mass communication theory considers effects, and hermeneutics considers reception' (1994: 131), distinguishing between United States and European scholarly reflection.

From this hermeneutic perspective on our media consuming, a viewer's ready-to-hand pre-reflective package of knowledge is seen as generic, enabling from informed horizons of identifying types of television the audience's tacitly constructing a narrative for a screen 'window on the world'. Habitual action (walking) equally exemplifies a genre of ready-to-hand body knowledge, implicitly implementing appropriate activity, while a carpenter's use of tools instantiates a different modality: ready-to-hand behaviour in malls embodies another type of tacitly actualising appropriate activity. Accomplishing a practice 'has a unique style that relates it to the individual' (Tan et al., 2009: 8).

In projecting meaning, a practice's construction of intelligibility around us—its 'primordial' product (Watson and Shove, 2008)—is enabled by equipment, the very mall itself or use of screens: they enhance or elide participating in 'being-with-others'. Later in the chapter, we draw on narrative presented during discussion with consumers to consider how visitors to a cavernous shopping mall engaged in practices that marketing can visually celebrate. These practices contribute to—or indeed, mark out—the consumer's habituated 'life-world—a person or group's day-to-day world of taken-for-grantedness' (Seamon, 2007). Authorial interviewing reflects upon life-worlds.

Hermeneutics, then, argues for our human 'understanding' as being primarily *how*: first and foremost it is tacitly incorporated in behaviour, projecting therein a narrative meaning. Consumer practice is said to be 'primordially' (Heidegger, 1962) unreflective: only secondarily and subsequently is it considered in propositional statements of understanding *that*. In organisations, how is a reflectively examined life underwritten by the 'texts' (Ricoeur, 1981b) members compose through their tacit habituated implicit understanding-in-practice? What is the relationship of our embodied understanding incorporated in practices to celebratory or critical moments and the contributions to focus groups and interviews to which Thompson and others frequently and prescriptively refer in consumer marketing research? Exploring modes of pre-reflective and reflective consumption *in situ* and subsequently, the chapter extends work on mall aesthetics and 'embodied experiences' [Biehl-Missal and Saren (2012)], the 'embodied practices' of visitors immersed in 'designed urban environments' (Degen et al., 2010).

From a hermeneutic practices perspective, this research reveals horizons of generic understanding *implicit* in habituated action from which people project and produce participatory modes of 'being-with-others'. The work of analysis is to conceptually explore, exhibiting these horizons *explicitly*.

Hermeneutic practices theory enlarges upon Heidegger's early thesis in *Being and Time* that human habit is the scarcely reflected upon, ready-to-hand *substratum* of everyday living. Equipped and embodied, we tacitly articulate narrative of being-with-others, both off and on screen. Knowing how is incorporated in every action, projecting and producing participation—or separating absence.

The threefold purpose of this chapter is to substantiate a hermeneutic practices perspective with its accompanying spatio-temporal concepts, so further enabling exploring of scholarly writing self-defining as practices theory. These pages further endeavour to identify and conceptually augment hermeneutic theory employed by interpretive consumer and marketing research through a brief empirical study.

Practices Theory as Hermeneutic: Understanding as the Tacit Actioning of Enablement

From the perspective of hermeneutic practices analyses and theory, our fundamental mode of understanding 'entities' (Heidegger) is incorporated in behaviour, enabled by 'equipment' (ibid.). 'Knowing how' precedes reflective 'knowing that'. Understanding is first and foremost instantiated in using (Heidegger, as noted, illustrated this epistemological assertion for the priority of practical knowing with a hammer). From what wider horizon of assumptions—research can enquire—does a person's behaviour issue, whether during focus group, interview or beyond? How is understanding-in-practice projecting meaning, produced in public narrative, assembled in participatory activity?

A hermeneutics of human behaviour discloses for discussion tacit (little reflected on) routine phenomena of understanding-in-practice(s)—shaping spaces (and times) of anticipated and attained intelligibility. Manifested from apple choosing to watching television, understanding is a 'ready-to-hand' (Heidegger, 1962) equipped embodied practice of 'projecting' (ibid.) meaning, our exercising intelligibility from 'horizons of expectation' (Jauss, 1982b), a 'form(ing) of life' (Wittgenstein, 1991). Yet understanding is 'naturalised out of everyday awareness' (Couldry and McCarthy, 2004: 5).

In the preceding chapter, we considered how philosophical hermeneutics connected to social practice theories: both are concerned with analysing our understanding-in-use embodying horizons of understanding. For the idea of 'practices' is 'foundational' across interdisciplinary analyses: 'they are meaning-making, identity-forming, and order-producing activities' (Nicolini, 2011: 602). Earlier, he emphasises practices as the tacit or minimally considered routine deployment of understanding and establishes their study as initiated by philosophical hermeneutics:

> As authors such as Heidegger and Wittgenstein made clear, *practice* constitutes the unspoken and scarcely notable background of everyday life. Practices therefore always need to be drawn to the fore.
>
> (Nicolini, 2009: 1392; emphasis added)

In his defining article 'Toward a Theory of Social Practices' (2002a), Reckwitz, as we have seen, claims the same historical continuity between philosophical hermeneutics and practice theory, citing Wittgenstein's later works and Heidegger's early writing. We 'find everything that is original in practice theory already in the work of these authors' (250).

From the perspective of Heidegger's hermeneutic phenomenology—as shown—people are always already engaging in practices, ready-to-hand projects, therein producing a meaning for entities (apples, narrative) as equipment from collective horizons of understanding. Schatzki follows as a more societally oriented practices theorist (2001a), arguing that the 'social is a field of embodied, materially interwoven practices centrally organised around shared practical understandings' (12). Similarly, in his particularly lucid paper, Warde posits practices theorising as emphasising 'doing over thinking, the material over the symbolic, and embodied practical competence over expressive virtuosity in the fashioned presentation of self' (2014: 286). Hermeneutics begets practices theory.

Familiarity, as Pavlickova pointed out (2013), is the fulcrum or the 'underlying dynamic of hermeneutics' (37). For this philosophy of human behaviour reflects on how consumers' horizons of understanding are woven into (and weave together) 'activities that have become routine' (Tuomela, 2004: 79), practices for which a person's reflective attention is usually not required.

Hermeneutically—that is, in producing meaning—we engage with entities (apples, narrative, tools) around us as equipment: our behaviour (dis)enables modes of being-with-others (consenting, complaining). Reiterating this philosophical account in contemporary consumer theory, a practice's 'specific elements' are presented as 'procedures, understandings, and engagements' (Echeverri and Skålén, 2011: 352, following the work of Schau et al., 2009: 31): a practice involves our 'implicit or tacit knowledge' shaping 'specific forms of practical judgements' (Echeverri et al., 2012: 429). Or to conclude this brief post-Heideggerian definitional story by reiterating Shove's concisely stated definition, a practice's 'constitutive elements' are 'meanings, competences, materials' (Shove, 2014a: 419). A short history of hermeneutics (en)frames practice studies as focussed on understanding-in-use.

A frequently floated criticism of hermeneutic phenomenology is that it is too individualistic, referring little in its analyses to the social and political context of understanding, and hence unable to underwrite practices theory. Phenomenological approaches, wrote Askegaard and Linnet (2011), must now transcend the 'overly individualist focus of some consumption research relying mainly on psychological or mental context' (390). However, they concede in their much cited paper that this is not necessarily phenomenology's 'direction' (391)—a point underlined by brief email to the present author: 'you are absolutely right in seeing that we are criticising a particular stance on existential phenomenology in (Consumer Culture Theory) rather than phenomenology as such—as you also correctly read into our paper' (22.12.11). Indeed, hermeneutic philosophy is explicitly absolved:

> within the hermeneutic endeavour of interpretation, they are more attentive than other phenomenological approaches to the (. . .) detailed description of experience, but also refer to extra-experiential contexts on theoretical and methodological grounds.
>
> (394)

In attending to the tacit—unreflected upon—behavioural consumer construction of meaning, this chapter expressly avoids a focus on 'psychological or mental context' (ibid). Moreover, arguing that activity is always already shaped by consumers' shared (often ideologically inflected) horizons of understanding their circumstances, hermeneutics embraces a political and social context. Here Ricoeur argues for a critical or 'depth' hermeneutics engaged in 'distanciation' (1981a).

Hermeneutic Marketing and Media Theory: Reflecting on Knowing How/Knowing That

In the earlier sections of the chapter, we retraced a hermeneutic social practices perspective (initiated by Heidegger and critically continued by Gadamer, Ricoeur, Reckwitz, Schatzki et al.). Research claiming to be anchored methodologically and theoretically by 'hermeneutics' is found within media (Wilson, 1993, 2004, 2009) as well as marketing scholarship (Thompson, 1991, 1997, 1998; Thompson et al., 1994; Thompson and Hirschman, 1995, 1998; Wilson, 2011, 2012). Arnold and Fischer (1994) provide a helpful discussion in a *Journal of Consumer Research* contribution, 'Hermeneutics and Consumer Research'. A hermeneutic of equipped and habituated (hence tacit) practices wherein people project and produce participatory narrative has been recently pursued in analyses of media users (Couldry, 2004, 2012; Moores, 2012, 2013; Wilson, 2015). Projecting of a narrative meaning for 'brand personality' is a further topic in marketing (Ivens and Valta, 2012).

In advancing its critique of dualism (or Descartes' separation of mind and body), mobilising the hermeneutic perspective in marketing has been concerned to look beyond mental processing and embed analyses in consumers' habituated use of equipment. In denying dualism, audience cognitive perspectives are considered implicit in behaviour—perhaps subsequently becoming explicit in focus groups. So, for instance, Arnould and Thompson asked of embodied understanding: 'can individuals use consumer culture to transcend the internalised or habituated orientations that emanate from their socialisation in class, gender, ethnicity, and other dimensions of social structuring?' (2007: 11) Here the 'Cartesian cut' between mind/body is superseded by speculating on 'agential cut' (Barad, 2003). Thus considered as equipment, can consumer culture enable consumer reflection?

The hermeneutic emphasis from its Heideggerian origins has indeed been on understanding-in-practices *preceding* understanding-in-propositions. As Purvis and Purvis write in their article 'Knowing How and Knowing What' (transcending wider absence in marketing of this epistemological succession), in hermeneutic thought, 'for Heidegger, readiness-to-hand comes first and is primary; presence-at-hand understanding (objective knowledge) comes later' (2012: 1630). Arnould equally signalled a recognition of this hermeneutic perspective on practices in marketing thought when he argues that 'rudiments' constituting the latter, 'consist of discursive knowledge and tacit knowledge sometimes grouped together as competences, materials and affective engagements' (2014: 129).

In marketing, moreover, Thompson's work is often cited in respect of hermeneutic inquiry. Thus 'hermeneutic research focuses on the symbolic meanings and processes by which individuals construct a coherent sense of self-identity' (Thompson, 1996: 389). Writing one year after Wilson's

(1993) contribution to media studies on 'hermeneutics, reception and popular culture', Thompson et al.'s paper (1994) references Heidegger's *Being and Time* (1962) in arguing epistemologically that understanding underwrites scientific study: 'interpretation is taken to be a necessary and inevitable aspect of scientific understanding', 'preconceptions provide a necessary frame of reference rather than act as distorting "biases" that hinder understanding' (433). At this conjuncture, the consumer's 'horizons of understanding' (Heidegger) from which practices theory asserts meaning is projected receive first recognition as a topological metaphor for exploring the construction of our intelligible experience. Nonetheless, no mention is made of Heideggerian phenomenology's equally fundamental claim in dismissing Cartesian dualism that humanity primordially understands entities as equipment (*Zeug*). '*Zeug* basically means "things" or "stuff", and in Heidegger's use more specifically "something for such-and-such an activity or use."' (Parkes, 1992: 112) Our core awareness is tacit and teleological: 'temporality and the spatiality of human activity are teleological phenomena' (Schatzki, 2009: 38).

Given marketing's main orientation to addressing the consumer as user, this is an important omission. A paper by Thompson and Hirschman the following year (1995) on the 'socialised body' ironically discusses the 'several multi-billion-dollar industries that have an explicit body focus, such as diet programs, fitness *equipment* and services' (139, emphasis added). Oriented hermeneutically, such equipment with a 'body focus' can be regarded as accessible to habituated, routine use where attention is distracted: 'products take part as mediators in activity' (Raff and Melles, 2010: 150).

Thompson's subsequent (1997) article 'Interpreting Consumers: A Hermeneutical Framework for Deriving Marketing Insights from the Texts of Consumers' Consumption Stories' neglects such a habituated tacit deploying or understanding of equipment use to refer only to the hermeneutic circle and 'historically established understanding' (443). When Betty (a research participant) discusses her habit of dining out ['I usually do it (eat out for dinner) on days when I've just been working so hard and the thought of having to come home and to just work harder still is just more than I can take'], analysis of her 'narrative frames' (445) or horizons of understanding considers only her *subsequent* reflection in talking to Thompson. Yet this narrative also involves reflection upon the activity *within* her accustomed practice—to 'eat out for dinner'—a 'thought' of avoiding her further engaging with equipment—to 'work harder still' (cf. Wilson, 2012). It is not difficult to imagine restaurant pictorial marketing celebrating such liberating consumer reflection.

In the following section, we discuss by considering an empirical example—our much visited mall—the temporal placing of reflection in our 'tool-being' (Thrift, 2008) to address the question, 'can individuals use consumer culture to transcend' (Arnould and Thompson, 2007: 11) habituated behaviour, with 'new forms of embodied cultural capital'

(Thompson and Ustuner, 2015: 240)? Routine, it seems, is disturbed by reflexive attention in crises, celebration and research contribution.

Hermeneutics in Organisation Studies: Beyond 'Ready-to-Hand' and 'Reflected Upon'

A comparison of business school disciplines reveals mobilising of a cogent hermeneutic or Heideggerian practices perspective in management and organisation study, notably by Yanow and Tsoukas (2009); Nicolini (2012) and Robinson and Kerr (2015). In conceptual discussion, Yanow and Tsoukas (2009) present an important distinction between 'reflection-on-action' (such as when participants discuss *preceding* events in focus groups) and 'reflection-in-action'—a celebratory or critical reflecting 'in the midst of' habitual behaviour. Considering the latter assumes an adequate account of routine activity. Aligning with a hermeneutic account of habituated practices as socially emplaced, embodied and equipped, the authors present their thesis that the 'phenomenological view of reflection-in-action, such as the one we propose here, emphasises its embedded (social), engaged (practice), and embodied (material) aspects' (1342).

Distinguishing between these modes of reflecting on/in action, then, is underwritten by the profoundly practices concept of 'embodied' or habituated understanding. As the authors argue, their presentation of 'reflection-in-action' points to momentary challenging of 'ready-to hand' (Heidegger, 1962) accustomed activity in a 'further theorising of the character of surprise' (1339). Yanow and Tsoukas approach management study from a hermeneutic perspective incorporating understanding-in-practice. Likewise, Lai et al. (2007) are 'challenging the dominant dualist influence of Cartesian philosophy in marketing' from a 'hermeneutic perspective' incorporating the 'embodied self'.

Where marketing theory neglects the embodied and little reflected on habituated *substratum* of consumption as a site of narrative production in favour of 'historically established understanding' (Thompson, 1997), consumer reflective thought shaped by tradition, it is unlikely to accommodate 'ready-to-hand' understanding incorporated in behaviour or consumer reflection-in-practices. Yet the latter can be seen as a significant challenge to the hermeneutic dualism of 'ready-to-hand' and 'reflected on' or 'presented-at-hand' (Heidegger, 1962). Illustrating such an inclusion, we can turn empirically to enlarge upon the Malaysian mall research project anchoring the previous chapter's theoretical considerations. Here, as we have noted, consumer reflection occurs both momentarily within a practice (cell phone photography) presented by a visitor as accustomed and subsequently, prompted by the material occasion of being in the mall. 'We can have access to (habits) and reflect on them, *while they are operating*' (Kilpinen, 2009: 122, emphasis in original). The present chapter furthers studies of multi-cultural motivation by consumers engaging with shopping spaces (Farrag et al., 2010) in considering visitor reflections on their practices.

Our tacit routine embodied projection (aiming and constitution) of meaning is presumed to congeal, not collide, with surroundings, to intertwine without issue, sustained by the world. Nicolini remarks on hermeneutic phenomenology's practices perspective (following Heidegger's analysis of understanding and interpretation in his *Being and Time*) that 'for reflexive, investigative, theoretical knowledge to come into play, something previously usable must become unusable' (Nicolini, 2012: 34; Nicolini et al., 2003: 9). 'Reflexive understanding arises at moments of breakdown' (ibid.: 10). But functional entities can also enable enlightening (*Lichtung*), offering liminal possibility (Turner, 1967) beyond habituated understanding, of 'identity exploration, self-focus, instability' (Marchant and O'Donohue, 2014). The previous chapter illuminated a mall visitor's reflective self-focus.

Everyday activity is immersively goal directed, not least in producing intelligible meaning: 'humans are always operating within an horizon of projection and concerns (*Besorgen*); that is, they are absorbed and caught up with things to do and achieve' (Nicolini, 2012: 36). We can pass beyond unreflectively employing entities merely as functional equipment to momentarily regarding them as supporting celebration. In this complex behavioural play of switching meaning—crossing borders—the liminal (Küpers, 2011) is foregrounded, the 'edges' in transitory modes of consumer experience.

Seeking to evaluate this hermeneutic practices perspective on empirical research data, a pilot project exploring the liminal interface—or interweaving—of consumer ready-to-hand and reflected-upon experience was arranged in a large suburban mall. This multi-level building with its wide walk ways contains among its many shops, around one hundred and fifty food and beverage outlets along with ten entertainment clubs, bowling and gym sports facilities, as well as a cinema complex. Space is distinguished by considerable investment in seasonal celebrations (e.g. for Chinese New Year).

Rather than interrupting consumer activities or walking along with mall visitors (Lowrey et al., 2005), a small booth was established with the kind permission of management where passing consumers were invited by students staffing the stand to share mall photographs and so participate in this project of consumer research. Potential contributors were invited to talk at a later date about the cell phone photos which they had *previously* taken, and in so doing respond to the topic, 'what does the mall mean to you?' Visitor photography of this architecturally splendid mall is widespread—a habituated practice evident on social media sites particularly concerned with pictures.

As Jansson argues, 'media consumption weaves together with other forms of consumption, thus exposing the inseparability of these two domains' (2002: 6–7). Likewise, mobile phones have been previously cast as an 'emergent technology' for use in marketing research among consumers (e.g. Hein et al., 2011; see also 'participant-led photography', Penaloza, 1998; Vince and Warren, 2012; Warren, 2002). Screen immersion in shopping malls is ubiquitous.

This initial phase of inviting people to participate in media-led reflection on visiting the massive mall occupied a weekend. A subsequent four-week correspondence online ensued thereafter, arranging a mutually convenient meeting between consumers and the researchers. Participants discussed twenty-five photographs, individually and as a group (six persons): female and male, ranging in ages from twenty to fifty-one, Chinese, Indian and Malay, contributors included new graduates as well as an account executive, management trainee and teacher. In group discussion, sometimes known to organisation research as 'thematic workshops' (Svahn et al., 2009: 2), people were asked to consider the earlier photographs they had taken as signalling 'themes' they wished to consider (e.g. 'bonding'). Where consumers met a researcher individually, discussion revolved around 'feelings', specific memories prompted by the pictures and short descriptions of their content.

Subsequent to these 'face-to-face' meetings between mall visitors and researchers, a further twelve online as virtual *Facebook* and *WhatsApp* 'chat' were arranged with a research assistant in three groups discussing their photographs taken of memorable moments in the mall. Participants of both genders were exclusively Chinese, with one exception (Bidayuh) and included a business man, dentists, doctor, housewife, students and lecturers: they were recruited as friends of friends. The contributions to both 'real' and virtual meetings were all fully transcribed by a research assistant.

Talking here provided accounts of customary consumer visits to the mall, or in hermeneutic terms, enabled narrative 'presencing' pre-reflective or 'ready-to-hand' (Heidegger, 1962) behaviour. Reference was made to concurrent reflection, enlightened moments, a 'clearing' (ibid.) or *Lichtung* in our mall consumers' everyday awareness. Distributed across genres or modes of immersion in the mall (such as 'enjoying the crowd', the 'health option', taking pictures), reflection-on/in-practices occurred spontaneously. Or it could take shape in remembering, participant response to photographs—arguably themselves a mode of behavioural reflecting—prompted by this mall's being 'lighted up', celebrating the nation's diverse multi-cultural festivals—'spectacle' (Sherry et al., 2001). Here mall spatial design and themes (Fırat et al., 2011; Van Marrewijka and Broosa, 2012) prevailed:

> At 'Chinese New Year, the lights . . . erm now look at this (photograph) is just that, I think it just, just brightens the day with the lights and . . . with the lanterns, so it is like more of a . . . like leading the path kind of stuff, showing the way because it's lighted up', an older male Indian responds, recognising the mall's decorating as illuminating.

Captured visually, consumer reflection on/in cell phone practice is discussed. 'I love candid shots. It seems to capture a moment in time, a real moment:)' (male, Chinese visitor). Or as female Chinese mall visitors enthused, a 'precious moment', a 'remarkable moment'. We have considered at length (concluding the previous chapter) taking such pictures as an embodied habituated practice suspended momentarily in consumers' celebratory reflecting on their participatory 'being there'. 'I remember at this moment when we took the picture it was something that you want it to last', here signalling a reflective clearing, a fresh horizon, distinct from mundane appreciation of mall photos, 'those pictures'. Reflecting subsequently in response to (or reception of) the mall is also a generic practice, building embodied narratives of understanding-in-use, incorporating a wider horizon of interpretation. Narratives 'act in people's lives in ways that matter deeply' (Smith, 2016: 202).

Practices can be conceptually internally interlinked as where shared generic understanding of a Chinese Reunion Dinner generates consensus on the meaning of tossing *Yee Sang* as a practice. Analytically, one could consider such cases as culturally related constituent 'practices-in-a-practice' open to a triple hermeneutic of researchers regarding the meaning of a reunion shaping its elements. On the other hand, the seasonal festival celebratory function of a mall can be viewed as pleasurable or profitable from *disparate* horizons of understanding embedded in the consumer and management practices. Here the mall becomes a loosely defined 'boundary object' (Carlile, 2002: 442), focus for 'negotiation' of rewards through juxtaposing the cost of assembly with crowds drawn and responses in focus group research. The functioning boundary object enables practices with distinct horizons of understanding to 'co-ordinate'—if not to achieve consensus on the pleasurable/profitable identity or significance of—annual commemorative or religious festival displays in a large shopping mall.

> 'Boundary objects are a sort of arrangement that allow different groups to work together without consensus' on meaning, permitting connotative 'interpretive flexibility' which is consistent with agreed denotation of the object. The material arrangement 'is worked on by local groups who maintain its vaguer identity as a common object, while making it more specific, more tailored to local use within a social world'. 'New participants (in groups) acquire a naturalised familiarity with its objects as they become members.'
>
> (Star, 2010: 602, 604–605, 611)

Consumer Reflection on Practices: Disclosing Generic Understanding-in-Use

A practice (or *praxis*) is a little reflected on embodied generic narrative of understanding-in-use, incorporating horizons of understanding. In focus group or research interview, participants can reflect upon or explore those sometimes distant horizons of understanding. Practices as equipped (tool-bearing), evading attention (tacit) and exercising generic expectation may be considered.

We discussed in the preceding chapters how philosophical hermeneutics prefigured elements of practice theories. Philosophy and theory can be conjoined as a hermeneutic practices perspective. Viewed from this vantage point, practices (such as walking in malls/watching movies) can be read as tacitly integrating a 'fore-understanding' (Heidegger, 1962) of their genre with 'facticity' (ibid.).

Bringing hermeneutics to bear on behavioural analysis, a practice:

i. is pre-reflectively 'fore-structured' (ibid.) prior to participant attention (disclosed in discussion);
ii. presumes 'fore-having' (ibid.) enabling equipment (e.g. Heidegger's available hammer);
iii. projects or tacitly 'fore-sees' (ibid.) from generic 'horizons of understanding' (anticipates hammering);
iv. produces or assembles from such 'fore-conceptions' (ibid.) embodied narrative (hammering);
v. participates in 'being-with-others' (co-ordinating the particular behavioural narrative). Here our (vi) appropriation (Gadamer, 1975) or learning of possible perspective (e.g. on purchasing) in participating may shape
vii. alignment and formation of our identity or
viii. alienation occurs, distanciated criticism of the practice (Ricoeur, 1981a). Aligning with material possession, purchasing, consumers produce an 'extended self' (Belk, 1988), mark(et)ing out identity, given the 'ego stretching ability of earthly possessions' (Ludik et al., 2015: 200) to affirm or alienate class, ethnic, gender positioning.

The practices perspective integrates individualistic, cultural, material and structural aspects of consuming read as embodied tacit narrative establishing intelligibility. Thus a shared horizon of understanding, embedded in practice, can contextualise a common, if tacit, conviction about 'how-to-do'. To take two individualised examples from the analysis of fore-structured behaviour in a shopping mall:

(a) 'My boyfriend (now my husband) is always by my side and accompanies me, to even look at the shoes and the cosmetics. Hihi. I know some men will not want to accompany their girlfriends' [female, Chinese, celebrating equipment enabling modes of 'being-with-others' (Heidegger)].

This mall narrative departs from a generic horizon of understanding from where masculine behaviour is fore-seen ('I know some men will not want to accompany their girlfriends'), allowing distinctive fore-conception of her husband as being 'always by my side (. . .) to even look at the shoes and the cosmetics', producing a narrative of shopping behaviour wherein he 'accompanies me'.

(b) '(The mall) used to be my rendezvous with a bunch of friends who have the same liking for retail therapy. Whenever I needed a break, I used to sit by the brink and observe other shoppers. Good old times! . . . I would start gossiping with my friends while doing our observation' (female, Chinese, reflecting on multiple modes of ludic participation in mall narrative as 'retail therapy').

Fore-seeing 'retail therapy', the mall as a 'rendezvous with a bunch of friends' is perceived from habituated horizons of understanding. Materially positioned, 'our' conceptions of participatory 'observation' and 'gossiping with friends' are co-ordinated sitting 'by the brink'. Shared activity is shaped individually (with 'fore-sight') and societally (conforming to 'retail therapy').

Reflecting on the décor, their delight or disenchantment in the shopping mall, consumers are aligned with content and appropriate narrative or are alienated from the processes of consuming. 'What does the mall mean to you?' These 'rhythms', captured in mobile media photo (Wilken and Goggin, 2012), of rallying, reunion and rekindling articulated consumer answers in activities. Declaring their behaviour to be a habitually 'continuous business', but while walking, appreciating 'in terms of the décor, in terms of the look and feel' the mall's prompting reflecting-on/in-practices, a male Indian tells how visitors cross its threshold from everyday life, sharing a managed ludicity:

> it is a vast contrast (with other malls) when you (are) walking in terms of the décor, in terms of the look and feel. So people appreciate that and they will come back and (it) is a continuous business.
>
> (Male, Indian)

Here this research participant speaks of consumers walking, aligned in appreciation of the mall's 'decor, in terms of the look and feel'. They may well appropriate (Gadamer, 1975) aspects of its marketing to shape their identity, inflecting brand narrative towards their own stories, for as Urry remarks in his 'pedestrian observations', there are 'many ways to walk' (2006: 362). Consumers in this mall 'sustain ludic consumption community experiences' (Seregina and Weijo, 2017: 140) for brands 'forge collective identities' (Cayla and Eckhardt, 2008: 217).

Reflecting on the mall, of course, is not always an easy evincing of celebratory behaviour. For its visiting consumers can evoke a 'necessary disenchantment' (Couldry, 2013) when remembering a placed habituated gaze. Here a would-be seller's ready-to-hand looking is recognised, presented-at-hand:

> 'sometimes, like for us, we are the younger generation, so sometimes when we go into certain shops they look at us as if we don't have money to buy . . . I think that is just the negative side'.
>
> (Female, Malay)

Addressing the 'negative side' of selling, this visitor to 'certain shops' is clearly alienated. 'Critique rests on the moment of *distanciation*' (Ricoeur, 1991a: 35) (emphasis in original). More specifically, our consumer 'interaction as process (practice?) disrupts place when certain actions, events, and situations undermine users' convenience, comfort, and trust' (Seamon, 2018).

Convenient use is not always represented in cell phone practices: 'the free toilet is really, I would say . . . .' (male, Chinese). Nonetheless, celebration and criticism—alignment and alienation—are eloquently evident in consumer practices, their behavioural reception of this massive mall.

Marketing and Organisation Theory: A Hermeneutics of Reflection-On/In-Practices

> You mean this sort of thing goes on all the time?
>
> (Question at recent business school conference)

Hermeneutics is the philosophical narrative of how humanity processes understanding being in the world, their understanding-in-practice(s) making continual sense of their surroundings. People are always already active in constructing or projecting meaning—seeing chairs, tables around them, not sense-data without significance. The processing wherein such entities are recognised and their properties (tacitly) anticipated, arriving at material culture, is as argued, 'ready-to-hand' (Heidegger, 1962), receiving little attention. In a person's 'primordially' producing meaning, 'being is projected upon (. . .) significance' (ibid.: 187). Ubiquitous understanding is goal oriented both in achieving a meaningful world and in its habitual purchase on an environment of entities as 'tools' (ibid). Thus '(competent) actors' need to '"keep in touch" with why they act as they do' (Giddens, 1981b: 36).

Embodied beings, people fundamentally understand an entity in terms of actual or potential usage as 'equipment'—that is, as Heidegger wrote, projecting 'its service*ability*, its us*ability*, and its detriment*ality*' (1962: 184, emphasis in original). Mundane teleological understanding is 'invisible-in-use' (Takayama, 2011), little reflected on, implicit in practice unless celebratory, critical or it is considered in discussion.

Hermeneutic philosophy as an account of our arriving at meaning has underwritten media and reader reception studies (Wilson, 2009). Viewing from the 'perspectival diversity' (Kozinets et al., 2004: 661) of varied (if limiting) horizons of understanding screen content, we project—expect and establish—distinct narrative. As reviewed throughout this chapter, hermeneutics has informed a narrative of our everyday consumption in marketing theory and emphasising constructing meaning as equipment enabled, reflection on our material culture. In the last, making sense of manufactured environments is seen as projected and produced in consumer participation. Managers equally 'make up an organisation' and its meaning—a further focus for business research (Granot et al., 2012: 548).

Knowing is evident in consumer behaviour (here flowing through a mall), manifested where entities are comprehended corporeally as equipping people, an understanding 'embodied rather than brought to consciousness as a thought or an idea' (Dant, 2005: 86). Hermeneutics argues that 'how the material world exists for us is constituted in our practical actions and how we make use of the things around us' (ibid.: 85), as through behaviour generating material culture in a shopping mall. 'The use of the object (. . .) integrates the object into social lives' (Dant, 2000: 665).

In this conceptual contribution to thinking about consumers (briefly empirically displayed), a hermeneutic practices perspective was set out—from which philosophical orientation on everyday activity, mobility marketing can be considered. How may it present and appropriately address material interaction among consumers in the mall? For such activity—having coffee, purchasing goods—is habitual, yet may be also a passing bearer of celebratory or critical considering, a characteristic we recognised here and valued by referring to this visiting behaviour as 'place ballet' (Seamon, 1979). In activity so evaluated by agents, its incorporated practical treatment or understanding of entities as 'equipment' (from apples to smartphones) is reflected upon either simultaneously or subsequently.

Where place ballet is represented in reflection—consideration of routine, rather than its challenging collapse—meaning generating practices are evident, their horizons of understanding foregrounded. Its mediated mobility as material culture may be captured in photographs, presented in discussion as a visual meta-text bearing reflective behaviour and, indeed, promoted in appropriate marketing.

Mobility is constituted by practices [exemplified from car driving to mall visiting whether local or expatriate (Butler and Hannam, 2014)]. Practices are primordial. So a seemingly stationary gaze is projected, produced, and participatory. Mobilities (whether ready-to-hand or reflected upon) are molecular practices. Mobilities 'encompasses both the embodied practice of movement and the representations, ideologies and meanings attached to both movement and stillness' (Sheller, n.d.)

Research structured by critical hermeneutics (Heidegger, Gadamer, Ricoeur), taking shape as reception or practices analyses, may be moving to a significant role in marketing theory. Indeed, much earlier, productively appropriating a hermeneutic reception theory for consumer studies was initiated by Scott (1994a, 1994b) and Stern (1989). In this 'meaning-based model' (Mick and Buhl, 1992), as media users, we play perceptually (Stern et al., 2005). A decade later, Keller and Halkier (2014) remarked on the 'recent interest in practice theoretical approaches' (36) to marketing.

'Hermeneutic and semiotic approaches are widely used in mainstream-marketing' (Cova et al., 2013: 216). Considering hermeneutic references across both research and theory, a search for its shaping of ideas in *Consumption, Markets, Culture* located its presence in thirty-five articles as well as thirty papers in the *European Journal of Marketing*. Only slightly fewer articles in *Marketing Theory* (twenty-nine) contained references as did twenty-eight papers in *Qualitative Market Research*, along with thirty in the *Journal of Marketing Management*. Hermeneutic philosophy—celebrated, cited or critiqued—underwrites significant contribution to marketing thought. As Sitz (2008) succinctly summarised some years ago, albeit arguing for the difference of 'discourse analysis', 'analyses of consumers' narratives mainly rely on semiotic, psycho-cognitive, hermeneutic or phenomenological approaches' (177).

'In a society that attaches particular value to "abstract knowledge", the details of practice have come to be seen as nonessential, unimportant' (Brown and Duguid, 1991: 40). Instead, this chapter has endeavoured to further hermeneutic theory of practices following Reckwitz (2002a) by (re)turning to core concepts in its philosophical underwriting, allowing the author to think through marketing and organisational theory discussion of a behaviourally evident understanding in action and speech. Habituated consumption functions both as the tacit condition of meaning making (e.g. strolling through a familiar mall) and—as a focus for reflection-on/in-practices—its narrative content (e.g. on cell phone). Interactive spaces are thereby 'made meaningful and lively by embodied social practices' (Larsen, 2005: 420) where visitors presume, project and produce behavioural narrative in modes of being-with-others, so evincing celebratory alignment or critical detached alienation.

Summary so far: The chapter has considered consumer reflection—foregrounding their horizons of understanding around 'habituated orientations' (Arnould and Thompson, 2007: 11) or behaviour. In doing so, we discussed at length how 'individuals use consumer culture to transcend' (ibid.) habit. Context is clearly particularly important in hermeneutic studies of organisations (Prasad, 2002: 24).

Consumer culture theory has much acknowledged interweaving of marketing and material culture. The chapter has explored whether considering this dialectic from our hermeneutic practices perspective enhances research and marketing activity. From such a viewpoint, consumers engage in equipped, embodied mobility, habituated, hence tacit practices—as entered from little reflected-upon horizons of understanding yielding to self-monitoring moments of celebration and criticism. Their subsequent reflection on a practice (such as ubiquitous photography in a mall) may be initiated and supported in a focus group exploring horizons of understanding and their social embeddedness—tacitly 'embedded and enmeshed in practice' (Ajjawi and Higgs, 2007: 613), (in)forming behaviour. 'Cultural categories are constantly substantiated by human practice' (1986: 73), argued McCracken.

Immersion in recurrent behaviour is tacitly recognised from our horizons of understanding-in-use. Drawing upon a hermeneutic perspective on practices, we can be said to implicitly

> presume 'fore-having'—or we have—appropriate equipment
> project or 'fore-see' a type (genre) of behaviour and rules
> produce from such 'fore-conceptions', behavioural narratives, articulated in participatory action, in which appropriation of possible perspective, alignment or alienation may result.

Embodied horizon of understanding—as with geographical boundaries—can be a focus both of consensus or sustained contestation. From a political economy perspective on culture (Fornas, 2008: 897), as intertwining 'materiality and meaning' (ibid.: 901), a mall marketed as (reified) shopping 'adventure' in buying, can be regarded by visitors in a distanciated reading of such positioning as their preferred place for 'bonding'. As with the participation programmes (talk shows) involving an 'active citizen-viewer' discussed by Carpentier (2001), so in this mall promenading, 'power relations are also always two way relations, even if the power of one actor (or party) is limited compared to the other' (212).

Referring to interviews and focus groups with mall visitors, this chapter has sought to affirm a practices perspective empirically through including their contributions in discussion with a local facilitator:

i. 'dwelling' or immersed in a familiar mall, consumers' ready-to-hand understanding (unreflected on/incorporated in practices) is of entities as 'equipment' (*Zeug*) rather than objects *simpliciter*;
ii. celebratory or critical consumer reflecting within practices (*Lichtung* or a momentary clearing in the mundane) may be enabled by refreshing displays or be spontaneous, a passing self-awareness;
iii. creating this momentary clearing in otherwise unreflective everyday awareness is manifested in participatory behavioural reflecting ('doings and sayings'), captured in consumers' photography;
iv. rather than seamless narratives of self-reporting by our participants in research categorised as being 'hermeneutic', contributors should

> be encouraged to present celebratory and critical moments within habituated practices. 'I remember at this moment when we took the picture it was something that you want it to last.' For these can constitute remarkable images embodying our reflection.

Incorporated in circulating around their mega-mall, consumer narrative practices construct a diverse material culture of response to concretised display in which personal and professional goals are integrated—or occasionally involved in challenge. From a marketing perspective, its perceived promise of festive decorating, 'great innovative ideas on each festive celebration', 'creativity comes every festive season' (male, Chinese visitor) is particularly encouraging of mobile practices where 'making know-how known' (Chia and Holt, 2006: 642) is clearly understood and achieved.

As with a London 'concrete (mall) megastructure', this Kuala Lumpur 'complex of material and spatial phenomena (. . .) offers the possibility of multiple readings and meanings to different groups of people, framed by the cultural conditions of any given moment' (Melhuish, 2005: 28) in an embodied acquisition and assertion of meaning. Like social media such as *Facebook*, visitors are addressed both as buyers and bonding, sources of profit and sustaining friendship. The mall enables their ready-to-hand immersion and reflection-in-practices, with visitors momentarily switching in a liminal crossing between these modes of experience, as well as subsequent reflexive consideration. Here we have conjoined hermeneutic philosophy with consumer theory in a practices perspective, suggesting in passing an alternative mode of audience advertising address to a reflective consumer.

Finally, in respect of 'reflection', this chapter uses the German term *Lichtung* as denoting a 'clearing' and 'enlightening' in Heideggerian philosophy. While *Being and Time* was published in 1927, its most frequently used English translation is in 1962. Capobianco writes (2010):

> By the 1960s Heidegger had fully purged his understanding of *die Lichtung* of any relation to *Licht*, so the translation of *Lichtung* as 'clearing' in his statements of the 1960s is much more in line with his explicit intentions. Even so, we should keep in mind that the German word *Lichtung* in the sense of 'clearing' does have a linguistic relation to *Licht/lichten* in the sense of 'lighting' and 'brightening'.
>
> (2010: 116)

4 Consuming Psychology: Interpretative Phenomenological Analysis

Thematic Understanding in Hermeneutic Practices

Project

Earlier chapters reviewed hermeneutic philosophy and practice theories aiming not only to point out their parallel theses but also to argue for their synthesis in a hermeneutic practices perspective. A third chapter sought to review hermeneutic marketing studies from this horizon of understanding. In the present chapter, we reflect on psychology's Interpretative Phenomenological Analysis (IPA), suggesting that its thematic studies of research participants' narratives be integrated as establishing the latter's presenting hermeneutic practices, shaped by necessary features of understanding life. We can see—following textual concerns of earlier chapters—a wide-ranging literacy in people's 'reading' experience, their anticipatory prefiguring, articulating or configuring narrative, subsequently being refigured or interpreted through application to personal circumstance in a storied sense-making.

IPA, from the first, acknowledged its underwriting as qualitative psychology by hermeneutic philosophy. A focus on practices would enable IPA to bring the hermeneutic spatio-temporal model of generic understanding informing practices to bear on coming to terms with participant narrative. In this chapter, we consider how people recounting their stories (often of difficulty) can be viewed as referring to embodied generic understanding-in-use of equipment, emplacing (or putting in place) evaluative 'horizons' or perspectives on that behaviour, seen distantly in retrospective reflection. A recollected practice (e.g. of caring) contains implicit reference to constraint and enablements shaped by embodied social role with its shared generic rules and directives for competent enactment. In so far as IPA is underwritten by hermeneutic philosophy offering a 'horizon of understanding', we can accept 'when we are trying to understand another person or a text, we need to have some idea of the horizon in which the subject matter is intelligible to the author or speaker' (Vessey, 2009: 539).

IPA—Researcher 'Themes' as Participant Practices of Understanding Life

> Doing IPA inevitably involves being hermeneutic in the general sense; doing it well involves more particular hermeneutics.
>
> (Smith, 2011a: 58)

Integrating hermeneutic (Heidegger, Gadamer, Ricoeur) philosophy's narrative of consumer understanding with a not too distant social theory of practices (Reckwitz, Schatzki, Shove), we can now see hermeneutic practices as being culturally embedded behaviour with core universal aspects—*embodied* generic narrative of *equipment* understanding-in-use, *emplacing* (incorporating) affective perspectives or horizons of concerned understanding, aligning with or alienated from other points of view. Everyday meaning creating (hermeneutic) productive practice can range from our walking in a mall to watching television, little reflected on routines. There, we tacitly articulate assumption (presupposing) and anticipation (projecting) with actual event in a hermeneutic circle of (sometimes defeated) understanding. Understanding as a practice is thereby primarily implicit and instrumental, a practice from which one can infer broader participant perspectives or less immediate horizons of contextual interpretive understanding: to determine 'a horizon means being able to see beyond what is close at hand' (Laverty, 2003: 25). Research foregrounds core aspects of such tacit understanding—the co-ordinates or points in their horizon of comprehension from which participants tacitly (albeit most clearly) have assigned immediate meaning to their experience from care giving to coping with chronic pain. 'I always thought you had pain to tell you when there was something wrong.' (female, reflecting on her body as dysfunctional 'equipment' in Osborn and Smith, 1998: 69)

'We must each have a certain repertoire of discursive and practical skills for living in each mode of being', 'social, personal and corporeal' (Harre, 1993: 2). Being thus skilfully equipped to effect embodied discursive perspectives is a required 'universal feature of all forms of human life' (ibid.), from apple selection as signalling gendered competence to shaking hands expressing friendship.

Are practices with these multiple unfolding aspects or 'moments' equally revealed through Interpretative Phenomenological Analysis (IPA) of the 'themes' that research participants present in their narrative discourse, reflecting idiographically or individually on lived experience (Smith et al., 1995)? Can these perpetual aspects of consumer practice be also an acceptable focus for questions shaping culturally embedded discussion in focus group/ interview, aspects acknowledged as generic or thematic (e.g. where mall visiting emphasises shared horizons of understanding)? Can a *temporal* production of our embodied, equipped *being*, putting into play and emplacing perspectives, be then a core concern for a *hermeneutic* IPA? 'Time is an ever present horizon for us' (Finlay, 2011). Here IPA seeks its answers 'through interpretive engagement with transcripts' (Flowers et al., 1998: 411), acknowledging (and thereby distancing itself from Husserl) the ineluctable 'fore-understanding' of the researcher in making sense of data—an alignment with Heidegger which has been termed 'new phenomenology' within some nursing studies (Dowling, 2007: 137).

In practices, people engage tacitly or unreflectively with entities understood as 'equipment' or *Zeug* (Heidegger, 1962). Or as Van Manen writes, 'we first of all understand the world through the equipment and practices within which we dwell' (2007: 17). The focus group participant whom we considered in Chapter 1, primarily understood entities (the apples!) as being equipment (rather than just objects), in selecting fruit 'with no flaws'. Uncertainty over a precise account ('something like this') when she comes to narrate her activity for the benefit of a focus group suggests that she is foregrounding, rendering explicit, a practice normally lacking concurrent consideration, monitoring: here it is pre-reflective or tacit. Yet it is a practice which has also shaped her identity-defining mode of gendered being-with-others—'the guys', who 'just grab and go!' Hermeneutic understanding-in-use incorporates evaluative viewpoints, affective horizons of understanding generic activity. 'We understand things from certain framework conditions' (Davidsen, 2013: 323).

Likewise, a female Chinese frequent mall visitor told us in a focus group that, 'basically, I expect good security from the mall'. We noted her anticipating can be interpreted hermeneutically as referring to both the material and metaphorical affective horizon of expectation from which she enters the mall—projecting thereupon 'good security'. Her presuming is evident as projected by her mode of habitual being in the mall, visible in behaviour (e.g. how she carries a bag)—exhibiting her tacit (not concurrently considered) view of this mall as equipped to deter 'snatch thieves'. Walking securely in the mall instantiates a generic, enabled, embodied practice or behavioural cognition—a tacit process of immersive presuming, projecting, producing an ambulatory participatory narrative. Her visiting this mall thereby incorporates and emplaces an affective horizon of understanding its space, habituated 'pre-reflective, pre-linguistic understanding' (Boden and Eatough, 2014: 161) of the vast place as 'secure', a horizon of perceived engaging shaping actual and possible experience.

> (Embodied) horizons are the conditions that provide the meaning for (experience), conditions which need to be made conscious for a proper understanding of the (experience). As providing the key to understanding our perceptions they draw us forward, inspiring investigation.
>
> (Vessey, 2009: 536)

Given their generic accomplishment practices are goal directed and rule governed, just as in the aesthetic practice of constructing type-conforming melodramas or a romantic film narrative. 'To submit production to genres (is) to produce an individual' (Ricoeur, 1981a: 136), whether a story or choosing an apple. Practices are routine, embodied equipped generic understanding-in-use, evident in tacitly generating individual activity, with little self-monitoring, as in walking securely at a mall: 'our individuality' is 'bound up with the fact of embodiment' (Harre, 1993: 1).

In practices, behaviour emplaces or puts in place our little reflected on, hence '*horizons* of understanding' (Gadamer, 1975), affective perceptions of their value as activity (avoiding 'flaws' with health issues, enjoying relaxing 'security'). Such cognitive horizons can be regarded as 'fused' with existing (Gadamer) or far from ['distanciated' (Ricoeur)] alternative perspectives (such as the 'guys' for whose non-selective perception of the apples, 'it's just the same. Just grab and go').

Practice theorists (Reckwitz, Schatzki, Shove), we noted, followed hermeneutic theory in arguing for the generic status of practices as tacit embodied, equipped teleological routine. That is, practices are patterned: they 'necessarily imply certain routinised ways of understanding the world, of desiring something, of knowing how to do something' (Reckwitz, 2002a: 251). Purpose is thus embodied in practices: their epistemologically equipped character is at their core. Practices, parallel with cinema or a literary genre, are said to be 'nexuses of human activity, open-ended sets of doings and sayings organised by understandings, rules, and teleoaffectivities' (Schatzki, 2015: 2). A further set of theorists also asserts that, like conventions shaping activity for cinematic genres, conventions for practices such as walking are 'sensitive to culture and situation' (Shove and Pantzar, 2005: 47). For a conjoined hermeneutic practices perspective on enabling our understanding-in-use, 'genre' is a central concept connecting the emphasis of philosophers and social theorists on tacit achievement. Practical understanding exercises—with little reflection—an establishing of prior behavioural genre. 'Genres', like themes, 'represent some level of patterned response' (Braun and Clarke, 2006: 82).

Interpretative Phenomenological Analysis, asserts its author, is 'strongly connected to the interpretive or hermeneutic tradition' (J.A. Smith, 2004: 40), so acknowledging both a hermeneutics of restoring meaning and 'hermeneutics of questioning, of critical engagement' (ibid.: 46). Here, we discuss whether such connecting enables participant narrative—established as 'themed' following discussion with researchers—to further disclose its referencing generic hermeneutic practices. We go some way to address Chamberlain's (2011) concern with IPA over the limited consideration of,

> its philosophical and theoretical background, and above all, discussion on how IPA is positioned, epistemologically and theoretically as phenomenological and hermeneutic in nature . . . (More significantly)

> the lack of discussion (. . .) around the critical connection between the analytic methods of IPA and the researcher's engagement in hermeneutic analysis limits the possibilities for moving beyond themes. (53, 51)

As Norlyk and Harder argue in their review of nursing studies (2010), 'there is a need for clarifying how the principles of the phenomenological philosophy are implemented in a particular study': this 'research could be strengthened by greater attention to its philosophical underpinnings' (420, 427). We now consider if attention to 'philosophical underpinnings' is sufficiently realised by analysing participant narrative themes as generic embodied equipped practical understanding, an interpretive interest tacitly emplacing a wider horizon of understanding. Does the research discussion with the 'person-in-context' (Larkin and Thompson, 2012: 102) reflect on her or his hermeneutic practices?

From Participant Practices to Philosophical Underpinning: (1) A Hermeneutic Re-view of IPA Research in Health Psychology

Introducing Interpretative Phenomenological Analysis in 1996, contributing to the cross-disciplinary 1990's (re)development of an applied hermeneutics (Thompson, 1991; Wilson, 1993), Smith wrote on health psychology, developing a research route between the quantitative measuring linking participant attitudes to behaviour (cf. Wilson, 2011) and qualitative analysis of participants constructing social positions in discursive contributions to focus groups and interviews. Instead, the 'aim of IPA is to explore the participant's view of the world', albeit recognising that 'access is both dependent on, and complicated by, the researcher's own conceptions' (1996: 264). Producing interpretations of the participant's primary sense-making is denoted a 'double hermeneutic' (Smith, 2011b: 10).

IPA follows hermeneutics, subscribing to its epistemology where 'for human affairs, the model of scientific theory, which is adequate to an object, is replaced by that of understanding, seen as a fusion of horizons' (Taylor, 2002: 136). Understanding is essentially perspectival, explored in the hermeneutics of understanding-in-use we consider by semi-structured interview (Smith, 1995). Translation from participant into researcher language can complicate this double hermeneutic. Yet 'thinking processes', anticipatory, accompanying, after practices are recorded (Smith et al., 2002). Care recipients' 'meaning-making processes' are given voice (Gough and Deatrick, 2015: 291). A double hermeneutic can become triple where, for instance, the researcher interviews co-ordinators reflecting on intervention strategies for the disabled, where the latter's viewpoint is also referenced, as in the case of one university 'student who had difficulties with, anxiety with presentations, so we had to discuss that and see what the anxieties were', then seek solutions (Koca-Atabey, 2017: 141).

IPA 'interprets within the terms of the text which the participant has produced' (Smith et al., 2009: 37), allowing thereby a 'restoration of meaning' (Smith, 2004: 46). From a hermeneutic perspective, a participant's 'terms' can be further analysed within IPA. How do those terms display understanding to be embodied or cast within a wider 'horizon of understanding'? IPA also 'allows a hermeneutics of questioning, of critical engagement' as a researcher 'may well ask questions and posit readings which the participants would be unlikely, unable or unwilling to see or acknowledge' (ibid.).

Illustrating 'IPA in practice' (1996), Smith considers hospital haemodialysis where machines replace the function of damaged kidneys (267–270). A participant reflects on being 'really fed up with the repetition' of routine 'passive' involvement with the practice. From a hermeneutic stance, one sees in her account of 'becoming part of this machine', embodiment and equipment unhappily merge, incorporating a narrative of understanding-in-use. Perception of her desired spatio-temporal distance (not being 'tethered to one place') are evoked from an affective horizon of understanding, thereby emplaced: a 'dialysing at home would be—I'm still being myself. I've still got my identity but I'm just giving myself some treatment', actively engaging equipment. '(It's) under my control and I use it'. Less 'alien' equipment understanding-in-use would emerge (Yardley, 2002: 19). The bodily 'battle for agency' is evoked further in poetry discussed by Spiers and Smith (2012: 122). Embodiment can be challenged by equipping as where a patient comments on the large size of an HIV tablet: 'you feel it on your chest and it is like you're going to throw up' (in Spiers et al., 2016).

Embodied understanding of eating behaviour—where food is the equipment used or refused—as a mode of 'control' or 'power over their external (as opposed to internal) environment' is seen by Jarman et al. (1997) to be regarded as a core characteristic in the diagnosis of anorexia nervosa (142). As a therapist comments, 'it is a sort of, as a protest about not having other ways to protest'. Likewise, Eatough and Smith (2006) argue regarding the experience of anger that it can be said to be a mode of bodily engagement with the world: 'bodily change is a key aspect of what anger feels like; being angry is an experience which is *lived* through the body' (494, emphasis in original).

Coping with chronic pain, equally, is a corporeal practice. Here such intensity of embodied experience can suppress life's 'meaning to the sufferer' (Osborn and Smith, 1998: 65). Immediate suffering may displace a richer interest in existence to the horizons of interpretive understanding. Research participants 'remained preoccupied with a sense of confusion, loss and threat' (ibid.: 76). Interviewees searching for explanations suggest pain is construed as signifying failed 'equipment'. 'I always thought you had pain to tell you when there was something wrong.' (female; ibid.: 69)

Hermeneutic practices constituted by embodied narratives of equipped understanding-in-use can be counter-factual or considered as potential but not actual events. Smith et al. (1999) discuss 'doing interpretive phenomenological analysis' in contributing to qualitative health psychology. A participant during their research on chronic back pain comments:

> you always think well there's loads of people far, far worse off than you, you know so you try to think of other people who are permanently in wheel chairs, and it's supposed to make you feel better, which in a way it does. But basically it's frightening.

Contemplating being 'permanently in wheel chairs' as an everyday practice or one's generic mode of equipped understanding-in-use when moving emplaces conflicting perspectives: 'you feel better' 'but basically it's frightening'. Such *de facto* 'disembodiment' is viewed by this contributor to pain research from dissonant affective horizons of understanding potential experience.

In the same chapter (1999) Smith et al. consider the experience of paediatric nurses caring for patients with anorexia nervosa. One of these nurses narrates her experience of 'wanting to help':

> I just feel frustrated I think. I just wish that I could help 'em more and you know sort out what's happened. I could become more involved actually if I let myself.

In this nurse's apparently repeated response or practice of wishing to 'help 'em more' a meaningful pattern or behavioural minigenre emerges, a set of personal narratives incorporating her seemingly uncertain or tacit horizon of understanding the experience as feeling 'frustrated I think'. Seeking to overcome this disharmony with her patients (or narrative disequilibrium), she then speculates on a resolution, a hermeneutic circle of resolving frustration: 'I could become more involved actually'.

Hermeneutic modeling of 'understanding' embodied in practices from reading to our routine activity as a 'fusion of horizons' (Gadamer, 1975) asserts its spatio-temporal character. For Ricoeur, as we have seen, occupying a distant horizon of understanding enables political criticism (1981a). In research associated with Interpretative Phenomenological Analysis, perceptual distance allows critique of an embodied self. Smith and Osborn (2007) consider 'pain as an assault upon the self', a narrative implicitly constructing separation between source and sufferer of pain—the same person. A participant discusses 'being mean': 'it's the pain, it's me, but it is me, me doing it but not me do you understand what I'm saying?' Here, cause and critique of 'being mean' issue from one source, conceived as 'not me' reflected upon (by 'me') from a distanced affective horizon of understanding. Another participant emphasises a spatio-temporal distance—a disjunction of selves comprehending pain behaviourally: 'It's like living with this guy who follows you around all the time.'

Disjunction or distance between horizons of understanding behavioural narrative can occur with 'contested diagnosis between CFS (chronic fatigue syndrome) and depression' (Dickson et al., 2007: 856). Confronted with his doctor's diagnosis of depressive behaviour (e.g. not sleeping), one research participant asserts, 'I said "It's not depression, I know my own body and I know how I'm feeling and I know this is not depression."' Source and subject of his reflecting are the same self.

The body tells a story, incorporating (often) visually evident anticipating and articulation of narrative, exercised within generic horizons of practical understanding as in walking, confident of security, through a shopping mall. In their article on 'Making Sense of Risk', Senior et al. (2002) discuss research in which participants 'reported acting in ways consonant with the perception of an increased risk of heart attack' (157). Poor diet is perceived as culminating in high cholesterol levels, emplacing wider perceptions: 'part of it is through family plus me diet, bad diet, bad lifestyle. Bad, bad lifestyle' (male; ibid.: 161). Behaviour is here being understood as culpable narrative.

Reflections on embodied narrative evincing affective concern construct an identity for the speaking subject tracing out a sometimes disputed or submerged horizon of self-understanding. In doing so, alternative (power-bearing) perspectives can be refused: 'It's not depression.' De Visser and Smith (2006) discuss 'mister in-between', an Indian student viewing cultural horizons offering varying behavioural insight. Within this discursive structure exist routes to 'being masculine' (ibid.: 686), wherein men can 'align themselves with particular discourses and to monitor their behaviour accordingly' (ibid.: 687)—ways appropriated distinctively, challenging conformity (ibid.: 694).

De Visser and Smith (2007) consider generic male behaviour when equipped with—or using—alcohol as constructions of the 'self', as positioning within horizons of acceptable masculinity. To map the latter, 'participants were asked to define and discuss concepts such as "masculinity" and "health"', elucidating emplaced 'ideologies of masculinity and drinking' (ibid.: 599). A participant, for instance, referred pointedly to those popular culture 'characters who are regarded as . . . really icons of masculinity who go out and booze, and get in fights' (ibid.: 601), perpetuating a practice.

In their Interpretative Phenomenological Analysis of 'anger and anger-related aggression in the context of the lives of individual women', Eatough et al. present 'three analytic themes':

> (i) subjective experience of anger, which includes the perceptual confusion and bodily change felt by the women when angry'; (ii) multiple 'forms and contexts of aggression, paying particular attention

> to the range of aggressive strategies used'; (iii) 'anger as moral judgment, in particular perceptions of injustice and unfairness.
>
> (2008: 1767)

Here anger-in-practice involves (i) embodied perceptual narrative (ii) equipped 'aggressive strategies' of generic understanding-in-use (iii) emplacing 'moral judgement'. Thus 'being angry is an experience that is lived through the body', tooled or equipped as 'pre-reflective engagement with the objects and events given to us in our world' (ibid.: 1791). Anger puts in place judgement. 'The bullying and her perceptions of unfair treatment by her parents are woven into Debbie's meaning-making narratives of anger' (ibid.: 1787), incorporated as an affective horizon of understanding.

'Anger is rarely about a single instigating event; rather, it carries the weight of the past and intentions for the future' (ibid.: 1793). Anger as embodied generic narrative instigates a pattern of remembered and anticipated practice—or habituated Husserlian 'retention' and 'protention'. Time and place structures ubiquitous practical understanding of circumstances—meaning (Willig, 2001).

Moving to a desert island, a chronic pain sufferer in Smith and Osborn's (2008) research would

> still be a miserable old git but it wouldn't matter, it's only when other people come around that it matters, if you can just be yourself it doesn't matter what you do, I'd probably shout and swear all day but it wouldn't matter I wouldn't have to put on that front so it'd be easier.
>
> (73)

Newly equipped by life alone on an island, his practice of 'practical coping' (Heidegger) 'all day' would emplace 'easier' horizons of understanding: 'just be yourself it doesn't matter what you do'. Smith and Osborn assert thematically, 'self/identity and relationships define pain experience'. An understanding-in-practice of physical pain assumes and articulates 'the corporeal nature of the pain' (Snelgrove and Liossi, 2009: 737), recording a narrative of malfunctioning equipment, a body.

Horizons of affective understanding can themselves be determined from 'divergent points on the path to change' (Penny et al., 2009: 969) in understanding treatment of 'first-episode psychosis': embodiment 'fell outside of culturally accepted limits' (ibid.: 976). So overcoming the illness could take social routes such as the 'sport thing, where she can keep the mind busy' (female, interviewee) or a marriage, 'maybe he will get better, a wife's love is different' (female, married) (ibid.: 978).

From a hermeneutic perspective, thematic analyses can be regarded as exploring otherwise little regarded 'horizons of understanding' (Gadamer, 1975) practices. In Ahmad and Talaei's article on research 'understanding chronic pain' (2012), one 'patient' comments on a discernible habituated social practice in response to chronic pain. Reflecting on this spatially equipped routine, she asserts—'I'll avoid light . . . noise, too many people around get me upset . . . I keeping myself alone, control myself in the room, I like to be alone' (114). She presents this wider perspective on routine practice embodying understanding-in-use of the room, here designated as 'keeping myself alone'.

Narrative genres are characteristically structured by an 'equilibrium' or calm followed by a disruption or 'disequilibrium', which eventually returns to a 're-equilibrium' (Todorov, 1990). Here, her getting 'upset' by 'light', noise', 'too many people' (the disequilibrium) finds later resolution (as an equilibrium) in 'liking to be alone'. A horizon of understanding chronic pain takes material shape here, instantiated through moving to a place where she can 'control myself in the room'. Her vividly told account reflects on achieving her 'attuned' (Heidegger, 1962) embodied anticipation—through a 'hermeneutic circle' (Gadamer, 1975) of such understanding-in-practice, returning to her sanctuary.

Affective, shifting horizons of understanding equally take not only metaphorical but material shape in Smith and Rhodes (2015) discussion of depression. As the authors comment, 'one can see the (research) participants powerfully describing a diminution or breaching of their previously taken for granted spatial place in the world (. . .) spoliations of the topography of the life-world'. Here a participant remarks on the experience of divorce, 'reversing out of my drive, knowing that I wasn't coming back to the house' (207). His horizons—literal and shared—are fundamentally reconstituted. Another participant speaks of understanding his depression as embodiment in a separating 'bubble', an 'aloneness' he knows is 'bad for you', disenabling his recovery (201).

Crossing horizons of understanding chronic pain in support group attending is considered by Finlay and Elander (2016), a practice they conceptually construct as a 'pain toolkit' (666)—equipped 'progressive pain management' entered after 'conjecture' as emplacing 'comparative friendship' (660). 'Horizons' are implicit in shaping the 'foreign', a cultural distance from 'your own language':

> the only way you could describe it really is being a foreigner in a foreign country and suddenly finding somebody who spoke your own language and you could relate.
>
> (Male)

Vangeli and West (2012) discuss research participants moving across horizons of embodied self-understanding from 'smoker' to 'non-smoker', mediated by stopping smoking in a group or an identity as 'team stop-smoker' (176). Perspectives on smoking could be hierarchically related: 'isn't it awful to say but you know I quite look down on people that smoke' (laughs) (female). For some, the equipment—cigarettes—remain enabling, if evaded, 'a nice relaxing thing' (male), suggesting a cognitive distance between the surface 'self-label' and a deeper 'experienced self-concept' (181). In such a narrative delivering self-identity, enhancing reconstruction can be evident (Smith, 1994).

Emphasising changed routines in his everyday life, a participant in Nolan's (2013) research on men with spinal cord injury, refers to issues with his body as equipment failing in performance. 'I've come to think of my body as part of me and I accept that it doesn't do things that it could in the past.' However, he hopes for a future independence. I 'will do everything to return, I will give everything, you know, to make a step on my own legs'. Here, 'a step on my own legs' would be an accomplished understanding-in-use, putting in place a distant future affective horizon of embodied comprehension to which 'I will do everything to return'—an equilibrium. Shaping an equipped and goal-directed generic practice, this thematic horizon of understanding can be extended or shared by other participants in this Interpretative Phenomenological Analysis research on 'masculinity lost'. Dickson et al. (2008) discuss spinal cord injury in similar terms of equipment—the body—failing, their 'participants' inability to control their bodies' (413). 'You can't move. You wake up, you go to get up and you can't. You can't move. And that's hard.' (male, research participant)

In their (2013) philosophically grounded consideration of care-giving practices in 'Meanings and Manifestations of Care: A Celebration of Hermeneutic Multiplicity in Heidegger', Tomkins and Eatough (2013) establish thematic genres or behavioural types of caring idiographic narrative: 'Care as Intervention', 'Care as Anticipation', 'Care as Advocacy' and 'Care as Intersubjectivity'. Caring can thereby involve varying equilibria or disequilibria (achievement or a failure in realising a goal). Care giving (in)formed by 'anticipation', for instance, 'involves (a caregiver) thinking ahead of the care recipient to try to predict and prevent problems' (ibid.: 12). Behaviour in each genre embodies a different perspective or tacit horizon from which caring (e.g. for a disabled young adult) is viewed or understood. 'Care as Intersubjectivity' 'honours personhood and independence' (ibid.: 15). These horizons of understanding are 'contextual frameworks' of generic action (Morris, 2005: 701).

Such caring genres particularly exemplify a hermeneutic account of the *a priori* or necessary aspects ('moments') of human understanding. For it is fundamentally ('primordially') characterised by practical concerns, 'concernful, practical dealings' (Moran, 2000: 231) with possibility.

> To live means to care. What we care for and about, what care adheres to, is equivalent to what is meaningful. *Meaningfulness* is a categorial

> determination of the world; the objects of a world—'worldly' or 'world-some' objects—are lived inasmuch as they embody the character of meaningfulness.
>
> (Heidegger, 2001 in Sheehan, 2014: 254)

Delineating 'what we care for and about' establishes the horizons of understanding. Caring, as we have seen, is equally embodied and equipped, fundamental features for the hermeneutic view of understanding. Understanding-in-use emplaces points of view, preceding any interpretation: our reflection on a practice discloses conceptual themes, here genres of caring. IPA considers otherwise tacit thematic horizons of understanding structuring participant concerned engaging with events.

So a caregiver presumes 'fore-having' (Heidegger, 1962) equipment ('tools' in Heidegger's broad sense of this term), negotiates with care recipients a 'project' (or hermeneutically, engages in 'projecting' a course of appropriate action) and in time produces results. Embodied actualising, or producing, puts into play—emplacing—a range of underlying tacit thematic perspectives, occupied horizons of understanding, a concernful 'dwelling' (ibid.) recoverable in research and reflecting.

In their paper on 'community-dwelling adults' living with multiple sclerosis, Preston et al. (2014) emphasise interviewees' focus on embodiment rather than wider horizons of understanding, yet disrupted 'habituation' 'contributes to the development of identity' (485). So participants 'often became absorbed in their illness experience, focusing primarily on the burden of symptoms' (489).

The researchers established thematic 'constructs' for interpreting their interviews—namely, the 'reality of living with MS' (its embodiment such as 'changing abilities), 'mastering MS' (body as equipment) and 'implications for personal identity' or participants' time-structured perspectives (as in 'living with unwanted self') (ibid.: 486). 'I'm not the man I used to be, that's how I feel.'

Habituated, routine behaviour is also a reference point in Glasscoe and Smith's (2010) paper on the parenting of a child with cystic fibrosis, a behavioural complexity researchers consider from the perspective of their thematic constructs: 'trying to keep things normal' and 'when things become difficult'. The research participant's reflectively addressing disturbance to routine is discussed from their further interpretive horizon of understanding, 'the complexity of decision making' (279). Her goal—despite complexity—is allowing her son to be a 'normal little boy like any other' (mother). As the authors comment on a conflictful reality aspiring to routine, 'not only does this mother describe the challenge as overwhelming she also says this is their life and therefore it is normal' (ibid.: 292).

The complexity of decision making in this behavioural biography is heightened by the dual—conflicting—perspectives implicit in the research participant's response to health issues. Here tacit thematic horizons of understanding 'create dilemmas' in dealing with difficulties:

> What complicates things for this mother is that she has two distinct frames of reference or roles that overlap and seem to aggravate one another. These are 'self as mother' and 'self as caregiver'. The former refers to her intimate relationship with her son and is governed by her emotional binding while the latter links more to her professional role governed by logic, reason and practicality. These dual horizons create dilemmas for her particularly when decisions about complex interventions are necessary.
>
> (Ibid.: 294)

Habituated behaviour, in this case by obese participants, also forms the topic of research for Chang et al. (2009) where individuals in their focus groups were 'not contemplating to lose weight at the time of the study' (259). From an investigative perspective, contributors' routine interpretive practice of understanding their situation incorporated conceptual formations around equipment ('lack of know how', 'failed attempts', 'difficulty to resist eating') as well as embodiment ('ugly', 'shameful', 'frustrations', 'less effective'), albeit that the concerns were not emplaced or reiterated more widely. The 'majority claimed that they did not experience any anti-overweight or anti-obesity discrimination' (ibid.: 261). These researchers' instantiation of understanding's core configurations of experience as equipped, embodied and emplacing shared perspectives (e.g. 'lack of know how', being 'ugly', or 'discrimination') integrated the detailed coding of Malaysian participant responses, ordering 'otherwise scattered aspects of the world into new configurations' (Friedman, 2010: 167).

Contributing a further Malaysian perspective in the health psychology research genre, Rofil et al. (2015) discuss their sense of belonging and identity emerging from the everyday practice of '*jamu* (herbal medicine) consumption among Malay women of Javanese descent' (61). Traditional health-care practices functioning hermeneutically or as communal meaning-making involve:

i. 'Javanese-Malay *bomoh* (traditional healers)' (65) embodied generic narratives of
ii. equipped understanding-in-use [e.g. they 'chant Koranic verses while preparing the herbal medicines' (ibid.)]
iii. emplacing [or 'reinforcing' (ibid.)] an affective shared horizon of understanding—a 'sense of belonging to their communities' (61), the 'cultural identity of Javanese community' (71).

In short,

> *jamu*, as an element of the Javanese health-care practices, turns out to be an instrumental site of identity negotiation for these diaspora women, . . . the cultural aspects of *jamu* including its practices, knowledge and cultural beliefs provide them a space to imagine their sense of belonging. (71–72)

A Malaysian context is also present in the discussion of 'Mothers of Children with "A-U-T-I-S-M" in Malaysia' (Ilias et al., 2016). Their experience is thematically presented metaphorically as 'climbing Mount Kinabalu, which is Malaysia's highest peak' (9), a clearly embodied 'resilient overcoming' (6). Narratives incorporate this culturally located understanding-in-use as enabled and equipped 'coping strategies' (ibid.), emplacing a wider affective 'sense of being "proactive" to help their children': 'I say if you have the heart, you will find a way' (10). Autism is seen as a 'voyage', with 'lack of resources' and 'worries for the future' (6).

From Participant Practices to Philosophical Underpinning: (2) A Hermeneutic Re-view of Interdisciplinary IPA Research

Interpretative Phenomenological Analysis is a transcendental pursuit, asking the question, 'what are the conditions of our experiencing the world?' In Ahmad and Talaei's article on research 'understanding chronic pain' (2012), discussed earlier, a participant's embodied experience of her room is as enabling self-organised survival: I 'control myself in the room'. Implicit in the practice—its 'primordial' structure—is equipped construal of circumstances from a horizon of understanding. Likewise, we can ask, 'what are the conditions of our experiencing the world as consumers?' Here, as with consumers experiencing sports coaching (Callary et al., 2015), embodiment is central to how people construe the 'social categories in which they belong' (Chryssochoou, 2000: 404). As Larkin and Griffiths (2004) position their analysis of taking risk in dangerous sports and recreational drug use, these manifestly equipped consumers are 'embodied beings, situated within an interdependent framework of cultural resources and social relationships' (216), a horizon of interpretive insights. These Interpretative Phenomenological Analysis researchers were 'keen' that some 'key issues', themes within the core area of equipped understanding, were addressed by participants, notably the latter's 'concept of "addiction"' (218). Clarifying contributor narrative (McWilliam, 2010) is at the heart of this hermeneutic approach.

Discussing their Interpretative Phenomenological Analysis of consumer interaction with car ownership and use, Mann and Abraham (2006) relate equipment (transport) to embodiment through the theme of 'personal space' in private transport. Research participant narratives emplace personal space within a temporal horizon of understanding as 'time alone without intrusions' as well as being the 'feeling of ownership of space' (164). 'It's my own space' (P17). 'My car is my car and it's my area inside' (P6). 'I need my own space and my car is my own space' (P5). Yet such owned personal space could be constructed from the shared places in public transport through further employing of equipment: so 'I'd take my personal CD player with me . . . I like to have my own music and have my own space and just be myself' (P5). Here, achieving personal space is a behavioural project.

Consumer embodiment is equally at the core of Scott et al.'s 'Selling Pain to the Saturated Self' (2017). Using such pain-inducing 'equipment' as 'electric shocks, fire, and freezing water' during endurance events embodies a horizon of understanding resulting 'wounds and marks', enabling the 'participants (to) stitch together the narrative of a fulfilled life' (22, 29).

Embodied participant narrative negotiates meaning within a horizon of wider understanding, marking out a particular viewpoint. Genetic testing 'raises questions about individuals' perceptions of their own bodies' (Chapman and Smith, 2002: 126). Mundane behaviour, buying apples, walking in malls, exercises a personal perspective on human health and security, defining cultural horizons.

Timotijevic and Breakwell (2000) discuss how migrants from a troubled nation draw on a 'system of group categorisations and cultural values in order to retain their sense of self-efficacy, continuity, distinctiveness and self-esteem' (355). Horizons both material and metaphorical are renewed. Minor equipment (a suitcase)—'I actually had enough time to pack my stuff'—shapes a major narrative of embodied disruption. 'Everything else I had left there, now it is all gone.' (female, Bosnia) A horizon of reflective understanding is established: 'We are stronger and more prepared to sacrifice and value things in life.' (female, Serbia) Implicit in future anticipating is actualising past memory.

As in such interviews so across disciplines, the 'use of hermeneutic phenomenology enables the exploration of participants' texts and experiences with further abstraction and interpretation by the researchers based on researchers' theoretical and personal knowledge' (Deris et al., 2016: 3). In learning to understand experience (as these researchers indicate), a heuristic 'scaffolding' (ibid.) is constructed, whereupon participants access conceptual 'equipment', embodying wider perspectives.

From a hermeneutic perspective, aspects or 'moments' in the process of understanding can be re-presented, as we have seen, by spatio-temporal images or metaphors such as our 'projection of meaning', 'fusion of horizons', 'aligning' or 'distancing'. Smith et al. (2009) assert of a researcher theme that it should best 'contain enough particularity to be grounded and enough abstraction to be conceptual' (92). Using a hermeneutic spatial metaphor, such thematics can be said to be looking at how foregrounded particular participant narratives are contextualised or being framed by broader perspectives—an 'expanded' (Geanellos, 2000: 114) formerly tacit horizon of understanding.

Pursuing further a spatial metaphor for conceptual abstraction as distance from particularity, the more distant 'above' participant accounts a cultural horizon of understanding is being located, the more abstract or broader the perspective or viewpoint, open to including further contributor narrative. 'Caring' is a very wide horizon of understanding, allowing its emplacing in multiple research accounts. It could be regarded as at the summit of a conceptual hierarchy framing or including less abstract themes. As embodied across social practices from institutionally wide to more specifically focussed, caring can 'sustain' 'hierarchical structures' and is 'fulfilled in them' (Taylor, 1985: 23).

In short, participant activities can be interpreted, perceived, seen, thematised within a broad—or narrower—horizon of understanding. Thematic conceptualising, as with slowly climbing a hill or building a hierarchy, moves from the grounded particular to forming a distant abstract idea. In reflexively recognising this hierarchy, researchers are 'recognising the impact of their horizons of meaning on their eventual interpretations' (Shaw and DeForge, 2014: 1573). Rather than providing a concluding menu of interview participant narrative themes (a potentially lengthy list), researchers can map these diverse perceptions as articulating the core aspects of understanding as an embodied, equipped, emplacing practice—thereby 'connecting ontologically-based philosophy with practical research' (Conroy, 2003: 37). Here investigative results are 'read' through systematising theory.

A hermeneutic practices perspective sees inhabiting our everyday life-world as an embodied narrative affectively configuring human identities. Shaw et al. (2016) similarly present their view of this life-world as a 'set of interrelated dimensions'—'spatiality, temporality, intersubjectivity, mood, identity, and embodiment' (2). Shareable visions of understanding-in-practice receive emphasis.

As we have noted articulated in our analysis throughout this volume hermeneutic philosophy provides spatio-temporal concepts (e.g. embodied 'horizons of understanding', a 'fusion of horizons', participant 'projection' of possibility and 'refiguring' narrative)—shown to enable analysis of shared dimensions of meaning and materiality in participant narrative. Participant contributions to Shaw et al. (2016) writing on 'extra care' housing for older adults equally respond to hermeneutic theorising.

These narrative practices incorporating 'refigured' (Ricoeur) identities, shaped by 'coming to terms with having what feels a little bit invasive', 'four walls to see, four walls closing in on me', or 'sit(ting) on the chairs outside, my hat on, and people com(ing) past', map out embodied horizons of understanding affordance or 'equipment' (Heidegger)—materially (dis)enabling conditions of living in community housing. These are evidently 'prefigured' (Ricoeur), anticipatory accounts of habituated formed 'fore-understanding' (Heidegger). 'And this is like your cabin and you come out you see and you've got everything there for you'. 'I do like to do a little walk about each day . . . around the perimeter'.

From Participant Practices to Philosophical Underpinning: (3) Embodied, Equipped Understanding Emplacing Thematic Horizons

Smith asserts from the outset 'interpretive phenomenological researchers' recognition of the importance of context and language in helping to shape participants' responses' (1996: 264). Here a philosophy of hermeneutic practices offers a set of metaphorical concepts assisting IPA's 'thematic' close analysis of participant narratives, showing cultural adaption, images and identity in reflective accounts. The IPA relationship between systematising 'superordinate concepts' and 'themes' can be represented as being an interpretive hierarchy of 'horizons' (Gadamer), from wider to specific views of participant accounts, shaping 'fine-grained analyses of individual lived experiences' (Eatough and Smith, 2008: 186) in meaning-making. Initial ideas concerning the latter (a 'very particular form of meaning' (Smith et al., 2009: 22)) can be subsumed within broader conceptualisations or horizons of understanding.

Such a hierarchy from the core formations or universal configurations of 'understanding' as embodied, equipped and emplacing cultural horizons or perspectives to more local conceptions of contributors' thematic preoccupations is philosophically analytical. As Smith wrote (in 1999), 'The researcher's analytic endeavour is required to make sense of the participants' accounts' (409). Thus researchers can work within core formations of understanding to introduce conceptual constructions—themes—integrating a 'coal face' coding or initial notes on participant narrative. Indeed the latter contain their own reflective conceptualisation—such as of religion (Golsworthy and Coyle, 2001).

Considering theoretical models to guide nursing assessment with caregivers of people with dementia, Carradice et al. (2002) note how their 'tentative themes represented the beginning of the conceptualisation process', integrating coded embodied 'changes in the person with dementia' (19).

> The nurses described how behavioural and cognitive changes in the person with dementia due to the disease such as incontinence, aggression and memory problems, make demands on the carer which cause stress. (20)

A researcher theme (such as aggressive behaviour in dementia) establishes a viewpoint, a horizon of understanding, from which coded act of aggression can be placed in context and listed or mapped. Dementia interpreted as embodied locates the illness within a core configuration of understanding.

Consistent with our earlier analyses of research participants' narrative, Smith writes, 'I think there is considerable scope for developing, and extending hermeneutic theory to help its application to the activities of researchers in the human sciences'(2007: 4). Not only can a research participant's narrative themes be explored during an interview as 'configuring' (Ricoeur) a position on 'horizons of understanding' (Gadamer) but also, following Schleiermacher who 'suddenly sounds contemporary', Smith points out that participants as 'authors' of their activity may be consulted on the significance of their experience, so hearing 'what the person is intending to tell me about the experience they are undergoing' (ibid.: 5). Extending further hermeneutic 'metaphors of movement' (ibid.: 7), a person's account can be integrated in a 'hermeneutic circle of understanding' (Gadamer), enabling researcher insight across a 'fusion of horizons' (Gadamer), albeit not necessarily agreeing, yet ensuring that the listener's 'fore-conceptions' (Heidegger) do not distort narrative analysis.

Smith claims, justifiably, 'IPA clearly has theoretical underpinnings in phenomenology and hermeneutics.' (2010: 187) Connecting with these 'underpinnings', IPA avoids a criticism of being 'superficial' (Giorgi, 2011). In short, hermeneutic IPA can, as Larkin et al. (2011) also later claim, 'make a useful contribution to the development' of research on equipped 'embodied active situated cognition' (319), emplacing our understanding.

Interpretative Phenomenological Analysis can be further (in)formed analytically, drawing on this hermeneutic narrative of 'understanding' as 'practical engagement with the world', involving 'self-reflection and sociality, affective concern, and a temporal, existential location' (Smith et al., 2009: 17). For these are core ideas in coming to terms with any research participant contributions. Following the example of 'metaphysics' examining the fundamental categories of material being (causality, space, time, etc.), such hermeneutic 'metathemes' can be said to denote the ineliminable features or basic characteristics of 'understanding' considered as a practice of producing meaning. Understanding is metathematic not only in its 'codification of content' but 'maintenance of social relationships' (Jensen, 2013: 8). Metathematic membership, or our being able to exercise practical components of ubiquitous understanding, enables all the 'complexity and subtlety of what we call upon in our everyday knowing in order to make sense of our (. . .) experiences' (Eatough and Smith, 2006: 496).

Metathemes in a hermeneutic account of understanding as embodied, equipped, emplacing shared assumptions can be further detailed: these core aspects ('moments') in comprehension of the world: (i) show human identity to be purposive or teleological (ii) amongst temporal-spatial entities considered to be instrumental, albeit that (iii) impediments can be unreflectively taken for granted. Further ontological features of the material world necessarily presupposed by a hermeneutic theory of its understanding include (iv) the ability of equipment to extend a generic practice or habituated routine (v) whose disruption can prompt reflection (vi) generating further ready-to-hand practices.

Understanding is primarily practical, hence embodied and equipped: emplaces pre-reflective yet shareable affective perceptions, and as a temporal process, behaviourally presumes, projects and produces narrative. For hermeneutics, thus for IPA, these are three core configurations. While IPA 'does not test hypotheses, and prior assumptions are avoided' (Reid et al., 2005: 20), research with this method, focussed on participant sense-making, presumes *a priori* moments of understanding.

> The '*a priori* indicates completely formal and necessary concepts and judgments that are prior to and anterior from the experiences they manufacture. These *a priori* are housed within the subject. They are employed in the generation of the understanding of the world'.
>
> (Berman, 2009: 147)

When 'understanding' enters our research as embodied, equipped and emplacing perspectives, these given characteristics can be 'fleshed out' with specific themes discoverable in respondent discourse. Equipment may be assessed thematically or categorised by contributors in terms of their control: 'If you don't get it right, then the rope's too heavy' (contributor in Larkin and Griffiths, 2004: 226).

The thematic structuring of participant discourse displayed by its researchers should thus be grounded or underpinned by pointing to its instantiating the universal or 'primordial' shaping of our understanding by metathemes anchoring the mundane and momentous practice of interpreting our circumstances. As core themes, they are thus recognised to be 'all perspectives or analytical moments of a larger whole which is the situated embodiment of the human individual' (Ashworth, 2003: 151). Referring to these epistemological metathemes can generate 'situated insights' (Cope, 2011: 608): they constitute categories of bodily incorporated, instrumental and implicit understanding. So, for instance, Macleod et al. (2002) reflect on 'three key areas (. . .) explored with each' participant in genetic counselling: 'perceptions of their genetic situation' (embodiment); 'how they had tried to cope' (equipment or support) and the emplaced 'perceptions of their genetic consultation' evident perhaps in prior behaviour (147). 'We've got a doctor that said "it's not hereditary" but it is and we knew that before we went to the genetics clinic.' (female, counselee; ibid.: 148)

Snelgrove and Liossi (2009) present as 'superordinate themes' in living with chronic low back pain, 'maintaining integrity', 'crucial nature of the pain' and 'managing the pain' (739). That these denote core metathematic moments of understanding pain as failure of equipment, embodied and emplacing perspectives is evident from their 'sub-themes' such as (respectively) 'work-related incidents' or 'bio-mechanical failure', the pain's 'sensory or biological core' and patient 'relationship with health professionals: losing faith/retaining faith' (ibid.: 739–740). Notably, participant 'bodies were referred to as "letting them down"' (ibid.: 741), conjoining dysfunctional bodies/ equipment.

Where research focusses on a practice as embodied, equipped generic narrative, embedding horizons of understanding (e.g. 'care as advocacy'), the following prompts to group discussion or questions to participants are pivotal. From a hermeneutic perspective, they issue from core aspects of comprehending *any* experience and so accommodate, allowing 'people to describe in their own words their experiences, feelings and thoughts rather than responding to predefined categories' (De Visser and McDonald, 2007: 462). Within the subjective subtleties of Visser and McDonald's own paper, this is evident through exploring 'swinging' couples' conceptual horizons in understanding intimate sexual activity: 'this (swinging) isn't being unfaithful' (Cate, swinging for just over a year).

Methodologically, prompts pursuing a tacit construction of social practice can be as follows:

1. The Practice as Embodied Generic Narrative—'Tell us about (the practice)—based on your knowledge of (this practice) what did you assume would take place?' 'Did it?'
2. The Practice as Equipped—'What enabled/ changed/ prevented achieving (the practice)?'
3. The Practice as Emplacing Horizons of Understanding (Thematic)—'Why, more widely, do you engage in (this practice)?' 'Do other (ethnic/ gender/ generational) groups differ?'

References to embodied, equipped narrative emplacing views are to core characteristics—or metathemes—in the participant responses. Such core concerns or 'constitutive structure' (Willig, 2007: 221) enables the very possibility of our understanding—containing (shaping) more specific themes. They constitute 'requisite conditions for all understanding' (Chang and Horrocks, 2008: 386) and are therefore source of a 'higher-order structure for the analysis' (Smith and Rhodes, 2015: 199).

Practices as generic embodied, equipped narratives embedding thematic understanding we have noted can be arranged hierarchically. Drawing on a previously cited example of Chinese New Year Reunion Dinners as instantiating the behavioural genre of 'reunions', where 'my brother-in-law is a Muslim', a practice sub-genre is initiated whereby 'my sister will sit on a separate table which is still together (with the family)'—family reunion is celebrated, differently embodied and equipped.

More widely, this chapter has reflectively considered employing hermeneutic philosophy in our analyses of participant narratives. IPA research establishing 'conceptual themes' (De Visser and Smith, 2006: 688) can thereby disclose culturally distinctive discourses which instantiate universal 'moments' (emphasising the temporal) in embodied understanding's varied practices. An *a priori* epistemology underpins empirical studies [Holloway and Todres (2003: 355): Shinebourne (2011: 16)]. As Finlay writes when debating methods (2009), beyond IPA's focus on idiographic narrative in qualitative psychology research, 'phenomenological method is sound if it links appropriately to some phenomenological philosophy' (8), 'integrating phenomenological concepts' (2014: 133).

Integrating these philosophical concepts within consumer psychology, we have explored the theme, evident, as we have noted, in visitor narratives, of caring about a massive mall as a 'home from home' or a 'second home'. This theme was played out by student research participants in embodied, equipped behaviour, emplacing these tacit horizons of understanding discovered in our focus group. Temporally, such implicit assumption is evident in anticipation (or inference), articulated in activity. Beyond the 'multiplicity of meanings' (Jarman et al., 1997: 137) evident in such narrative, there is a shared horizon of generic understanding. *People* behaviourally—tacitly—project perspectives.

In the present chapter, we have endeavoured to exhibit these *a priori* universal hermeneutic moments as immanent also within participant discourses heard in health psychology, 'presented as *both* a priori and essential *and* concrete and variable' (Tomkins and Eatough, 2013: 4, emphasis in original). Focus groups and semi-structured interviewing display these epistemological moments in responses, so initiating our 'consideration of emergent core constructs in IPA' (Brocki and Wearden, 2006: 100) as being equipped, embodied narrative, emplacing horizons of concerned understanding.

Being reflective entails relating findings back to core aspects of understanding experience as a 'practical engagement with the world', involving an 'affective concern' (Smith et al., 2009: 17). So, for instance, a participant's perspective is located within wider evaluative horizons of understanding or their trial and error can be shown to return participants to habituated 'ready-to-hand' (Heidegger) experience—thus instantiating the 'constitutive structure' (Willig, 2007: 221) of understanding.

As noted earlier, participant narrative reference to 'needs' (failure or success in satisfaction), 'control' (or its failure) and affective perspective signal core categories of embodied, equipped and emplaced understanding. Research respondent accounts anticipate functioning of equipment, report embodied articulation of meaning and align with or distance themselves from a cultural horizon of understanding. In their narratives, 'reality is comprehended through embodied experience' (Starks and Trinidad, 2007: 1374) choosing apples, walking through the mall, withstanding pain, securing cognitive horizons. An 'experience of voice hearing' as auditory verbal hallucination is nonetheless embodied, where the voice can be understood as enabling, even equipping, 'positive, supportive and assisting', 'to get a new direction' (respondent) 'to a functioning state' (ibid.)' (Rácz et al., 2017: 3).

From an occupational perspective on health, Wilcock writes, 'Existentialist philosophers such as Hegel, Heidegger, and Sartre have also considered the concept of being' (2006: 114). Heidegger, we have maintained, argues that our being present in the world is fundamentally understanding-in-practice, realising informed projection, or 'becoming' enabled/limited by 'belonging' (familiarity). Within a hermeneutic perspective, generic understanding-in-use instantiates behavioural possibility. We are 'being(s) to whom an understanding of their own Being belongs' (Mulhall, 2005: 39), living through conceptual or 'discursive structures' (Willig, 2007: 214) which enable and elide experience.

Assisting research participants to present narrative interpretive practices instantiating these abstract structuring categories—principally the 'overarching cognitive framework' (Macleod et al., 2002: 147) of understanding—would philosophically underwrite qualitative psychological research (Gough and Lyons, 2016). How, for instance, framing questions in these core concepts, one can ask does patient 'awareness in early stage Alzheimer's disease' present as their 'managing threat to self' (Clare, 2003), as interpretive practice engaging with dysfunction through 'self-maintaining' or 'self-adjusting' behaviour responding to 'memory (equipment) difficulties'? How often do participants in reflective health psychology research 'struggle' (Howes et al., 2005: 132) across 'daily physical and mental challenges' (Bramley and Eatough, 2005: 232) to eventually attain—securing—a horizon of concerned understanding, a wider eufunctional emplacing of confronting issues? 'Finding your own place' (Rodriguez and Smith, 2014) projects and produces an embodied narrative, tacitly putting in place a deepening cultural perspective in understanding, heard, seen and recorded in IPA research.

Practices competently performed are generic instantiations of achievement. They incorporate as wider structural reference points cultural horizons of understanding, eliding or enabling activity: 'This (swinging) isn't being unfaithful'. Integrating human agency and societal structure through a hermeneutic practices perspective, 'a truly cultural psychological view of agency emphasises the dependence which agency has on social relations' (Ratner, 2000: 430).

Summary so far: Regarded from a hermeneutic philosophical viewpoint, understanding necessarily frames or fore-structures human experience within 'meaning-structures' (Svenaeus, 2011: 337)—a 'framework of categories' (Schmidt, 2010)—as equipped, embodied and emplacing wider affective perspectives (horizons of understanding), so constituting ubiquitous interpretive practices. We have re-viewed recent research on participant practices where elucidating their meaning is core focus in studies undertaken by qualitative (IPA) psychologists—arguing for a philosophical underpinning by recognising understanding-in-use as materially enabled, or equipped, practice putting in place IPA's hermeneutic hierarchy, established analytically as thematic 'horizons of understanding' (Gadamer).

Research participant contributions constitute discursive narrative 'particularity' (Smith et al., 2009: 92) rather than 'raw data', *prima facie* open to being conceptualised, placed within themes, rather than nomologically contained within generalisations. Contributors reflect on their being always already immersed in generic practices—routine, tacit, little reflected-upon understanding *how*—from which meaning accrues to an environment of entities construed as equipment. Here IPA's phenomenology is radically distant from positivism's separating culturally detached subject contemplating objects.

Smith et al. (2009) show how IPA is (in)formed by the philosophically hermeneutic narrative of 'understanding' as embodied, equipped 'practical engagement' occasioning 'self-reflection' amid shareable 'affective concern' (17). This definition establishes core concepts, high in the hierarchy of IPA's interpretive horizons of understanding or its researchers' tier(s) of themes and equally abstract or distant from the particularity of research participant contributions. Attuned to these superordinate concepts, lower order themes are characterised by sufficient 'abstraction to be conceptual' but also 'contain enough particularity to be grounded' (ibid.: 92). Where researchers code and conceptualise, thus establishing thematic perspectives in participant discourse, these horizons of understanding can be shaped and integrated by their relationship to 'peak' perspectives within IPA as a defined practice theory. Hence, for instance, 'affective concern' is a core idea in IPA's thinking about research as well as implicit in conceptualising a particular participant's understanding of their experience. Analysis sees, notes particularities, seeking cognitive frameworks rather than furthering their generalisation.

These concepts at the peak of the analytical pyramid deconstructing a participant's particular process of narrative 'understanding', on the one hand define the approach as a practices perspective, while on the other distinguish IPA from other qualitative strategies, thereby shaping the trajectory of research from its anticipatory outset in first engaging with narrative particularity. Introducing theory external to Interpretative Phenomenological Analysis to illuminate its findings is a separate concern.

The mundane practice of understanding configures the material world as equipment or tool, primordially through embodied use, tacitly embedding shareable cultural horizons of understanding. Practices are generic, equipped, embodied, putting in place behaviourally incorporated perspectives, presuming, projecting and producing narrative resolving disequilibria, from 'flaws' to insecurity. In its analyses, IPA relates this basic interpreting of the world at the heart of understanding as a practice to less abstract conceptual constructions serving to integrate coding or a researcher's first notes on participant narrative response as an interview progresses. IPA studies exemplify understanding as an ubiquitous interpretive practice whose fundamental 'grip' on entities is as equipment: embodied use tacitly maintains a horizon of affective understanding. Here a researcher's conceptual categorising (in 'themes') instantiates this model of 'understanding'.

Wide-ranging theory such as Interpretative Phenomenological Analysis constitutes an epistemological 'form of life' (Wittgenstein, 1991) where abstract formulae like an 'affective concern' (Smith et al., 2009: 17) internally inform interpretation of the more concrete narrative particularity provided by a participant. So interview data are seen as presenting 'particularity and texture of the experience for the participants' (Smith, 2011b: 21). Their narratives exhibit practices emplacing thematic horizons of understanding, pre-reflective behaviour constructively enabled as well as being constrained by occupying social roles, signifying a complex 'interrelationship between agency and structure' (Houston and Mullan-Jensen, 2012: 270)—open to being further considered from a hermeneutic perspective of critical distanciation (Ricoeur, 1981a). 'Coming to an understanding' (Rolfe, 2015: 150) perceives practices as socially situated.

5 Consumer Practices Viewing Screens

A Hermeneutic Perspective on Constructing Identities

Project

In this fifth chapter, we consider the interpretive employment of media equipment—the screen, with its customarily unreflected upon tacit types of understanding-in-use. Reference to the study of television as 'non-media-centric' in recent literature signals authorial primary emphasis on the embodied practice of its deployment (*how* it is viewed) in understanding, constructing identities for audience as well as content. Following the chapters on marketing and psychological perceptions of consumer hermeneutic disclosure, discussion here first reviews some earlier studies of televisual consuming as audience practices producing identities. Engaged in 'decentring and contextualising media and communication research' (Hepp, 2010: 42), this chapter on media use is avowedly 'non-media-centric' (Morley, 2009) for it emphasises the generic behavioural practices of engaging with media prior to considering their tacitly deploying a horizon of understanding—or their representing an external world, albeit across differing narrational modes of media access.

Hermeneutically, we have seen that a practice of consuming is (i) embodied knowledge-in-use, exhibiting cultural competence and (ii) equipped by 'tools' (in a very inclusive sense). A practice thereby (tacitly) prefigures or anticipates narrative, behaviourally configuring its telling (e.g. apple buying), a process open to being refigured or applied by participants in construction of self-identity. Guys 'just grab and go': but 'we, we, we (women) pick the apple that looks nicer with no flaws'. In this compressed narrative, a 'formative horizon of (her) identity' (Taylor, 2004: 55) emerges.

Consuming's fore-understood behavioural producing of generic narrative (iii) emplaces or puts in place our little reflected on perspectives, tacitly establishing (iv) our aligning or alienation. Such embedded horizons of concerned understanding are perhaps (v) considered subsequently (as in focus groups), viewed comparatively for a moment: 'Normally, (guys) would say, "It's just the same. Just grab and go" '. Practices imbricate affective perceptions, sometimes functioning later as a foregrounded focus for research. Establishing the embodied horizon of participant understanding—with its configurative narrative—is contextualising or grounding the analysis of a hermeneutic practice in behaviour and broader outlook. Instantiated by a participant's culturally competent activity, generic practices equally articulate understanding of an institution's (e.g. supermarket's) rules and values.

In short, from a hermeneutic practices perspective, understanding is *a priori* (necessarily):

(i) *anticipatory* (Heidegger)—informed by generic fore-conception and thereby temporal;
(ii) *applicative* (Gadamer)—embodied narratival knowing *how* preceding knowing *that*;
(iii) *aligning or alienating* (Ricoeur)—with/ from wider affective horizons of understanding.

Incorporated in generic, albeit ubiquitous practices, understanding is continually constituted through people presuming, projecting and producing narrative meaning across a 'terrain of habitual use', 'trajectories' (Couldry, 2009b: 439, 442) deploying enabling artefacts from shopping to screen. Meaning evolves from our informed anticipation reconciled with actuality, or the 'situated interplay of experience, practice and structure' (Lewis, 1992: 283) across our embodied making narrative. In media use, programme preferred narrative perspectives on the world may (like 'frames') function as 'structural manifestations which order the interpretation of reality' (Carter, 2013: 5) reviewed or re-organised and perhaps resisted by audiences configuring meaning from horizons of understanding. Seen from a philosophical stance of Franco-German hermeneutics, the non-media-centric analyses (Moores, Morley), which we consider in this chapter foreground behavioural generic understanding-in-use (e.g. domestic) of media before reflective concern with users' embodied affective 'horizons of understanding' (Gadamer) their screen narrative representing of material world. The 'mediated and discursive "self" is yoked to the body' in 'acculturated physicality' (Durham, 2016: 117, 118).

Audiences, Consumers and Watching Television: Hermeneutic Practices in Media Use

We have seen in the previous chapter on psychology's Interpretative Phenomenological Analysis that Smith et al. (2009) have provided a hermeneutic or interpretive practices account of 'being-in-the-world'. Human understanding is a 'practical engagement with the world'—involving our 'self-reflection and sociality, affective concern, and a temporal, existential location' (17). This is a short yet succinct summary of the *a priori* metathemes or core characteristics—that is, the 'primordial' features (Heidegger, 1962)—of understanding as we enact the practice every minute of our lives. Even being a researcher is a 'part of human, embodied existence' (Schuster, 2013: 195).

We assume as well as confirm these core characteristics or 'moments' of understanding in continually experiencing our surroundings. Hence it appears categorically inappropriate to treat the claim for their status as a hypothesis, asking for 'evidence', when the process of gaining evidence would itself instantiate 'understanding' as an equipped, embodied process of knowing how—tacitly putting in place a wider horizon of understanding open to our potential reflection. Can we speak of 'evidence' for metathematic aspects of understanding which enable our very human existence?

Fundamental features or the metathematic moments in the 'temporal, existential' practice of consuming are instantiated in particular culturally shaped sequences: the universal is imbricated in the local. It is of course appropriate to ask for evidence in respect of research claims about *specific* themes (or responses) in understanding which may—or may not—be present in participant accounts. When a marketing study claims that a continuing theme in audience understanding of an advertising narrative is its chaotic construction, this needs support by verbal data (e.g. 'it is quite a chaos').

It is equally productive to reflect upon culturally inflected versions of global metathemes in the continually exercised practice of understanding. We discussed in Chapter 2 the account of a particular family's Chinese New Year Reunion Dinner provided by a participant. Here one can see embedded in their story also a philosophical narrative. In the latter, core features or metathemes of a family reunion as their understanding how to engage in a practical (embodied, equipped) routine are present—so putting in place an 'affective concern' (Smith et al., 2009: 17), their collective thematic temporally shaped horizon of understanding 'sharing' open to reflective gazing in cultural research:

> 'the most important, the significant part of it, is because you see after a year's (sic) of hard work that we come together, and we have dinner and then we can share all the things among ourselves, family members especially': 'things' (a dinner) importantly 'equip' (Heidegger) this family reunion.

In short, in regard to *a priori* aspects (or in phenomenology's technical terms, 'moments') of understanding which underwrite our ubiquitous experience as interpretive, our requesting empirical evidence is to misunderstand their epistemological status. For these core aspects of comprehending are already present in understanding the claim. Nonetheless, research on our hermeneutic practices can valuably enquire as to how such 'moments' are manifested in multi-cultural participants talking about activity. What is the evidence for particular thematic responses being present, so instantiating core aspects of understanding? Is such structuring of research participant subjectivity (Gough and Madill, 2012) satisfactory? Recognising 'questions of interdisciplinarity' as 'influencing the ways audience research establishes its place within the wider research landscape' (Mathieu et al., 2016: 463), in this chapter we shall reflect upon twenty-five years of media studies 'fleshing out' audience understanding, articulating the 'actual central focus of audience research: the question of meaning-making—interpretation' (Pavlickova and Kleut, 2016: 351) as embodied practice in which objects enable *and* constrain. Media clearly need analysis 'as technologies including infrastructures *and* as processes of sense-making' (Couldry and Hepp, 2017: 5, emphasis in original).

Moores wrote in1990 that the time has come to 'consolidate' media studies' theoretical and methodological insights by 'refusing to see texts, readers and contexts as separable elements' (24). From shopping malls to social media, culturally inscribed concrete to materially located cyberspace, *texts* are considered in the present chapters as 'tools' enabling embodied (hence socially positioned) users, who thereby tacitly emplace wider horizons of understanding. Apples, we have noted, can be 'read' as 'flawed', potentially disenabling users, a visibly evident embodied reading which affirms a horizon of feminine competent looking: '(guys) would say, "It's just the same. Just grab and go."'

More recently, Morley emphasises the status of media technology as 'tool' perceived by its users as (ir)relevant to their equipped understanding-in-practices, when he states in an interview:

> The question is how particular people, in particular contexts, perceive the relevance (or irrelevance) of specific media technologies for their lives, and how they then choose to use those technologies or ignore them, or indeed 'bend' them in some way, to a purpose for which they were not intended.
>
> (Morley, 2011: 128 interviewed by Jin)

From a hermeneutic practices perspective, everyday media use is visibly embodied as in our domestic television viewing (Morley, 1986) and equipped [for instance, by radio (Moores, 1988) or public screens (Krajina, 2014)], emplacing or putting in place our tacit understanding of 'everyday social relations' (Moores in Krajina et al., 2014). 'Teleoaffective' (Schatzki, 2015: 2) generic action (Ricoeur, 1981a: 136) engaging with media is behaviourally 'played out' (Moores in Krajina et al., 2014)—'fore-understood' (Heidegger, 1962), presumed, projected and produced around technology, integrating 'meanings, competences, materials' (Shove, 2014a: 419). A generic approach to screen use integrates an investigation of forms of viewing as goal-directed or purposive practices of producing narrative with a study of programme form. Reflective moments interrupting habituated practices—or a 'ready-to-hand' (Heidegger, 1962) practice presented by participants for attention—can emerge when 'investigating the "invisibility" of the ordinary' (Krajina in Krajina et al., 2014)—or its pre-reflective 'horizon of understanding' (Gadamer, 1975). In an earlier chapter, narrative recollecting of mundane mall visiting exhibited a moment of heightened bonding in practical understanding: 'I remember at this moment when we took the picture it was something that you want it to last'.

> The 'ever deeper embedding of our lives in media' may be addressed by the 'particular contribution to media and communications research of social theory'.
>
> (Couldry, 2015a: 1)

In this chapter, recognising 'transmedial' (Hepp, 2013: 616) digital research on the process of mediatization, we turn to ubiquitous practices in using media (in)forming everyday life. 'Media logic' (ibid.: 618) is clearly equipped, embodied (in production and reception) and emplaces wider communication, cultural and political horizons of understanding. The earlier chapter considered a media logic implicit in cell phone use, taking pictures of a seasonally celebrating South-East Asian mall with visitors' reflective 'thematic framing of a mediatized world' (ibid.: 622). A practice is an embodied, equipped narrative configuring of meaning emplacing such horizons of understanding. Here we reflect on audience practices in viewing television and using the Internet, thus telling the 'story of the stories' (Fotopoulou and Couldry, 2015) wherein audiences configure identities. This narrative has been recently echoed in discussing the 'challenge of grasping (children's) practice':

> children's knowledge of (their media use routines) were embodied and situated, they moved around, turned on and off devices and engaged in various person-environment-technology relations with little reflection.
>
> (Storm-Mathisen, 2016: 85)

Cultural Power, Practices and Domestic Television: Habituated Horizons of Understanding—A Reflective Hermeneutics

'Television remains the bedrock of the media diet for many of us' (Dill, 2013: 3). Present engaging with Internet research clearly occurs in the context of a continuing viewer immersion in legacy media, television and its video derivatives. Hermeneutic practices are equally sustained.

In his monograph *Family Television: Cultural Power and Domestic Leisure* (1986), Morley considers the gendered power implicit in practices of watching television in the home. Perspectives embedded in familial behaviour, sometimes hidden horizons of nonetheless consensual and shared understanding are visited, viewed and evaluated in reflection. Equipped by television's technology, embodying 'social (and primarily familial) relations within which viewing is conducted', 'viewers make sense of the materials they view' (ibid.: 1), projecting and producing meaningful content on screen, thereby emplacing wider frameworks of understanding. Morley investigates 'questions of interpretation and questions of use' 'in relation to each other' (ibid.) in the family. Making sense of texts is always already contextualised, shaped by circumstances of—focussed, distracted—viewing. Here there are aligned—or conceivably antagonistic—hermeneutic practices, an embodied narrative of family use shaping a tacit narrative of their meaning-making on screen.

Bringing the body into media user research, Morley writes, reflecting on his earlier studies,

> that 'my focus of interest has thus shifted from the analysis of the pattern of differential audience "readings" of particular programme materials, to the analysis of the domestic viewing context itself—as the framework within which "readings" of programmes are (ordinarily) made'.
>
> (Ibid.: 2)

Embodied material and temporal arrangements in consuming television emplace domestic power, the age and gendered related social capacity to decide how, when and whether to view a programme 'on the box', to anticipate articulating pleasurable content. In a practice—domestic or more widely—social roles are a generative mechanism, enabling and constraining action:

> Thus, to consider the ways in which viewing is performed within the social relations of the family is also, inevitably, to consider the ways in which viewing is performed within the context of power relations and the differential power afforded to members of the family in different roles—whether in terms of gender or in terms of age.
>
> (Ibid.: 25)

In short, 'viewing of television is itself conducted as a social activity' (ibid.: 20). Moreover specific competences (associated with gender or generation, for instance) will be required in using certain forms of cultural equipment [such as the continuous serial (i.e. soap opera) or current affairs television] to make narrative sense out of content (ibid.: 33), emplacing ideological assumption. But more fundamentally, Morley's study 'prioritises' asking why particular televisual programme genres of cultural equipment are seen by viewers as being relevant, the 'pertinence or salience of different types of programme material to different family members' or across social groups (ibid.: 35). Yet a use-value can be uncertain, suggested as emplacing indeterminate horizons of understanding:

> Well, I don't think they can understand it all . . . I think they understand what they want to understand. They paint their own pictures, so to speak. They twist it round.
>
> (Father, Family 1: ibid.: 46)

Using television routinely can emplace a 'fusion of (viewer/viewed) horizons' (Gadamer, 1975: 306) wherein a horizon of understanding 'telly' can become all-encircling, enabling personal identity as euphoric:

Woman: 'To me, I think telly's real life.'
Man: 'That's what I'm saying, telly's taken over your life.'
Woman: 'Well, I don't mind it taking over my life. It keeps me happy.'
(Family 6: ibid.: 73)

Gendered use of media equipment—television's programming in education or entertainment—can be differentially embodied, accompanied by 'nattering' or signal a male preference for silence: 'I'd rather watch on me own—if it's just something I want to watch, I like to watch everything with no talking at all' (male, Family 9: ibid.: 103). Morley's family television viewing, then, exemplifies 'constitutive structures' (Willig, 2007: 221) of 'understanding' as equipped individualised practice, contained within wider—and distinct—horizons of understanding of a home as 'for men' a 'site of leisure' and 'for women' a 'sphere of work' (Morley, 1986: 140). So writing more than twenty years later on 'qualitatively different experiences of time', Wajcman (2008) asserts 'housework is unpaid and never done', and its accomplishing distant from the 'temporalities of paid labour' (65). Television's use, its status as equipment or relevance, shapes establishing a sense for its texts. Morley considers the 'media territory of a specific practice' (Tosoni and Ciancia, 2017: 44), establishing meaning.

In his subsequent (1992) collection of published research after *Family Television*, *Television, Audiences and Cultural Studies*, Morley argues for a wide-ranging media studies agenda in which structures enunciating domestic powers are placed within a broader political dimension of inquiry. Here media equipped audiences (i) configuring (Ricoeur) genres of content in (ii) practices which emplace wider societal horizons of understanding (Gadamer) domestic ritual become the focus of hermeneutic inquiry. The objective in such a politics of power in media use should be

> production of analyses of the specific relationships of particular audiences to particular types of media content which are located within

> the broader framework of an analysis of media consumption and domestic ritual.
>
> (265)

Making sense of media narrative is shaped differently by (intense, intermittent) modes of role-related viewing. Essentially embodied family behaviour in generic equipment use—'texts' on television, but increasingly everyday engaging with a diversity of media 'tools'—is located within wider horizons of ideological understanding distributing ability. In such ubiquitous 'gendering of space' (Morley, 2000: 1), available opportunity (such as Morley's early example of controlling the channel selector) naturalises power where even the 'most minute details of bodily deportment and language can reproduce larger patterns of social ordering' (Couldry, 2003: 50).

Practices constituting understanding-in-use (from choosing apples to watching programmes) emplace affective horizons of understanding their behavioural accomplishing of roles. As Morley's male viewer (noted earlier) defined his exercise of competence: 'I like to watch everything with no talking at all.' Audience agency is enabled and encircled not only by 'readings' of programmes but also equally by familial social structure across class, gender, generational and racial groups. Being a member of a television audience means generating role-related (child, parent), goal-driven interpretive narrative, varying in content even among simultaneous viewers of the same programme.

Practices instantiate 'doing' negotiated through everyday culture in the 'social formation of agency' (Ratner, 2000: 421). Working through social practices shapes particular identities. From a hermeneutic perspective, media equipped meaning construction can be placed philosophically and practically within habituated horizon of understanding. Reflecting on earlier *Parenting for a Digital Future* research, the 'key to understanding childhood or adolescence lay in the meanings we could ascribe to routine' (Sefton-Green, 2016). As Pavlickova (2012) claims in her 'At the Crossroads of Hermeneutic Philosophy and Reception Studies',

> Gadamer's account of interpretative understanding (can help) to comprehend the reader—text encounters as an active negotiation of meaning and to place the cross-media use within the broader context of the users' everyday lives, and 'routines', instead of focusing on isolated uses of the particular media or media content.
>
> (29)

In social practices—prefigured accomplishing of habituated routines—behaviour is configured and subsequently refigured in emplacing identity ('I don't mind (telly's) taking over my life'). Theory's coming to terms with an audience's media practice is underwritten by philosophy, a 'negotiation of epistemology' (Murru, 2016: 393) far from empiricism's focus on mental contents simply imitating a mundane world. For it is rather with a philosophical focus on our hermeneutic practices, 'habitual, meaningful practices and movements of everyday living' (Moores, 2017), that one can situate a media user's tacit meaningful comprehension of text and contribution of content, narrative representation disclosed in research.

Viewed from a hermeneutic perspective, the prefigured, configured and refigured (Ricoeur)—or audience identity defining—construction of television narrative content can be positioned within a more than media-centred considering of such generic embodied, equipped practices (Heidegger). For such practices—from even minimal attention to remembering to switch off sets—tacitly affirm or emplace our wider habituated horizon of affective understanding (Gadamer) daily life. Pink and Mackley (2013) write in their ethnographic-hermeneutics of understanding as embodied, equipped and emplacing perspective: 'Through mundane and not usually spoken about routines of everyday living, media are engaged for affective and embodied ways of making the home "feel right"' (678).

Audience Practices (Knowing How) and the Construction of Identities: Absorbed, Aligned and Alienated Viewers

Practices and the exercise of power within 'interpersonal relationships of viewing' domestic television emplacing the audience's affective horizon of understanding narrative are considered in Wilson's (1990) reflection on the British breakfast programme, 'TV-am and the Politics of Caring'.

As always, 'an audience's use of a text presupposes and indeed produces particular interpretations of its content. Consumption generates its own epistemology' (ibid.: 125). Here presumed viewers of altruistic individualistic narrative (such as a cinematic star celebrating a sick child's birthday) do 'care about *caring*' (ibid.: 133, emphasis in original). While immediately admirable, its consequence as a narrative is 'repression of political division with a consensus established around caring' (ibid.: 134). A consensus built along these lines puts in place a depoliticising horizon of understanding the world which in a hegemonic marginalising of structural social inequality may be construed as being 'profoundly political' (Keane, 1982: 162). Televised narrative can maintain 'asymmetrical relations of power' (Thompson, 1986: 66) if unchallenged in a 'politics of the present' (Scannell, 2004: 583).

> The key question in the analysis of the ideological character of the media is how the messages of the media are taken up by their recipients, made sense of by them and incorporated into other aspects of their life and culture.
>
> (Thompson, 1986: 78)

Hence the 'real significance' of programmes is the focus of interpretive analysis (Dahlgren, 1988a: 287) or a distanced hermeneutic unpacking (Ricoeur, 1981a) of their ideological import articulated within familiar and unproblematic horizons of existence. Research with audiences discloses media use—'messages' 'taken up by their recipients'—within embodied (perhaps familial) wider horizons of affective understanding—a close aligning, conspicuous alienation, even apathy. The '"epistemic gap" between assumed horizon of an intended audience and the horizon of an empirical or "real" audience' (Weissmann, 2013: 143) can result in rejection of authorial preferred reading.

On the following pages, we consider media consumer prefigurative or tacitly anticipatory practices, a making sense of programmes through embodied, equipped immersive cognitive play, emplacing wider horizons of understanding. For reception theorists, the relationship between text and reader is characterised by an 'ease of play', a 'to-and-fro movement' in which the latter moves back and forth over the instrumental text with an incorporated holistic construction of its meaning. Exploring the metaphor of embodied 'play' in analysing audience activity, Silverstone draws upon the hermeneutic phenomenology of play theorists such as Huizinga (1970) for media study (1999).

In the London School of Economics blog, *Parenting for a Digital Future* 'What is "Play" and "Playfulness"?' Sefton-Green refers (2017) to Sutton-Smith's *The Ambiguity of Play* (1997). The latter presents a history of ideas where 'a major philosophical source for the modern rhetorics of the self as player has been historical phenomenology (. . .) major philosophers in this tradition have been Husserl, Heidegger and Gadamer' (181).

Writing philosophically about the flow of (textual) meaning, hermeneutic philosophers such as Gadamer foreground the positioned practices of understanding. In embodied cognitive play, they assert, significance is created for 'all meaningful human activity' (Hans, 1980: 312). The concept of 'play' may be used to explore the multiple ways in which people constitute themselves as audiences, their cognitive, political and even physical behaviour in response to a screen's mediating meaning. Play's 'pervasiveness as a dispersed practice' generates cultural innovation (Roig et al., 2009: 93).

The viewer's ludic focus on content can vary in the intensity of its preoccupation with a text, playing from high absorption to being distracted by domestic context of consumption. Exemplifying the game-like quality of our everyday experience with the medium, watching is accompanied by a 'curious balance' between 'feelings of presence and absence' (Moores, 2000: 110).

Even where viewers (lacking in energy or time) casually engage in watching television as a 'secondary, relatively meaningless' activity (Hermes, 1993: 493, 498), they playfully integrate some understanding of programmes, albeit a relatively empty perception of content. Recollecting in focus groups provides evidence of how much those gazing or glancing at the screen find intelligible.

The playful audience is both passive and active. Absorbed by/in television, we are subjected to its generic requirements. Ludic theory of media engaging is a 'rules perspective' (Lull, 1990: 63). But as viewers, we construct narrative meaning. Screen text with its indeterminate content requires the 'serious fun' of comprehension (Huizinga, 1970). Playing, audiences produce plural responses.

As with involvement in a game, watching programmes requires attention in moving around within the diegetic space and time of a text, establishing a meaning for its content. Enjoying 'virtual participation' (Livingstone, 2000: 8), audiences are enabled, at least intermittently, to forget tedious surroundings. They play outside 'ordinary life-boundaries' (Nagel, 1998: 20)—in Schroder's (1988) phrase, television watching has an 'ecstatic dimension'. As one of his viewers realises in retrospect: the drama 'pulls you in, like you're almost right there'.

The embodied, equipped, emplacing generic practice of play (the ludic) has multiple aspects—or in phenomenological terms, 'moments'—enabling when applied to our media use a conceptual model or analytical framework integrating empirical research. Given the essentially ludic processes involved, consuming screen media is characterised by varying characteristics of play:

i. abstracting (or separating) oneself from one's (mundane) material surroundings;
ii. pursuing goals, whether virtually intrinsic or materially extrinsic (teleological);
iii. producing eudaemonic effects (constituted by player or media user 'well-being');
iv. experiencing aesthetic (dis)satisfaction with articulated screen narrative content.

We noted earlier an exchange where television viewing exemplifies these features, albeit that 'well-being' is a contested concept and in being 'happy' material/virtual separation is occluded. We see a close interaction between understanding (as 'real life') and use ('taking over my life'), in which meaning is domesticated, a meaning consequent upon an easy fusion of interpretive horizons.

Woman: 'To me, I think telly's real life.'
Man: 'That's what I'm saying, telly's taken over your life.'
Woman: 'Well, I don't mind it taking over my life. It keeps me happy.'
(Family 6: in Morley, 1986: 73)

Immersed in a programme, some distract themselves with pleasure from tiresome domestic contexts, achieving 'diversionary escape' (Lee, 1999: 345).

In an 'ecstasy of participating' (Schroder, 1989: 9), viewers are deterritorialised, 'lifted off' from their localities (Tomlinson, 1999: 137): they 'totally zone out from the day' (interviewee, Priest, 1995: 76), a 'pleasurable forgetfulness' (Hoijer, 2000: 201). Enthusiastically 'killing time' (Venter and van Vuuren, 2000: 11), audiences manifest prolonged attention to screen content. Television's naturalism, its accustomed patterns of content presentation, supports a 'visual vehicularity', 'easy escapism' from 'tiresome mundanities' (Siegel, 2002: 50). The apparent present tense of events on an electronic screen annuls their travel time to the audience's 'now'. In this 'game of creation' (Radovan, 2001: 231), or ludic achieving meaning, viewers enjoy the 'ecstasy of the immediate' (ibid.: 233). Absorption can be all-encompassing, as wholly engaging detachment from the mundane, an 'immersion into the "other worldliness" of the screen' (Morley, 1996: 324–325). Consuming/being consumed by content abstracts audiences from the secular, a 'liminal' encounter (Lie, 2000: 30), leaving behind 'daily experience' (Lie and Servaes, 2000: 311). Where those watching become fully focussed, epistemological change is occasioned, a prolonged audience involvement: taken up by television, 'the game plays you' (Sutton-Smith, 1997: 183. See Gadamer, 1975). Consuming television can be continual 'diversion' (Jensen, 1986: 227).

On the other hand, much television aesthetics assumes an address to an inattentive, playful audience, whose idling involvement is often intermittent. Forthcoming programmes are announced, again and again. Advertisements are continuously recycled. In televised drama for both global and local markets, information is circulated amongst characters, repeated or abbreviated. Media content is especially packaged for those only capable of a muted attempt at following narratives on screen, for viewers distracted by domesticity. Viewer participatory play, as semi-involvement in television, can be characterised by no more than a casual concern with content. Narrowly varying depictions in soap operas of viewers' lived experience can become tedious for the sense-making self.

Making meaning, media use/play as a hermeneutic practice, normally without scrutiny:

v. anticipates content (the player's fore-structured or prefiguring understanding);
vi. articulates textual detail (if only in an uncompleted hermeneutic circling);
vii. engages in structurally circumscribed [(dis)enabling rule-governed] behaviour;
viii. constructs personal or social identities thereby distributing political positioning.

Associated with accessing both screen and sports field are the intrinsic goals of cognitive escape from the mundane and the extrinsic (or instrumental) cultivation of material advancement and self-definition. The latter can eclipse the former, infringing play-like separation from surroundings.

Audience alignment or identification with character 'message' presupposes the unhindered viewing of a 'transparent' or 'veridical' media narrative that 'creates an impression of realism and produces a faith in the truth of the images, even in a fictional programme' (Bailey, 2002: 243). In conforming to a viewer's generic anticipation, construction (editing) of a veridical text is effaced, enabling its apparent access to an equally unrehearsed, unscripted reality.

Identifying with character or presenter, aligned audiences overcome an inevitable distance, integrating or extending their horizon of meaning construction. But cultural distance can also be alienating (as when advertising distorts a familial practice) where the viewer engages in analytical criticism. Identifying with, or marking out independence from, interpreted screen content (in)forms audience practices. For a viewer to identify with a character involves her or him appropriating one (or more of) that individual's role-constituted practices with its associated point of view on events—a horizon of understanding on which that viewer takes up a not too distant position. So a presumed audience for a televisual narrative wherein a cinematic star celebrates a sick child's birthday 'care about caring'—identify with the practice of altruism emplacing a horizon of concern with the world.

(I) Audience Play-in-Practice: Generic Projection and Production of Meaning. Assigning a meaning to 'specificities of play spaces' (Law and Crawford, 2016: 2) on screen requires viewers to integrate anticipating narrative with actual events, in a (re)creational play-like or ludic to-and-fro hermeneutic circle of story construction. An audience's tacit prefigurative expectation generated by assumptions about a programme's genre (such as drama) encountering perceived realities on screen may require a configurative revision with the goal of securing their understanding of a coherent narrative.

Screen narrative can confirm or undermine a viewer's horizon of understanding, maintaining or subverting their position, the broader beliefs or perceptions in terms of which they make sense of a programme, perceiving it to instantiate a genre and its population to exemplify types. Television is understood like the material world in communal intersubjectively obtaining categories of thought. A similar account to hermeneutic theorising of this domestic medium's reception can be found in film studies. Elsaesser argued, amongst others, for a 'matrix of expectations and anticipatory projections coexisting and fusing with the more primary matrix of the viewing situation itself' (1981: 279).

Horizons of viewing are the categories of understanding in terms of which our spectatorship allows meaning to emerge. In practices both within and between its texts, much television seeks to construct a life-world which in images and values family audiences can acknowledge as confirming in place its own cultural horizons of understanding the world, so enabling shared perspectives (even embodied in presenters) on events. In a news programme, the familiarity of presenters mediates the unfamiliar in a de-fusion of difference, an attempted effortless fusion of horizons with the assumed audience, together understanding a complicated world. Horizons of understanding associated with minority groups are here marginalised, registering only imbalance of power.

Hermeneutic focus groups or interviewing explores the affective horizons of awareness, the changing categories ('moving horizon') in terms of which (or from where) consumers identify what they see ('real life', 'telly') as they engage with a surrounding world, anticipating and actualising its meaning. Horizons—concretely material and constituting meaning—are shaped by history. Implicit within everyday recognition, participant horizons of understanding become explicit in research.

Already known but not much regarded horizons of understanding, their background generic awareness, inform knowing familiar phenomena, our sense of the already experienced. The passage of subjective time, remembering, generates assumptions about spatial content or event. Constituting thereby the shape of a life-world, cultural horizons are confirmed and occasionally challenged. For their background standing can conceal ideological construction, illicit awarding of generic power. Apparently natural, seeming inevitable, a cultural horizon's contingent status is rendered invisible, yet acquiescence in its connotative dimensions of understanding can deliver ideology to television and viewer, limiting justification. Language operates perspectivally in construing the world.

Morley's familial television viewing, we noted, involved equipped individualised practices, embodying wider horizons of understanding a home as a site of male leisure and female work:

> the core of practical consciousness consists not only, to use Ryle's terms, of 'knowing that' but also of 'knowing how'. (. . .) 'Ideas'—or (more accurately) signification—are inherently embroiled in what people *do*, in the texture of the practicalities of daily life.
>
> (Giddens, 1981b: 68; emphasis in original)

The real audience is defined by the inevitable distance between its cultural horizons enabling experientially defining the world as instantiating types and television's generic perceptions. Thus a complete closure of the epistemic 'gap' between text and 'empirical' reader is impossible for it would achieve a fictitious identity. Viewing is everywhere a fusion of horizons drawing on their difference, a perspectival assertion of meaning: some aspects are marginalised or new (in)sights foregrounded.

In television's attempt to efface the distance between the cognitive horizons of a speaker and listener, the television presenter's speech denies distance with the use of close-up, engaging viewers in direct verbal and visual address which appears to reject the possibility of a more distanced, even critical relationship with the text. The electronic immediacy of the screen asserts a closure between the spatio-temporal moment of a programme's discourse and the world of the viewer. This digitally produced 'presence' of textual content is a denial of mediation, functioning in consequence to assert that the audience has access to an undistorted truth. 'And we hope to see you again tomorrow.'

Participation, then, in the practice of understanding involves an active presence, generating meaning rather than being passive and textually determined. Assisted by television's familiarising discourse, audiences overcome (never wholly) a semiotic distance between programme and viewer through mediating fusion of horizons. The audience experience of similarity mediates encountering textual difference, shaping their always already occupied horizons of televisual understanding,

(II) Audience Aligning, Alienation or Apathy: Affirming Viewer Horizons of Understanding. While understanding involves a (usually extending) fusion of horizons, identification between an audience and character calls upon their aligning, their engaging with experience from the same perspective.

Viewers identify with role-inhabiting individuals in screen practices (from caring to consuming):

i. sharing interpretive interests (from pursuing altruism to purchasing apples with 'no flaws');
ii. selectively negotiating roles through similarity and difference (effacing distance);
iii. securing tacit horizons of such concerned understanding (from happiness to health) in place.

Audience 'chat' can focus on all three 'moments' of identifying: 'We always sit down and it's "do you think she's right last night, what she's done?"' Where identifying with individuals ends or it is impossible, a viewer's distanced consideration of text (drama, documentary) may commence.

Processes of identification in viewing television are articulated around (albeit not reducible to) goal-directed interpretive interest in the activity of sense-making. Arriving at an understanding of a drama provides viewers with experiences fundamental to being able to identify with characters. Both attempt to understand situations in which they find themselves. Projecting an interpretation of a situation and having it confirmed (or falsified) is not only implicit in a character's comprehending her or his world but present also in the audience's understanding of the drama.

In this way, further identification between viewer and character is always premised on the experience of managing a hermeneutic role. An audience can read narrative meaning into programme, while also extracting from them coherent significance for not infrequently fragmentary moments of daily existence. The cultural affinity with content—identification—can be consequent upon viewers reading programmes from an inventive horizon of interpretive understanding, perhaps reconstructing moral persuasion.

Generic awareness is a fundamental moment in viewer knowledge as well as of programme formation, producing audience expectations within the hermeneutic process of understanding a text. Awareness of a genre generates tacit anticipations, watching from a 'horizon of expectation' (Jauss, 1982b). Different genres and different forms of television generate multiple horizons of expectation. Being aware anticipation appropriate to the ending of serial episodes is inappropriate when directed at series is central to competent viewing. A camera's cutting to register conversational interchanges meets an audience's horizon of expectations. Further addressing a hermeneutic anticipation, editing can satisfy an audience's desire to see, to ascertain the accuracy of their narrative projection.

When a viewer's horizon of visual expectation is confirmed by a programme's practices, the result is a 'veridical' sequence of images: editing passes unremarked, in an apparently unmediated and reliable presentation of how things are. Unproblematically employing equipment—television—to access the world, attention is not on the process which escapes scrutiny but the goal. Audiences tacitly anticipating generic visual practice are oblivious to the text's mediation. The truth of these images is preserved from doubt by near transparency of access which they provide to the 'real', a precondition of viewer identifying with individual on screen. A veridical visual sequence, then, possesses apparently self-authenticating truth. 'Veridical' can be used to denote a certain form of experience available to the audience in which a programme genre functions in anticipated mode. The 'veridical effect' is product of television's aesthetic conformity to viewer expectations.

Finding only the anticipated flow, the audience notices little of the camera work or editing responsible for setting images within what is experienced as an uninterrupted sequence. They pass without our conscious scrutiny. Denying their status as a selective appropriation of event, veridical images enable understanding by television viewers whose horizon of expectation has been smoothly and unproblematically confirmed as none other than an accurate anticipating of the external world.

In the language of phenomenology, audience horizons of visual expectation are built from a past knowledge ('retentions') allowing anticipatory 'protentions' regarding editing. If protentions are confirmed without difficulty the viewer's experience becomes a veridical awareness of events. Thus presuming from continuity announcements that they '(fore-)have' before them (for instance) a media narrative, audiences tacitly project from a common cultural horizon or 'fore-see' possible identity of the emerging programme as being a news bulletin. This broad 'fore-conception' is rendered specific through viewing—habitually producing with little self-monitoring a narrative whose anticipation has been articulated with experienced veridical text, in a practice subsequently analysed by theorist.

Identification, premised on the fictitious status of the televisually seen (whether serial drama or soap opera) being forgotten, demands a visual image which is truthful to the point of invisibility, a transparent aperture on the 'real' itself. From a practices perspective, the veridical experience of an image supports the ontological moment of identifying as well as the cognitive. With the appearance of unmediated access to 'reality' the viewer is enabled to 'read herself/himself' into the text, moving from the hermeneutic role of reader to that of a narrative agent—immersed in the time and space of the programme, engaged in embodied understanding. 'It pulls you in, like you're almost right there. You feel . . . you can feel it.' Here identification with role-inhabiting individuals is enabled. Speech and activity articulate a range of social roles each associated with the discovery and knowledge of truth, positions of embodied cognitive insight which align the (implied) viewer. Situated within a programme's familiar horizon of understanding, information is rendered unproblematic.

'Veridical' is a historical concept: rules which underwrite the production of transparency will change through time. The apparently unmediated experiences of the 'real' which support identifying with individuals and their interpretive interests have no essential nature. Televisual forms of drama and documentary, for instance, allow an audience viewing experiences of the veridical which rest on different visual (camera, editing) practices. Audience projected perceptions can be challenged.

In dramatic narratives, as distinct from documentary, the construction of the discursive text precedes and determines the selective appropriation of the materially non-discursive. The narrative camera is interested in allowing the viewer to establish cause and effect sequences (perhaps of some complexity) and not in their detailed visual description. These sequences involve events, action and individuals' verbal responses to each other. The drama's generic practices of visual narration allow transparent image sequences to emerge in confirming an audience's equally generic anticipation.

In documentary, the non-discursive precedes and shapes the discursive, producing particular forms of camera practice. Camera work (such as tracking) through drawing attention to itself may undermine experiencing transparent (unmediated) access to the documented 'real'. Here television foregrounds description of an extra-textually 'real' rather than telling a story. Watching documentary television, the (implied) audience sees from a horizon of understanding constructed in commentary.

Occurring within the context of a discourse of interpretation, the moment of viewing functions as a time of 'named', discursively presented vision. But a documentary can be inflected by the narrative ambitions of entertainment, establishing in the process diegetic content with varying degree of pre-textual existence—and audience accusations of falsehood.

(III) Audience Defamiliarising/Distancing: Subverting Identification with a Character's Interpretive Interest. Television's texts (its variety of programme) may engage in strategies which render opaque the otherwise transparent access to the apparently real associated with veridical aesthetics, aiming at enhancing audience reflection. A first technique involves authoring voiceovers in contradiction—or allocating opposing characteristics to a programme's content, calling into question its functioning to unproblematically present the 'real'. Accounts of events are rendered indeterminate or in conflict. It upsets the claim of the image to give access to an uncontrovertibly self-evident identity.

A second strategy suspends the veridical effect of, for instance, documentary, by prefacing it with a continuity announcement casting doubt on the validity of its content. Here the—intended—viewer is to exercise a 'hermeneutics of suspicion' in understanding a genre associated with truth.

Pre-programme announcements construct intended audience interpretation of these television texts as involving authored ('personalised', 'personal viewpoint'), possible accounts of the world. Thus identifying with the text's 'author', a subject in the text, is undermined; apparently veridical support for their position is contextualised by advising a cautionary approach to its constructed account. If a documentary is announced as 'personal', the relationship between its discursive articulation of the visual and 'reality' itself exists for the intended viewers at the level of the speculative. Programmes introduced as 'personal viewpoint' explicitly acknowledge their source in subjectivity.

The third challenge to the veridical constructs a visual text as postmodernist: its status as a representation of reality is refused. Instead, its reference is taken to be simply to itself (as in music video), to other images in other texts (soap opera or situation comedy), or to images more widely.

From a postmodernist perspective, the visual 'layers' of a programme are 'open' and indeterminate with respect to the truth or falsity of the verbal discourses accompanying them. They provide no evidence by reference to which the veracity of what is said may be judged. For what is seen by the viewer is discredited as a transparent display of a non-discursive reality, a reality 'beyond' the text. Experiencing the programme is detached from knowledge of the real. Modernist faith in the visual as informing about an independent world is challenged.

Popular television's 'play and replay' of the types and forms of situation comedy, soap and talk show can be read as postmodernist pastiche, an exploration of the possibilities generated by the simulacra of generic variation rather than representing a social reality. Postmodernist music video undermines the confirming of visual assumptions which elsewhere enables the veridical effect, a sense of immediate access to reality beyond television. Postmodernism is valued in its asserting a cultural centrality for the image, not least the televisual image.

Television presenters or their horizons of understanding can be recognised so supporting viewers projecting meaning within the programme in constructing a narrative account of content. The medium, we have seen, construes the world through terms familiar to the assumed audience, perhaps effacing as it does so the more unfamiliar dictions of political differences. Here there is a hierarchy of familiarity. But Brechtian theory of drama can be employed to produce television representing the familiar as the unfamiliar open to detached analysis by a distanced audience. Here dramaturgical technique undermines the familiar, presenting it at hand as a subject for reflection.

An alienated or a 'distanciated' reading of a television text defamiliarises the cognitively familiar, placing it within the inverted commas of 'estrangement'. The distanced reader refuses the easy recognition of horizons of understanding on offer. Familiar discourse is no longer the unproblematic but is open for questioning. To simply 'see' the programme content rather than 'recognise' the familiar is to resist involvement in the processes of identification associated with television. So instead of the audience adopting familiar social roles displayed in documentary or drama, they become the focus of the active viewer's critical (political) attention. The alienation effect is a 'making strange' of the everyday so that its examination appears appropriate.

In television drama, unlike news and current affairs programmes, a direct address to the audience is unusual and therefore distancing. It produces not viewers easily aligning with 'truth' in reporting, but an (ideal) audience who is critically receptive of an unfamiliar communication. Situation comedies provide other instances of distanciation: a stereotyped or 'two-dimensional' character inhibits easy identification by viewers, alienating the latter from textual involvement. Analysis is enabled in a 'separation of the elements', a distancing from familiar positioning.

Undermining the status of television as transparent presenting of the real, distanciation suspends its hierarchy of truth, allowing critical intervention by the viewer. The familiarities of television practice are made strange. Concepts organising meaning within the programme are foregrounded for detached examination by the audiences to whom the text is addressed. Here 'alienation' is conceived of as undermining the complex and mutually confirming horizons of understanding and expectation from which the viewer engages with a programme, producing a defamiliarised analytical 'seeing' of assumption and content. Alienation, of course, occurs more widely where, for instance, inappropriate media marketing addresses consumers.

Images of the audience's life-worlds within marketing or media can be resisted, so yielding the difference between who you are and who television thinks you are, marking a distance between horizons of understanding everyday life. Whereas for Brecht distanciation is an artistic achievement originating in particular textual mechanisms, as we noted, the hermeneutic philosopher Ricoeur has argued that an alienated reading is made possible by virtue of spatio-temporal distance.

In a hermeneutics of television, viewing involves an overcoming of the cognitive difference between horizons of understanding, the cultural experiences of a separate 'otherness' and 'ownness' resulting from the differing histories of a text and reader. The distance between audience and textual perspective can be productively foregrounded for inspection, allowing critical separation of textual assertion to emerge. Viewer-initiated defamiliarisation refuses the text's construction of familiarity, its foregrounding of 'easy' speech and direct address to the audience.

Television's attempts, then, at producing a spoken discourse to reduce the cognitive distance between text and viewer do not always succeed. Familiarity characterising the 'neutral' diction of a presenter, for instance, may be alienated within a re-reading of it as classed and gendered discourse with a particular point of view. It will no longer be received as unproblematic framing of meaning or horizon of understanding within the text, the discourse of subjecting authoritative judgement.

Finally, putting behind us a horizon of suspicion, we need to record that watching television can involve a pleasurable recognition. Audience enjoyment also derives from achieving coherency and the solution of indeterminacies, or indeed from surprise, when a viewer's horizon of expectations is not substantiated. Attaining a coherent understanding is a cognitive activity which, where supported and guided by texts, is often more likely to meet with success than comparable activity in 'real life'.

In the next section, we explore audience/media user generic horizons of expectation, employing this idea from hermeneutic and literary theory to facilitate coming to terms with ubiquitous Internet use. We have seen how discussion using the Gadamerian spatio-temporal metaphor—'horizon of understanding'—can enable analysis of distant shaping of practices from cultural viewpoints resisted by consumers: yet 'important asymmetries of power get hardwired into the organisation of action and thought so that they become, precisely, difficult to see and articulate as power' (Couldry, 2008b: 104).

Internet Users Embodied Production of Meaning: Prefigured Construction of Generic Narrative

Early statements in my monograph's Preface referenced the British-European philosophical opposition between Locke's empiricist or representational theory of knowledge where the human mind was passive receptor of sense-impressions and a Heideggerian account of knowing as being the 'primordial' embodied, minimally monitored, exercise of our understanding-in-practices tacitly engaging 'equipment'. Here, yet again, modelling users' epistemological access to the 'Web can be thought of as a battleground between different conceptions of knowledge, ranging from the logical empiricism of Carnap to the (hermeneutic) focus on embodiment of Heidegger' (Halpin and Monnin, 2016).

This philosophical opposition is here furthered discussing our Internet access as (actively) making meaning online rather than constituted by its effect (as in so-called addiction studies) on users, a view originating in theory of legacy media's (television) causal consequence for audiences. Internet users invest energy and time in brandscapes (from *Facebook* to *Twitter* to name here but an (in)famous dynamic duo), activity (dis)enabled by algorithmic delivery of narrative items producing 'tension, actual or potential, between the aims that social actors are trying to achieve' (Couldry and Powell, 2014: 2) and constraint by horizons of online immersion not of their choosing. Here we can anticipate an 'emerging digital hermeneutics of new media users' (Livingstone, 2009: 7).

Earlier in the chapter, drawing on Ricoeur's hermeneutic account of narrative formation, we considered how television equipped audiences configured content genres, assigning meaning with which they immersively aligned or from which they were alienated, or just responded apathetically. Invoking a reader's informed anticipating, articulation and assigning of meaning to textual formats, Ricoeur's thinking through the 'configuration of narratives as a meaning-making practice takes into account how both structure (preunderstandings in narrative configuration) and agency (the act of configuration and refiguration) influence the construction and telling of narratives' (R. E. Wilson, 2015: 894). 'Preunderstandings' are personal positions on public shared horizons of understanding.

Media use, not least activity when 'going online', is likewise fulfilled by embodied generic practices incorporating anticipatory knowledge of screen narrative routines, themselves also generic: 'It is thought-provoking that, increasingly, without people's physical and hence visible participation in the process of communication, there will be neither text nor reception (of "new media") in the first place' (Livingstone, 2004: 85). By accessing the Internet, we engage through participatory equipped knowing-in-use, projecting, producing narrative emplacing affective shared (empathetic) horizons of understanding, refiguring identity of consumer and content. From apple buying to visiting shopping malls and social media, hermeneutic practices are generic. In so presenting Internet digital competence online we follow Ricoeur (1981a: 136) and Livingstone, also making the hermeneutically substantiating case

> that 'applying the notion of "genre" to conventionalised practices of participation may seem infelicitous, but it is useful for continuing the tradition in reception studies of conceptualising genre not as a property of the text *per se* but rather as emerging from the conventionalised or contractual interaction between text and audience. Thus, it concerns (. . .) the interface between audience and text, user and technology, agency and structure'.
>
> (Livingstone, 2012: 190–191)

Likewise, Das (2011b) is concerned with her 'youthful digital literacies on social networking sites—anticipations of genre and modes of interpretative engagement' (344) which are themselves generic.

More widely, consistent with our hermeneutic perspective, Pavlickova and Kleut (2016) claim for research on 'produser' practices in assembling digital narrative a continuity of theoretical shaping:

> What happens at the individual level, and the interpretation that comes before both usage and production, should be explored using and modifying already-developed concepts in audience reception studies.
>
> (355)

Hence we can ask questions such as 'how is particular produser content being pre-figuratively read and configured by audiences in a hermeneutic circle of understanding to produce coherent meaning, thereby refiguring their identities as consumers in the practice of media reception?' Integrating part with wider text to establish understanding can include an Internet author as source of intelligibility (Pavlickova, 2013). Yet comment Pavlickova and Kleut, 'rare is the research that asks what is (the) audiences' experience of produsage' (2016: 351). Embodied practice, facilitated by its online digital enablement, emplacing through tacit categorising and personal competence a background of cultural understanding, can be located within listening to (and observing) a media user traversing the 'whole range of media practices that a media user can undertake via their media repertoire, from watching, reading or listening to sharing, commenting and posting content' (Picone, 2017: 4).

Audience generic practices need not follow those of industry: so multiple types of television can be regarded as 'escapism' distinct from engaging with the latest news. Moreover, audiences can clearly be present where media are absent: people perform for others within and beyond the theatre (e.g. tossing *Yee Sang* at Chinese New Year Reunion Dinners). Audience hermeneutic practices may be both non-media-centric and, behaviourally engaged, not focussed on constructing representation.

Remembering the concept of 'genre' in furthering hermeneutic analysis of Internet consumer as well as their online content practices exemplifies a reflective modification of 'already-developed concepts in audience reception studies'. With this philosophically placed theoretical capital we can begin to address the call for 'more complex explorations of audience practices that take into account the vast range of online participation' (Bird, 2011: 505). Tacitly projecting appropriate content from a horizon of generic recognition, media users assemble narrative. How do our Internet user generic practices prefigure (project) and configure (produce) narrative from a content already generically structured? How does established (or habituated) individual Internet access interrelate embodied, equipped offline and online activity emplacing politically powerful wider perspectives? In generic practices, as we have seen (and shall further consider in the Conclusion), a human agency engages with (dis)enabling social structures: 'audiences, whether "produsers" or not, negotiate and manage the complex interaction of structural media power and individual/community agency' (ibid.: 509). Who/what does writing in *Facebook* or *Twitter* enable?

'Fake news' online cumulatively shapes a reader's 'optics' (Hirst, 2017: 87), 'horizons of understanding' narrative of notably political events. For sympathetic supporters aligned to such an account, an item enables a 'ready-to-hand' narrative practice, embodied in reiterated social media circulation, emplacing an increasingly potent ideology, generic as well as goal-oriented. The practice thereby digitally 'configures' identity, becoming a focus for subsequent celebratory/'distanciated' (Ricoeur) reflecting.

Information and communication technology use is importantly embodied and equipped (not least by the disabled): its deploying emplaces consensual—or contested—horizons of understanding. Wajcman writes in science and technology studies (STS), information and communication technologies can be 'conceived of as culturally and socially situated artefacts and systems': thus 'STS emphasises that human-machine interaction crucially depends on the locally-contingent meanings that people attribute to them' (2008: 67).

Internet users' embodied meaning production is clearly signalled online in the emoticon or emoji, an equipping cultural form or 'conduit for affective labour' (Stark and Crawford, 2015: 1). Such signals communicate the writer's affective perspective or preferred horizon of understanding preceding text, reflexive looking in a characteristically simple sign (such as the 'smiley' face).

'Genre', argues Wilson (2016), is a necessary reference point in writing about the parallel use of television and additional digital media to engage in discussion about programme content or 'viewing practices and second screen experience' (176). In developing 'nuanced understanding' of viewing habits mobile across media screens, she concludes 'genre is a key factor—more than age or gender—in determining how second screens are used, what they are used for' (175).

Generic audience behaviour in media use excludes a 'single mode of attention': 'sometimes viewing is distracted, and sometimes it is fully engaged' (182). 'Lean back' viewing characteristic of television watching contrasts here with 'lean forward' second screen attentive deployment. So

> although audiences are leaning back on couches, they are being encouraged to lean forward and engage actively via additional digital media to become more fully immersed in the primary TV text.
> (182)

A hermeneutic of generic second screen practices as embodied ('how second screens are used'), equipped ('what (second screens) are used for'), and as emplacing affective caring across horizons of understanding ('audience pleasure (and displeasures)' is present in Wilson's research. Generic competence and concern are evident in audience behaviour: focus groups or interviewing can succeed in tracing concerns to their location on a horizon of understanding.

In their conference paper (2016) 'Understanding Second Screen User's Motivations, User Patterns and Engagement in Singapore', Lin et al. further pursue an account of such generic activity consistent with a hermeneutic practices perspective. This habituated understanding-in-use of second screens is (i) evidently embodied (ii) equipped behaviour (engaging a 'second device'), tacitly (iii) emplacing (putting in place) a wider perspective ('horizon of understanding' (Gadamer))—'you will keep up' (immediacy). Activity presumes, projects and produces behavioural narrative wherein you 'validate your opinion'. Checking can constitute 'distanciation' (Ricoeur), alienation from 'primary screens': 'our generation is taught not to believe whatever the traditional media says' (female). On the other hand, opinions emerging from engaged use of primary screens are shareable in a 'fusion of horizons' (Gadamer): thus 'as long as you are posting and sharing with your other football fans, you feel like you are watching it together. It makes me more engaged (sic)' (male). Likewise celebrating consensus and identity: 'I see someone else posting his views on a particular news, I do feel a sense of community if I agree with him, as it validates my point of view' (male).

Generic hermeneutic practices are also situated at the core of Hepp's discussion of 'media-related pioneer communities' (2016)—namely, makers' 'practices of manufacturing', 'practices of the (quantified) self' and open data 'particular shared media-related practices of publicity' (925). These practices are equipped by technology (media), embodied (e.g. articulated in health practices) and implicitly cultivate wide horizons of understanding: 'all three share a belief in the possibility of a productive change of culture and society through digital media' (ibid.: 924).

In our addressing the question of whether theory developed shaping analyses of television audience behaviour can be a continuing resource for the 'age of the Internet' (Livingstone, 2004), 'genre' ranks as a central candidate for retaining. 'In both new and old media contexts, notions of genre organise texts and usage/reading practices' (Livingstone and Das, 2013: 110). Its application to embodied context and content of media use echoes hermeneutic preoccupation with our capacity to conform to 'fore-understood' meaning (Heidegger, 1962). Similarly, considering Internet use as like television, ludic—goal-directed abstraction from the mundane in 'virtual playground' (Mustafa and Hamzah, 2011), seeking well-being—appears appropriate. Digital media offer young people the 'choice when and where to disconnect from the often rule-bound and sometime conflictual world they find themselves in' (Livingstone, 2017: 60). As Corner writes, 'firm connection with a longer tradition of investigation and argument' can bring 'benefits' (2013: 1015) in coming to terms with empirical research on using digital sociology (Lupton, 2013).

While Internet practices (tacitly) negotiate understanding genre, they can be constrained by powerful algorithmic calculation, where mathematical prediction structures knowledge immediately available to audiences. Writing on the Netflix prize awarded for algorithmic achievement enabling the company to 'target' audiences with content viewers are most likely to download based on prior Internet selections, Hallinan and Striphas consider that to reflect upon the corporate significance of this prize 'lends insight, we believe, into how new meanings and practices can insinuate themselves into long-established routines', transforming habituated activity online (2016: 118).

Research fulfilling a qualitative ambition, pursued in particular from a hermeneutic practices perspective on generic Internet activity, needs to 'look very closely at the categorisations of practice that people themselves make' (Couldry, 2011: 217). Nonetheless, awareness of algorithmic shaping, that knowing is prefigured by other than personal selection, counsels a hermeneutics of suspicion in epistemological excavation of habituated horizons of access. For 'horizons (of media use) are being built, at the level of micro-adjustments of practice, into the habits of individual actors' (Couldry and Van Dijck, 2015: 2). Investigating Internet practice, embedded in corporate construct, should avoid a 'hermeneutic gap' 'between so-called quantitative and so-called qualitative data worlds' (Blok and Pedersen, 2014: 3) in a social analytics, thereby casting a clear eye on algorithmically (in)formed horizons. How do consumers view recurring mathematically initiated online marketing?

'Confrontations between anti-hermeneutical impulses (naive empiricism) and hermeneutical traditions' (Bolin and Schwarz, 2015: 2) are not productive. 'Computational research' must connect to 'broader analysis of human meanings' (Fuchs, 2017: 57)—reflecting upon corporate practices of 'data-driven targeting' from a wider horizon of understanding. For such 'production of experience' for consumers online (Hamilton and Bodle, 2017: 2) shapes a 'deep personalisation' (Couldry and Turow, 2014: 1711) of *de facto* constraining individuated digital 'informing'. In delivery of news online, 'algorithmically derived personalisation' can limit access to diversity (Carlson, 2017).

Looking from a hermeneutic practices perspective, how do 'social actors *themselves* deal with the increasing embedding of quantification, measurement and calculation in their everyday lives and practices' (Couldry et al., 2016: 120, emphasis in original)? Embodied use of an Internet platform (equipment) can emplace parameters of understanding shaped for corporate profit—that is, 'fundamental economic drivers' circulating 'cognitive and cultural frames' 'most readily available' on platforms where individual practices configure a 'wider myth of "us"' (Couldry, 2015b: 622). In our routine hermeneutic practices, 'we interact on the basis of habits adapted to these platforms with others whose habits are similarly adapted' (Couldry and Hepp, 2017: 124–125).

To cite Ricoeur (1981a) at this conjuncture, media users can distance themselves from these horizons, to '"negotiate" whether and how to appropriate them in their quotidian habits' (Van Dijck, 2013: 6). Yet while their immersive play-like practices in negotiating an online presence manifestly generate a personally rewarding outcome, their tracked activity (as datafied work) still culminates in latent corporate profit for 'powerful financescapes and brandscapes' (Firat and Dholakia, 2016: 15).

Competencies in 'digital cultural participation', argues Kanai, ought to be 'situated as social practices' (2016: 3). Interpreting these practices, the analytical purchase on generic process enabled by spatial metaphors of anticipated or 'projected' understanding, a cultural 'fusion of horizons' and the 'hermeneutic circle of understanding', continues to be appropriate in thinking about behaviour (Wilson, 2015). Authorial collaboration on configuring and refiguring a coherent narrative occurs within a shared horizon of understanding, embodied in equipped practices of contributing online. 'Shared meaning is both the precondition and outcome of the work that Twitter users do', in their 'collectively producing shared values and understandings' (Stephansen and Couldry, 2014: 1214). Yet users are 'part of a surplus-value generating class', 'exploited by capital' (Fuchs, 2017: 35). An unpaid post on *TripAdvisor* travels globally, enhancing this website's call to corporate advertisers: instantiating a pattern of searches, individual use generates a digital horizon of 'also recommended'. 'Web Analytics' and 'Big Data' collection and research have an ambivalent future. Will the

> emergence of this new resource provide us with a route to greater understanding and more rational, evidence-based decision and policy

> making (. . .) or will it lead merely to exploitation and control by powerful interests amid a 'fetishisation' and 'dictatorship of data'?
> (Bone et al., 2016: 4)

Relating to recent summative research discussing the present, past and a potential future for social media (Das and Ytre-Arne, 2017), a hermeneutic practices perspective on its *Audiences 2030* narratives can be outlined as follows. Developing a routine practical consciousness as 'small acts of engagement' in mediated 'sense-making' (ibid.: 25) is a continuous concern through 'audience ever new coping strategies' (ibid.), 'complex coping practices' (ibid.: 26), (in)formed by their horizon of understanding, temporally prefiguring digital media as 'intrusive' (ibid.: 25). Social media platforms constitute a boundary object structuring as well as structured by corporate/ consumer practices.

Media audiences 'negotiate different identities online' (ibid.: 26) across genres of narrative access, anticipating interpellation by algorithmic configuration of 'implied user practices' (ibid.: 27) in exercising competencies. Equipped (enabling 'social buttons') 'engagement practices' (ibid.: 28) emplace horizons of understanding in their generic, goal-driven 'commenting and debating' (ibid.) and small stories of 'identity construction' (ibid.: 29)—thereby mapping the 'social position of the producer' (ibid.) Yet a commodification of audience creativity is endemic across boundary objects (such as a *TripAdvisor* media platform) despite 'rapid changes in audience habits' (ibid.: 41) or their distancing to a horizon of understanding a 'media environment as too complex, too remote and too chaotic' (ibid.: 42, 66). Algorithmically generated horizons of understanding shape 'how we think about certain issues' (ibid.: 44), framing implied audiences commercially and politically. In short, 'emerging agency' (Clark et al., 2015) from *Twitter* to *Yahoo!* emplaces corporate contours.

Summary so far: In this chapter, we have reflected on media using practices from viewing television to visiting websites as embodied, instrumentally enabled, emplacing wide horizons of understanding. Considering the enduring concept of 'genre' or understanding as 'prefigured' (Ricoeur) to be a useful tool of analysis accedes to Marres and Gerlitz arguing that 'as social media enable social actors to engage through predefined activities, they render their activities analysable' (2016: 22). Online, we become 'captured' as well as creative coded and coding travellers, 'liking' yet not able to engage in critique.

Our digital travelling is shaped by little reflected on multiple consumer horizons of expectation. Corporate anticipating is sustained algorithmically. We build a narrative identity, generating profit driving with personal connectivity (Kitchin and Dodge, 2011). User tracking and its targeting curtails 'open data' (Gurstein, 2011), a digital limiting where the 'commons come into friction with capitalism's hegemony' (Allmer,

2015: 6), as algorithmically sponsoring the 'used user's' (Peacock, 2014) horizons of understanding. By our Internet use, we enable data mining of our engagement, so maintaining commercial and security database established from selling as well as suspicion oriented shaping of interpretation, this 'thinking about and categorising' our practices that 'embodies power relations within a society' (Miller, 2011: 125). Albeit based in a university Business School, Tadajewski writes critically that advertising 'tries to cognitively confine our patterns of thought' (2018: 6).

In these chapters, we are putting consumers in their philosophical place. Hermeneutic theory has (in)formed audience and health communication qualitative research: we have discussed work by Craig Thompson and Jonathan Smith. Shaun Moores' philosophically shaped enthusiasm for a 'type of media studies that's "non-representational" as well as non-media-centric' (in Krajina et al., 2014: 693) could enlist hermeneutics in its emphasis upon communication as primarily embodied—seeing its mediating or representing the external world as a secondary subject of study. Pink and Mackley similarly engage with 'non-media-centric, nonrepresentational and phenomenological approaches to media studies' (2013: 677). For non-media-centred communication researchers, consumers' habitual behavioural understanding *how* (to use cameras, computers, engage in purchasing, etc.) is first focus. Audience tacit understanding *that* (technology use, purchasing mode) have their wider implications, their 'horizon of understanding', can be explored subsequently as cultural perspective on the world. In presenting research participant narrative instantiating ineliminable aspects of 'understanding' as embodied, equipped, emplacing perspective, hermeneutic study can address claims that qualitative research is subjective, claims perennially posited by positivists. Narrative is generically 'framed' by audiences or producers [as 'prefigured', 'configured', 'refigured' (Ricoeur)]: its practice assumes the tacit equipping by 'tool' (Heidegger, 1962) or 'affordance' (Gibson, 1986), emplacing a habituated embodied 'horizon of understanding' (Gadamer, 1975) or cultural 'habitus' (Bourdieu, 1977).

In short, from the perspective of hermeneutic philosophy, 'it will be increasingly relevant to treat communicative practices rather than media as the central units of analysis in future media and communication studies' (Jensen and Helles, 2017: 18). Hermeneutic practices are ubiquitous.

Conclusion

Hermeneutic Practices: From Anthony Giddens to Algorithmically Generated 'Horizons of Understanding' (Hans-Georg Gadamer)

Project

In previous chapters, we have seen that within hermeneutic or interpretive practices theory, practices are equipped and embodied (Heidegger): they thereby tacitly emplace shareable 'horizons of understanding' (Gadamer). Power (or its construction) characterises these three 'moments'—not least hegemonic horizons embedding ideology from which distance may be achieved (Ricoeur). We have thereby sought to reflect empirically and philosophically upon the 'necessary embeddedness of human activity in social and material contexts' (Hui et al., 2017: 2). In a generic and implicitly goal-directed practice, consumers prefigure, configure and refigure identities (Ricoeur) of self as well as surroundings (e.g. as skilful purchaser and purchase), generating meaning. This concluding chapter briefly marks out a broad contribution of hermeneutic philosophy's perspective on diverse practices from architectural studies to science and theology, emplacing analysis across a wider scrutiny.

Fundamentally, however, we continue here a hermeneutic 'non-representational theoretical trajectory' (Warfield, 2016: 1) in constructing thinking about consumption, distinguishing between the 'clear consciousness found in the act of reflection and the sedimented certainties implicit in the course of the performances of action' across the 'practical embeddedness of the human being in his or her world' (Joas, 1987: 17, 22). 'Basically, I expect good security from the mall' our mall visitor considered, reflecting upon her 'sedimented certainties'. Audiences and consumers pursue narrative meaning (dis)enabled by tacit anticipation of generic structure. 'Practical consciousness' (Giddens) precedes representation—in subsequent thought, focus group, celebration or criticism. While we are encircled online by a datafied delivery of algorithmically delineated horizons of understanding, we are simultaneously engaged in a 'multiplicity of practices' (Rabinow and Rose, 2003: 15)—thereby embodying a hermeneutic circle of integrative understanding, crossing narrative perspective. Media are 'materialisations of practices of communication' (Hepp et al., 2018: 4).

Ubiquitous Hermeneutic Practices

Thinking about an individual's activity from a practices perspective enables its perception as a 'teleoaffective' (Schatzki) equipped embodied generic construction of narrative, itself generic. We can hear in a graduate thesis (Tiong, 2013) on digital media marketing illustrating the argument of Chapter 2 a respondent taking pleasure at her ease of configuring the branding narrative in a group of motorcycle videos on social media (*YouTube*): 'I am happy when watching the video', the 'feature of the video is just simple' (female, Chinese). Another participant refigures content to assert his essentially embodied shared identity: 'they are energetic like me' (male, Malay). Yet positioning himself at a distance from the sexualised content of another brand narrative—furthering his horizon of understanding—the same respondent in a dismissal of the images as 'Western style' refigures his reception as alienated: 'I'll distance. Cannot relate.' Anticipating or prefiguring narrative advertising content from a common prior knowledge of the motorcycle genre, a third is critical: not a 'lot about the performance' (male, Chinese) in another account demonstrating a media marketing of mobility. Integrating embodied narrative in a hermeneutic circle of understanding ('to and 'fro), they tacitly configure/are configured by an immanent or implicit structured generic practice (media branding).

One can attend to how their themes are presented through language considered as a tool or 'equipment'. Language has a 'vital, indeed inescapable purpose in helping us to understand human phenomena' (Neill, 2014: 430). Linguistic use considered as discursive tool maps out the speaker's tacit positioning on horizons of understanding: 'by looking at what has hitherto been hidden at the margins' 'we can begin to appreciate deeper cultural realities' (Amadasi and Holliday, 2017: 256).

The allegation that phenomenology does not situate experience in a sociocultural context was considered in Chapter 3 where we saw that Askegaard and Linnet (2011) allowed that in the 'hermeneutic endeavour of interpretation', it 'refers to extra-experiential contexts on theoretical and methodological grounds' (394). We later noted Smith et al. (2009) placing on record their definitive statement concerning hermeneutic Interpretative Phenomenological Analysis investigating categorical or core aspects of understanding, including our 'self-reflection and sociality, affective concern' (17). Practice theories (whose ranks, I argued, include a behaviourally oriented hermeneutic IPA) have been positioned by their proponents as reconciling individualist and holist accounts of society—so human agency is conceptualised as articulated within but also enabled by social structure—with a 'blending of enablement and constraint' (Bryant and Jary, 1991: 8).

Cultural (in)forming of our human activity has been resolutely advanced in the philosophy of science, where positivism's separating of contextualising theory from observational description was fundamentally challenged in Kuhn's epistemological *Structure of Scientific Revolutions*

(1962). 'Social and cognitive factors are inextricably linked in all science' (Anderson, 1986: 156). Chapter 5 acknowledged computing science's shaping cognition by 'algorithmic architectures' (Bucher, 2015: 2). Far from the '*positivist* nature of algorithmic ideology' (Kerssens, 2017: 220, emphasis in original), Google search results online are ordered from a corporate horizon of 'targeting' consumer markets: 'whenever we use a data-based tool, it is already using us' (Couldry and Hepp, 2017: 120). Tracking in 'Big Data' pursues our Internet hermeneutic navigation, digital use between choice and constraint, 'enfolding' (ibid.: 113) meaning construction in this time of algorithmic management as we engage with virtual platforms 'curated' for profit (ibid.: 141). Datafication quantifies our doing. In research instigating or interpreting quantified 'Big Data', investigators need to acknowledge the 'situatedness, positionality and politics of the social science being conducted' (Kitchin, 2014: 10).

Architectural studies of a more material cast have been informed by hermeneutic thinking as has theology's recognition of a cultural component in 'demythologising' their religious claims. Writing on 'Introducing Hermeneutics to an Architectural Audience' (2015), Coyne holds there are four core ideas linking architectural discourse and hermeneutic philosophy: 'interpretation', 'reception' (e.g. of buildings), design as employing the hermeneutic circle of understanding (so 'interpretation and creation coalesce') and the 'threshold' of buildings and initiating understanding. He 'would argue that understanding is spatial in any case', as indeed we have observed on these pages. Considering the 'work, or text, of architecture', Hancock (1995) draws on the hermeneutic distinction between reflective and practical consciousness to assert that 'any "objectifying" of the work is a curtailment of meaningful involvements that were already at work' (184).

In claiming to free the Christian New Testament from a previous age's mythology, Bultmann maintained its spiritual message is couched in core categories resembling the Heideggerian analysis of *Dasein*'s existence, requiring recognising rather than evading human responsibility in actualising possibility through a life inevitably mortal (Jones, 1989). Here hermeneutics becomes theological.

Gadamer's mapping the 'fusion of horizons' (as we discussed in Chapter 1) appears 'highly applicable to interreligious dialogue' (Hedges, 2016: 5). For comparative theology also 'it can be argued that its aim to open up new insights for Christian theology through looking at other religious traditions finds a firm basis in Gadamer' (ibid.: 5–6). Writing on hermeneutics and theology, Knotts argues that potentially inscribed within a 'fusion of horizons', 'no text is a "dead" text' (2014: 245).

Acknowledging the genesis of hermeneutics in understanding religious texts 'hermeneutical philosophy and biblical interpretation' can be considered to equally characterise a 'dual description of Ricoeur's intellectual identity' (Wallace, 2000: 302). Here hermeneutics may be 'pressed into the service of saturating faith with intelligibility' (ibid.: 304). Continuing Gadamer's thesis, its meaning accrues from the 'reader's interpretive construals' (ibid.: 306). Reflecting upon the Bible as written text, enabling a distanciated accruing of meaning we considered in Chapter 1, Ricoeur considers the 'theological consequence of the indissoluble correlation which we have discovered between the world of the text and appropriation' (1975: 32), constituting a theological hermeneutics.

Developing studies of media users presented in this book's previous chapter, the 'mediated construction of reality' (Couldry and Hepp, 2017) seen as 'communicative practices' (66) has been explored from a perspective akin to hermeneutic practices through postulating 'figurations' as being essentially equipped 'practices'. 'We cannot understand the practices of such figurations without the objects and technologies that we use in relation to them' (ibid.: 67).

Figurational practices are generic or 'types of action' (ibid.: 65). Drawing upon an example we have used earlier a Chinese New Year Reunion Dinner gathering is a generic social practice of embodied, equipped narrative, emplacing horizons of understanding, characterised accordingly by roles and rules (cf. Ricoeur on actions as 'texts' (1981b)). Likewise as 'figuration', it could be said to display 'characteristic roles in (the) figuration's actor constellation and the overall meanings that are thereby produced' (Couldry and Hepp, 2017: 64), emplaced or 'reinforced' (ibid.: 67).

Figurations and practices are goal directed or teleological. As with celebrating the extended family enabled by the reunion dinner, there is 'something that matters (is meaningful) to the actors concerned' (ibid.: 65), or their 'common orientation to a shared "purpose"' (ibid.: 66)—constituting their 'relevance-frame' (ibid.: 66). A metaphor can 'precisely capture a number of things' (ibid.: 65). Hence 'horizons of understanding' (Gadamer, 1975) could be regarded as being the shared 'overall constructions of meaning that orientate human action' (Couldry and Hepp, 2017: 62) or emplaced in behaviour. The 'boundaries of each figuration are defined by (their) shared meaning' (ibid.: 63)—or as in practices analysis an embodied 'horizon of understanding'—from which purpose is perceived, albeit with local variations in material and metaphorical point of view.

To further pursue our illustrative example of a Chinese Reunion Dinner, reflecting on their tacit 'practical consciousness' (Giddens, 1979: 2) of this family reunion, one participant remarks on its 'relevance-frame' or 'horizon of understanding': the 'most important, the significant part of it, is because you see after a year's of (sic) hard work that we come together, and we have dinner' (male). Using Ricoeur's (1988) terms, a generic hence anticipated or 'prefigured' narrative is behaviourally 'configured' and is here reflectively 'refigured' to establish participant identity: 'we come together'. Activities both configure the

Chinese New Year Reunion Dinner and are necessarily configured by its generic goal-directed being as a shared routine, albeit annual, practice after a year's 'hard work'. As a collective practice emplacing this group's embodied horizon of understanding it is equally an assembled 'figuration of individuals that share a certain meaningful belonging that provides a basis for action and orientation-in-common' (Couldry and Hepp, 2017: 153). Marketing a culinary item to these consumers addressing the 'boundary object' (Star, 2010), here being the reunion dinner, would be a practice varying in how individuals involved oriented their understanding.

Subsequently, Hepp and Hasebrink (2018) summarily assert that access is gained to (media-related) figurations by 'researching their (role-related) actor constellations, frames of relevance and communicative practices' (30). 'Figurations' appear analogous to an embodied narrative 'practice'—emplacing meaning constituting ideationally shaped 'frames' or 'horizons of understanding' (Gadamer, 1975). 'Frames of relevance', like interpretive 'horizons', culturally position a practice's purpose: 'figurations (are) connections of people through shared meanings and orientations' (Kuipers, 2018: 433).

Rather than regarding 'figurations' and 'practices' as similar, a holistic social theory appears appropriately advanced by considering arrangements of practices within an institution as '*con*figured'. Practices of 'caring' through a hospital may be said (optimistically) to be hierarchically configured, embodied, equipped, sharing a public horizon of understanding the organisation. As we have noted, caring can 'sustain' 'hierarchical structures' and is 'fulfilled in them' (Taylor, 1985: 23). Likewise, within a recreation and shopping mall, management and visitor practices can be considered as being configured, complementing and conflicting across this organisational 'boundary object' (Star, 2010).

In this brief book, we have thought about 'understanding' as primarily practical, 'hitch-free skilled practical activity' (Wheeler, 2005: 129), essentially embodied, prior to 'hitches' or its being reflectively considered in report, propositional reflective narrative. Within the frequently (albeit not always) habituated practice of understanding (practical understanding)—from being able to choose apples to celebrating Chinese New Year Reunions—we tacitly treat enabling entities (from apples to armchairs) as being 'equipment': 'equipmental meanings' (Olivier, 2017: 13) are evident in subsequent speech. People do not attend to behavioural routine involved in selection or sitting, for their focus is elsewhere: thus 'in order for our focus and attention to function, much of the world recedes into the background' (Farman, 2015: 1). Visibly evident in digital online practices is embodied goal-directed understanding-in-use far from focusing on the keyboard, albeit that in more complex employment of interfaces immersive 'hermeneutic attention' can oscillate with 'operative attention' (Frosh, 2018: 360).

Only should issue occur or when asked in a focus group is reflection required on process or purpose, contributions leading to a wider discourse or a horizon of practical understanding, perhaps pointing to participants' ethnicity, gender or religion, where their ethical or political perspectives on looking at the situation are located. 'Hermeneutical horizons are ultimately the horizons of practical action' (Shalin, 2007: 213). Reference to hermeneutic practices—embodied, equipped activity, thus emplacing a horizon of understanding—can provide a theoretical grounding across disciplines. Here philosophy is involved in constituting and shaping forms of knowing about our human lives. 'Social structures' are 'dependent in the last instance upon meaning for their shape' (Reed, 2008: 121, open to reflective analysis of thematic practice recollected in our research participant discursive accounts.

> Society, culture, institutions, interactions, and individuals are mutually constitutive and ultimately grounded in a hermeneutic ontology of *praxis* that generates the social world.
>
> (Vandenberghe, 2007: 296–297; emphasis in original)

A hermeneutic practices perspective can be variously incorporated by different theoretical groups where reflection succeeds or interrupts routine 'practical consciousness' (Giddens, 1979: 2). One of the people interviewed in the urban shopping mall, we have noted before, engaging in the habituated practice of taking pictures of herself and a friend with a cell phone camera, comments that 'it was a happy . . . happiness but is something more because I remember at this moment when we took the picture it was something that you want it to last' (female, Malay mall visitor). At this moment, her embodied 'pre-reflective grasp on environment' (Moores, 2009: 304) is interrupted.

A celebratory reflective instant emerged here in the midst of such a widespread practice, as this 'moment' suspending a pre-reflective process, an awareness clearly suffused by multiple 'affect, general understandings, linguistically articulated meaning and significance and (. . .) sociomateriality' (Hui et al., 2017: 3), or in terms used by IPA, 'self-reflection and sociality, affective concern, (celebrating) a temporal, existential location' (Smith et al., 2009: 17). In short, exhibiting materially enabled hermeneutic agency, she traced out her affective embodied 'horizon of understanding' (Gadamer, 1975) 'at this moment' of reflection.

Beyond 'bonding' through cell phone cameras in a shopping mall digital 'devices become variably embedded in multiple practices' (Hand and Gorea, 2018: 677), with reflecting during or subsequent to deployment generating complex configurations of practices-in-a-practice (such as self-tracking). Wider practices of data collection, metrics online, can inform, showing alignment, quantitative political positioning on contested horizons of understanding (Rogers, 2018).

In the preceding chapters, reflecting upon diverse academic practices, we have seen how:

i. literary and media theory's reader reception involves their hermeneutic processing (Iser, Jauss, Pavlickova);
ii. marketing and organisations study reflection on/in practices (Thompson, Yanow and Tsoukas);
iii. media audience/user practices are said to be (primarily) non-representational (Frisina, Moores, Morley);
iv. philosophically reflecting, social theory argues for hermeneutic practices (Reckwitz, Schatzki, Warde);
v. qualitative psychology asserts interpretative phenomenological analysis of participant practices (Smith, Flowers, Larkin), and I suggest (albeit not further argued here) that examination would show (vi) architectural perception, scientific paradigms, and theological interpretation of text are thoroughly hermeneutic. There is no doubt a wider penumbra, further areas and disciplinary niches wherein hermeneutics has a presence.

Where data-driven quantitative media analytics holds sway, a digital hermeneutics of modes of audience address (from algorithmic to vigorous response from Internet visitors) and generic user understanding is a necessary complement. Qualitative research is able to 'unpack' 'Big Data' (e.g. *Facebook* 'Likes') as consumer story where hermeneutic practice, an embodied narrative of 'rules and resources' (Giddens, 1979: 64), is 'refigured' (Ricoeur, 1988: 160) to affirm our affective identity.

As observed when introducing a previous volume (Wilson, 2015), *our* consumer and *their* corporate stories—participatory and promotional branding narratives—collaborate and compete for attention in the mall and beyond. Accounts circulate through the material world and cyberspatially on *Facebook*, *Twitter* and *YouTube*, eliding, extending horizons of immersive understanding.

References

Ahmad, A. and S. Talaei (2012) 'Understanding Chronic Pain', *Journal of Advanced Social Research* 2(2): 110–119.

Ajjawi, R. and J. Higgs (2007) 'Using Hermeneutic Phenomenology to Investigate How Experienced Practitioners Learn to Communicate Clinical Reasoning', *The Qualitative Report* 12(4): 612–638.

Allmer, T. (2015) *Critical Theory and Social Media: Between Emancipation and Commodification*. London and New York: Routledge.

Alvesson, M. and K. Skoldberg (2009) *Reflexive Methodology: New Vistas for Qualitative Research*. London: Sage.

Amadasi, S. and A. Holliday (2017) 'Block and Thread Intercultural Narratives and Positioning: Conversations with Newly Arrived Postgraduate Students', *Language and Intercultural Understanding* 17(3): 254–269.

Anderson, P.F. (1986) 'On Method in Consumer Research: A Critical Relativist Perspective', *Journal of Consumer Research* 13(2): 155–173.

Annas, J. (2012) 'Practical Expertise', in J. Bengson and M.A. Moffett (eds.) *Knowing How: Essays on Knowledge, Mind, and Action*. Oxford Scholarship Online <https://global.oup.com/academic/product/knowing-how-9780195389364?cc=my&lang=en&>.

Arnold, S.J. and E. Fischer (1994) 'Hermeneutics and Consumer Research', *Journal of Consumer Research* 21(June): 55–71.

Arnould, E. (2014) 'Rudiments of a Value Praxeology', *Marketing Theory* 14(1): 129–133.

Arnould, E. and C. Thompson (2007) 'Consumer Culture Theory (and We Really Mean Theoretics): Dilemmas and Opportunities Posed by an Academic Branding Strategy', in R.W. Belk and J.F. Sherry, Jr. (eds.) *Consumer Culture Theory: Research in Consumer Behavior*, Vol. 11, pp. 3–22. Amsterdam: Elsevier.

Arsel, Z. and C.J. Thompson (2011) 'Demythologizing Consumption Practices: How Consumers Protect Their Field-Dependent Identity Investments from Devaluing Marketplace Myths', *Journal of Consumer Research* 37(5): 791–806.

Ashworth, P. (2003) 'An Approach to Phenomenological Psychology: The Contingencies of the Life-World', *Journal of Phenomenological Psychology* 34(2): 145–156.

Askegaard, S. and J.T. Linnet (2011) 'Towards an Epistemology of Consumer Culture Theory: Phenomenology and the Context of Context', *Marketing Theory* 11(4): 381–404.

Bailey, S. (2002) 'Virtuality and the Television Audience: The Case of *Futurama*', *The Communication Review* 5: 239–257.

Barad, K. (2003) 'Posthumanist Performativity: Toward an Understanding of How Matter Comes to Matter', *Signs* 28(3): 801–831.

Barnes, B. (2001) 'Practice as Collective Action', in T.R. Schatzki, K.K. Cetina and E. Von Savigny (eds.) *The Practice Turn in Contemporary Theory*, pp. 25–36. London and New York: Routledge.

Belk, R.W. (1988) 'Possessions and the "Extended Self"', *Journal of Consumer Research* 15(2): 139–168.

Berman, M. (2009) 'Dufrenne and Merleau-Ponty: A Comparative Meditation on Phenomenology', in A.T. Tymieniecka (ed.) *Phenomenology and Existentialism in the Twentieth Century*, pp. 145–160. Netherlands: Springer.

Bettany, S. and H. Woodruffe-Burton (2009) 'Working the Limits of Method: The Possibilities of Critical Reflexive Practice in Marketing and Consumer Research', *Journal of Marketing Management* 25(7–8): 661–679.

Bevan, M.T. (2014) 'A Method of Phenomenological Interviewing', *Qualitative Health Research* 24(1): 136–144.

Biehl-Missal, B. and M. Saren (2012) 'Atmospheres of Seduction: A Critique of Aesthetic Marketing Practices', *Journal of Macromarketing* 32(2): 168–180.

Bilimoria, P. (1998) 'Towards a Creative Hermeneutic of Suspicion: Recovering Ricoeur's Intervention in the Gadamer-Habermas Debate', paper presented at the 20th World Philosophy Congress, Boston University.

Bird, S.E. (2011) 'Are We All Produsers Now? Convergence and Media Audience Practices', *Cultural Studies* 25(4–5): 502–516.

Bloch, P., N.M. Ridgway and S.A. Dawson (1994) 'The Shopping Mall as Consumer Habitat', *Journal of Retailing* 70(1): 23–42.

Blok, A. and M.A. Pedersen (2014) 'Complementary Social Science? Quali-Quantitative Experiments in a Big Data World', *Big Data and Society* July–December: 1–6.

Bloor, D. (2001) 'Wittgenstein and the Priority of Practice', in T.R. Schatzki, K.K. Cetina and E. Von Savigny (eds.) *The Practice Turn in Contemporary Theory*, pp. 103–114. London: Routledge.

Boden, Z. and V. Eatough (2014) 'Understanding More Fully: A Multimodal Hermeneutic-Phenomenological Approach', *Qualitative Research in Psychology* 11: 160–177.

Bolin, G. and J.A. Schwarz (2015) 'Heuristics of the Algorithm: Big Data, User Interpretation and Institutional Translation', *Big Data and Society*: 1–12.

Bone, J., D.E. Chukwuemeka, D. Emele, A. Abdul, G. Coghill and W. Pang (2016) 'The Social Sciences and the Web: From "Lurking" to Interdisciplinary "Big Data" Research', *Methodological Innovations* 9: 1–14.

Bordwell, D. (1991) *Making Meaning Inference and Rhetoric in the Interpretation of Cinema*. Cambridge, MA: Harvard University Press.

Borisenkova, A. (2010) 'Narrative Refiguration of Social Events Paul Ricoeur's Contribution to Rethinking the Social', *Ricoeur Studies* 1(1): 87–98.

Bourdieu, P. (1977) *Outline of a Theory of Practice*. Cambridge: Cambridge University Press.

Bourdieu, P. (1990) *The Logic of Practice*. Cambridge: Polity Press.

Bourdieu, P. (1998) *Practical Reason*. Cambridge: Polity Press.

Bramley, N. and V. Eatough (2005) 'The Experience of Living with Parkinson's Disease: An Interpretative Phenomenological Analysis Case Study', *Psychology and Health* 20(2): 223–235.

Braun, V. and V. Clarke (2006) 'Using Thematic Analysis in Psychology', *Qualitative Research in Psychology* 3(2): 77–101.

Brinkmann, S. (2008) 'Identity as Self-Interpretation', *Theory and Psychology* 18(3): 404–422.

Brocki, J.M. and A.J. Wearden (2006) 'A Critical Evaluation of the Use of Interpretative Phenomenological Analysis (IPA) in Health Psychology', *Psychology & Health* 21(1): 87–108.

Brook, J. (2010) 'An Elaboration of the Transformative Approach to Practical Theory: Its Connections with Gadamer's Philosophical Hermeneutics', *Communication Theory* 20: 405–426.

Brown, J.S. and P. Duguid (1991) 'Organizational Learning and Communities-of-Practice: Toward a Unified View of Working, Learning, and Innovation', *Organization Science* 2(1): 40–57.

Brown, J.S. and P. Duguid (2001) 'Knowledge and Organization: A Social-Practice Perspective', *Organization Science* 12(2): 198–213.

Bruns, G.L. (2004) 'On the Coherence of Hermeneutics and Ethics: An Essay on Gadamer and Levinas', in B. Krajewski (ed.) *Gadamer's Repercussions: Reconsidering Philosophical Hermeneutics*, pp. 30–54. Berkeley: University of California Press.

Bruun, H. (2010) 'Genre and Interpretation in Production: A Theoretical Approach', *Media, Culture and Society* 32(5): 723–737.

Bryant, C.G.A. and D. Jary (eds.) (1991) *Giddens Theory of Structuration: A Critical Appreciation*. London and New York: Routledge.

Bucher, T. (2015) 'Networking, or What the Social Means in Social Media', *Social Media and Society* April–June: 1–2.

Burchell, K. (2017) 'Everyday Communication Management and Perceptions of Use: How Media Users Limit and Shape Their Social World', *Convergence: The International Journal of Research into New Media Technologies*: 1–16.

Burkitt, I. (2002) 'Technologies of the Self: Habitus and Capacities', *Journal for the Theory of Social Behaviour* 32(2): 219–237.

Burles, M. and R. Thomas (2014) '"I Just Don't Think There's Any Other Image That Tells the Story Like (This) Picture Does": Researcher and Participant Reflections on the Use of Participant-Employed Photography in Social Research', *International Journal of Qualitative Methods* 13(1): 185–205.

Butler, G. and K. Hannam (2014) 'Performing Expatriate Mobilities in Kuala Lumpur', *Mobilities* 9(1): 1–20.

Cahill, K.M. (2016) '*The Habitus*, Coping Practices, and the Search for the Ground of Action', *Philosophy of the Social Sciences* 46(5): 498–524.

Callahan, C. (2011) 'Negotiating Adaptation: Perceptions of Culture and Communication among Cultural Sojourners', *Communication, Culture and Critique* 4: 314–332.

Callary, B., S. Rathwell and B.W. Young (2015) 'Insights on the Process of Using Interpretative Phenomenological Analysis in a Sport Coaching Research Project', *The Qualitative Report* 20(2): 63–75.

Canniford, R. and A. Shankar (2013) 'Purifying Practices: How Consumers Assemble Romantic Experiences of Nature', *Journal of Consumer Research* 39(February): 1051–1069.

Capobianco, R. (2010) *Engaging Heidegger*. Toronto: University of Toronto Press.

Carbaugh, D., E.V. Nuciforo, E. Molina-Markham and B. Van Over (2011) 'Discursive Reflexivity in the Ethnography of Communication: Cultural Discourse Analysis', *Cultural Studies ↔ Critical Methodologies* 20(10): 1–12.

Carlile, P.R. (2002) 'A Pragmatic View of Knowledge and Boundaries: Boundary Objects in New Product Development', *Organization Science* 13(4): 442–455.

Carlson, M. (2017) 'Automating Judgment? Algorithmic Judgment, News Knowledge, and Journalistic Professionalism', *New Media and Society* First Published 22 May 2017.

Carpentier, N. (2001) 'Managing Audience Participation: The Construction of Participation in an Audience Discussion Programme', *European Journal of Communication* 16(2): 209–232.

Carradice, A., M.C. Shankland and N. Beail (2002) 'A Qualitative Study of the Theoretical Models Used by UK Mental Health Nurses to Guide Their

Assessments with Family Caregivers of People with Dementia', *International Journal of Nursing Studies* 39(1): 17–26.
Carter, M.J. (2013) 'The Hermeneutics of Frames and Framing: An Examination of the Media's Construction of Reality', *SAGE Open* April–June: 1–12.
Caru, A. and B. Cova (2008) 'Small versus Big Stories in Framing Consumption Experiences', *Qualitative Market Research: An International Journal* 11(2): 166–176.
Cayla, J. and G.M. Eckhardt (2008) 'Asian Brands and the Shaping of a Transnational Imagined Community', *Journal of Communication Research* 35(2): 216–230.
Cetina, K.K. (2001) 'Objectual Practice', in T.R. Schatzki, K.K. Cetina and E. Von Savigny (eds.) *The Practice Turn in Contemporary Theory*, pp. 184–197. London and New York: Routledge.
Chamberlain, K. (2011) 'Troubling Methodology', *Health Psychology Review* 5(1): 48–54.
Chan, N.N., C. Walker and A. Gleaves (2015) 'An Exploration of Students' Lived Experiences of Using Smartphones in Diverse Learning Contexts Using a Hermeneutic Phenomenological Approach', *Computers & Education* 82: 96–106.
Chandler, D. (2014) 'An Introduction to Genre Theory' <http://visual-memory.co.uk/daniel/Documents/intgenre/intgenre1.html>.
Chang, C.T., K.H. Chang and W.L. Cheah (2009) 'Adults' Perceptions of Being Overweight or Obese: A Focus Group Study', *Asia Pacific Journal of Clinical Nutrition* 18(2): 257–264.
Chang, K.H. and S. Horrocks (2008) 'Is There a Place for Ontological Hermeneutics in Mental-Health Nursing Research? A Review of a Hermeneutic Study', *International Journal of Nursing Practice* 14: 383–390.
Chapman, E. and J.A. Smith (2002) 'Interpretative Phenomenological Analysis and the New Genetics', *Journal of Health Psychology* 7(2): 125–130.
Chia, R. and R. Holt (2006) 'Strategy as Practical Coping: A Heideggerian Perspective', *Organization Studies* 27(5): 635–655.
Chryssochoou, X. (2000) 'Memberships in a Superordinate Level: Re-Thinking European Union as a Multi-National Society', *Journal of Community and Applied Social Psychology* 10: 403–420.
Clare, L. (2003) 'Managing Threats to Self: Awareness in Early Stage Alzheimer's Disease', *Social Science and Medicine* 57(6): 1017–1029.
Clark, J. (2008) 'Philosophy, Understanding and the Consultation: A Fusion of Horizons', *British Journal of General Practice* January: 58–60.
Clark, W., N. Couldry, R. MacDonald and H.C. Stephansen (2015) 'Digital Platforms and Narrative Exchange: Hidden Constraints, Emerging Agency', *New Media and Society* 17(6): 919–938.
Coe, R.M. and A. Freedman (1998) 'Genre Theory: Australian and North American Approaches', in M.L. Kennedy (ed.) *Theorizing Composition: A Critical Sourcebook of Theory and Scholarship in Contemporary Composition Studies*, pp. 136–147. Westport, CT: Greenwood Press.
Collins, H.M. (2001) 'What Is Tacit Knowledge?', in T.R. Schatzki, K.K. Cetina and E. Von Savigny (eds.) *The Practice Turn in Contemporary Theory*, pp. 115–128. London and New York: Routledge.
Conroy, S.A. (2003) 'A Pathway for Interpretive Phenomenology', *International Journal of Qualitative Methods* 2(3): 36–62.
Cook, S.D.N. and J.S. Brown (1999) 'Bridging Epistemologies: The Generative Dance between Organizational Knowledge and Organizational Knowing', *Organization Science* 10(4): 381–400.
Cope, J. (2011) 'Entrepreneurial Learning from Failure: An Interpretative Phenomenological Analysis', *Journal of Business Venturing* 26(6): 604–623.

Corner, J. (2013) 'Is There a "Field" of Media Research? The "Fragmentation" Issue Revisited', *Media, Culture and Society* 35(8): 1011–1018.
Coskuner-Balli, G. and C.J. Thompson (2013) 'The Status Costs of Subordinate Cultural Capital: At-Home Fathers' Collective Pursuit of Cultural Legitimacy through Capitalizing Consumption Practices', *Journal of Consumer Research* 40(1): 19–41.
Couldry, N. (2003) *Media Rituals: A Critical Approach*. London and New York: Routledge.
Couldry, N. (2004) 'Theorising Media as Practice', *Social Semiotics* 14(2): 115–132.
Couldry, N. (2008a) 'Mediatization or Mediation? Alternative Understandings of the Emergent Space of Digital Storytelling', *New Media and Society* 10(3): 373–391.
Couldry, N. (2008b) 'Actor Network Theory and Media: Do They Connect and on What Terms?', in A. Hepp, F. Krotz, S. Moores and C. Winter (eds.) *Connectivity, Networks and Flows: Conceptualizing Contemporary Communications*, pp. 93–110. Cresskill, NJ: Hampton Press.
Couldry, N. (2009a) 'Rethinking the Politics of Voice', *Continuum: Journal of Media and Cultural Studies* 23(4): 579–582.
Couldry, N. (2009b) 'Does "the Media" Have a Future?', *European Journal of Communication* 24(4): 437–449.
Couldry, N. (2010) 'Theorising Media as Practice', in B. Brauchler and J. Postill (eds.) *Theorising Media and Practice*, pp. 35–54. New York: Berghahn Books.
Couldry, N. (2011) 'The Necessary Future of the Audience . . . and How to Research It', in V. Nightingale (ed.) *The Handbook of Media Audiences*, pp. 213–229. London: Wiley-Blackwell.
Couldry, N. (2012) *Media, Society, World: Social Theory and Digital Media Practice*. Cambridge: Polity Press.
Couldry, N. (2013) 'A Necessary Disenchantment: Myth, Agency and Injustice in a Digital World', Inaugural Lecture, Professor of Media Studies, London School of Economics and Political Science.
Couldry, N. (2015a) 'Social Media: Human Life', *Social Media and Society* April–June: 1–2.
Couldry, N. (2015b) 'The Myth of "Us": Digital Networks, Political Change and the Production of Collectivity', *Information, Communication and Society* 18(6): 608–626.
Couldry, N. and A. McCarthy (2004) 'Introduction: Orientations: Mapping Media Space', in N. Couldry and A. McCarthy (eds.) *MediaSpace: Place, Scale and Culture in a Media Age*, pp. 1–18. London and New York: Routledge.
Couldry, N. and A. Powell (2014) 'Big Data from the Bottom Up', *Big Data and Society* July–December: 1–5.
Couldry, N. and J. Turow (2014) 'Advertising, Big Data, and the Clearance of the Public Realm: Marketers' New Approaches to the Content Subsidy', *International Journal of Communication* 8: 1710–1726.
Couldry, N. and J. Van Dijck (2015) 'Researching Social Media as if the Social Mattered', *Social Media and Society* July–December: 1–7.
Couldry, N., A. Fotopoulou and L. Dickens (2016) 'Real Social Analytics: A Contribution towards a Phenomenology of a Digital World', *British Journal of Sociology* 67(1): 118–137.
Couldry, N. and A. Hepp (2017) *The Mediated Construction of Reality*. Cambridge: Polity Press.
Coulter, J. (2001) 'Human Practices and the Observability of the "Macro-Social"', in T.R. Schatzki, K.K. Cetina and E. Von Savigny (eds.) *The Practice Turn in Contemporary Theory*, pp. 37–49. London and New York: Routledge.

Cova, B., D. Dalli and D. Zwick (2011) 'Critical Perspectives on Consumers' Role as "Producers": Broadening the Debate on Value Co-Creation in Marketing Processes', *Marketing Theory* 11(3): 231–241.
Cova, B., P. Maclaran and A. Bradshaw (2013) 'Rethinking Consumer Culture Theory from the Postmodern to the Communist Horizon', *Marketing Theory* 13(2): 213–225.
Coyne, R. (2010) *The Tuning of Place: Sociable Spaces and Pervasive Digital Media*. Cambridge, US: MIT Press.
Coyne, R. (2015) 'Introducing Hermeneutics to an Architectural Audience', *Reflections on Technology, Media and Culture* <https://richardcoyne.com/2015/05/09/introducing-hermeneutics-to-an-architectural-audience/>.
Creswell, J.W. (2013) *Qualitative Inquiry and Research Design Choosing among Five Approaches*. London: Sage.
Crossley, N. (2001) 'The Phenomenological Habitus and Its Construction', *Theory and Society* 30(1): 81–120.
Culler, J.D. (1975) *Structuralist Poetics: Structuralism, Linguistics and the Study of Literature*. London: Routledge and Kegan Paul.
Curran, J. (1990) 'The New Revisionism in Mass Communication Research: A Reappraisal', *European Journal of Communication* 5: 135–164.
Dahlgren, P. (1988a) 'What's the Meaning of This? Viewers Plural Sense-Making of TV News', *Media, Culture and Society* 10(3): 285–301.
Dahlgren, P. (1988b) 'Crime News: The Fascination of the Mundane', *European Journal of Communication* 3: 189–206.
Dallmayr, F. (2009) 'Hermeneutics and Inter-Cultural Dialogue: Linking Theory and Practice', *Ethics and Global Politics* 2(1): 23–39.
Dandy, N. (2016) 'Woodland Neglect as Social Practice', *Environment and Planning A* 48(9): 1750–1766.
Dant, T. (2000) 'Consumption Caught in the "Cash Nexus"', *Sociology* 34(4): 655–670.
Dant, T. (2005) *Materiality and Society*. Maidenhead: Open University Press.
Dant, T. (2008) 'The "Pragmatics" of Material Interaction', *Journal of Consumer Culture* 8(1): 11–33.
Das, R. (2011a) *Interpretation from Audiences to Users*. Thesis submitted to the Department of Media and Communications of the London School of Economics for the degree of Doctor of Philosophy.
Das, R. (2011b) 'Converging Perspectives in Audience Studies and Digital Literacies: Youthful Interpretations of an Online Genre', *European Journal of Communication* 26(4): 343–360.
Das, R. (2016) '"I've Walked this Street": Readings of "Reality" in British Young People's Reception of Harry Potter', *Journal of Children and Media* 10(3): 341–354.
Das, R. (2017) 'Audiences: A Decade of Transformations-Reflections from the CEDAR Network on Emerging Directions in Audience Analysis', *Media, Culture and Society* 39(8): 1257–1267.
Das, R. and B. Ytre-Arne (eds.) (2017) *Audiences, towards 2030: Priorities for Audience Analysis*. Surrey: CEDAR.
Davey, N. (2006) *Unquiet Understanding Gadamer's Philosophical Hermeneutics*. Albany: State University of New York Press.
Davey, N. (2013) 'Aesthetic Reasoning: A Hermeneutic Approach', *Nordic Journal of Aesthetics* 46: 8–17.
Davidsen, A.S. (2013) 'Phenomenological Approaches in Psychology and Health Sciences', *Qualitative Research in Psychology* 10(3): 318–339.
De Certeau, M. (1984) *The Practice of Everyday Life*. Berkeley: University of California Press.

Degen, M., G. Rose and B. Basdas (2010) 'Bodies and Everyday Practices in Designed Urban Environments', *Science Studies: An Interdisciplinary Journal for Science and Technology Studies* 23(2): 60–76.
Deris, F.D., A.R. Salam, A.A. Rahman and R.T.H. Koon (2016) 'A Hermeneutic Phenomenology Inquiry on Teacher's E-Practices in the Online ESL Learning Environment', paper presented at the Qualitative Research Conference, Penang, Malaysia.
De Visser, R.O. and J.A. Smith (2006) 'Mister In-Between: A Case Study of Masculine Identity and Health-Related Behaviour', *Journal of Health Psychology* 11(5): 685–695.
De Visser, R.O. and D. McDonald (2007) 'Swings and Roundabouts: Management of Jealousy in Heterosexual "Swinging" Couples', *British Journal of Social Psychology* 46: 459–476.
De Visser, R.O. and J.A. Smith (2007) 'Alcohol Consumption and Masculine Identity among Young Men', *Psychology and Health* 22(5): 595–614.
Dhoest, A. (2015) 'Revisiting Reception Research: Case Study on Diasporic LGBTQs', *Participations Journal of Audience and Reception Studies* 12(2): 78–97.
Dickson, A., C. Knussen and P. Flowers (2007) 'Stigma and the Delegitimation Experience: An Interpretative Phenomenological Analysis of People Living with Chronic Fatigue Syndrome', *Psychology and Health* 22(7): 851–867.
Dickson, A., D. Allan and R. O'Carroll (2008) 'Biographical Disruption and the Experience of Loss Following a Spinal Cord Injury: An Interpretative Phenomenological Analysis', *Psychology and Health* 23(4): 407–425.
Dill, K.E. (ed.) (2013) *The Oxford Handbook of Media Psychology*. New York: Oxford University Press.
Dorairaj, A.J. (2000) 'Paul Ricoeur's Hermeneutics of the Text', *Indian Philosophical Quarterly* 27(4): 403–410.
Dotov, D.G., L. Nie and A. Chemero (2010) 'A Demonstration of the Transition from Ready-to-Hand to Unready-to-Hand', *PLoS One* 5(3).
Dowling, M. (2007) 'From Husserl to Van Manen: A Review of Different Phenomenological Approaches', *International Journal of Nursing Studies* 44: 131–142.
Dreyfus, H.L. (1991) *Being-in-the-World: A Commentary on Heidegger's Being and Time, Division I*. Boston, MA: MIT.
Dreyfus, H.L. (2001) 'How Heidegger Defends the Possibility of a Correspondence Theory of Truth with Respect to the Entities of Natural Science', in T.R. Schatzki, K.K. Cetina and E. Von Savigny (eds.) *The Practice Turn in Contemporary Theory*, pp. 159–171. London and New York: Routledge.
Durham, M.G. (2016) 'Children, the Media, and the Epistemic Imperative of Embodied Vulnerability', *Journal of Children and Media* 10(1): 115–122.
Eatough, V. and J.A. Smith (2006) '"I Was Like a Wild Wild Person": Understanding Feelings of Anger Using Interpretative Phenomenological Analysis', *British Journal of Psychology* 97: 483–498.
Eatough, V. and J.A. Smith (2008) 'Interpretative Phenomenological Analysis', in C. Willig and W. Stainton-Rogers (eds.) *The Sage Handbook of Qualitative Research in Psychology*, pp. 179–194. London: Sage.
Eatough, V., J.A. Smith and R.L. Shaw (2008) 'Women, Anger and Aggression: An Interpretative Phenomenological Analysis', *Journal of Interpersonal Violence* 23(12): 1767–1799.
Echeverri, P. and P. Skålén (2011) 'Co-Creation and Co-Destruction: A Practice-Theory Based Study of Interactive Value Formation', *Marketing Theory* 11(3): 351–373.
Echeverri, P., N. Salomonson and A. Aberg (2012) 'Dealing with Customer Misbehaviour: Employees' Tactics, Practical Judgement and Implicit Knowledge', *Marketing Theory* 12(4): 427–449.

Elsaesser, T. (1981) 'Narrative Cinema and Audience-Oriented Aesthetics', in T. Bennett, S. Boyd-Bowman, C. Mercer and J. Woollacott (eds.) *Popular Television and Film*, pp. 270–282. London: British Film Institute/Open University Press.
Epp, A.M. and L.L. Price (2010) 'The Storied Life of Singularized Objects: Forces of Agency and Network Transformation', *Journal of Consumer Research* 36(February): 820–837.
Everts, J., M. Lahr-Kurten and M. Watson (2011) 'Practice Matters! Geographical Inquiry and Theories of Practice', *Erdkunde* 65(4): 323–334.
Farman, J. (2015) 'Infrastructures of Mobile Social Media', *Social Media + Society* April–June: 1–2.
Farrag, D.A., I.M. El Sayed and R.W. Belk (2010) 'Mall Shopping Motives and Activities: A Multimethod Approach', *Journal of International Consumer Marketing* 22: 95–115.
Finlay, K.A. and J. Elander (2016) 'Reflecting the Transition from Pain Management Services to Chronic Pain Support Group Attendance: An Interpretative Phenomenological Analysis', *British Journal of Health Psychology* 21(3): 660–676.
Finlay, L. (2009) 'Debating Phenomenological Research Methods', *Phenomenology and Practice* 3(1): 6–25.
Finlay, L. (2011) *Phenomenology for Therapists: Researching the Lived World*. London: Wiley-Blackwell.
Finlay, L. (2014) 'Engaging Phenomenological Analysis', *Qualitative Research in Psychology* 11: 121–141.
Fırat, A.F. and M. Tadajewski (2009) 'Critical Marketing: Marketing in Critical Condition', in P. Maclaran, M. Saren, B. Stern and M. Tadajewski (eds.) *The Sage Handbook of Marketing Theory*, pp. 127–150. London: Sage.
Fırat, A.F., S. Pettigrew and R. Belk (2011) 'Themed Experiences and Spaces', *Consumption, Markets and Culture* 14(2): 123–124.
Fırat, A.F. and N. Dholakia (2016) 'From Consumer to Construer: Travels in Human Subjectivity', *Journal of Consumer Culture* January: 1–19.
Flowers, P., J.A. Smith, P. Sheeran and N. Beail (1998) '"Coming Out" and Sexual Debut: Understanding the Social Context of HIV Risk-Related Behaviour', *Journal of Community and Applied Social Psychology* 8: 409–421.
Flyvbjerg, B. (2001) *Making Social Science Matter*. Cambridge: Cambridge University Press.
Fornas, J. (2008) 'Bridging Gaps: Ten Crosscurrents in Media Studies', *Media, Culture and Society* 30(6): 895–905.
Fotopoulou, A. and N. Couldry (2015) 'Telling the Story of the Stories: Online Content Curation and Digital Engagement', *Information, Communication and Society* 18(2): 235–249.
Foucault, M. (1981/1988) '"Practicing Criticism" or "Is It Really Important to Think?" (May 30–31, 1981 Didier Eribon Interview), in L. Kritzman (ed.) *Michel Foucault, Politics, Philosophy, Culture: Interviews and Other Writings 1977–1984*, pp. 152–158. London and New York: Routledge.
Freeman, M. and M.D. Vagle (2013) 'Grafting the Intentional Relation of Hermeneutics and Phenomenology in Linguisticality', *Qualitative Inquiry* 19(9): 725–735.
Friedman, D. (2010) 'Writing on Film as Art through Ricoeur's Hermeneutics', *Journal of Writing in Creative Practice* 3(2): 161–170.
Frisina, W.G. (2002) *The Unity of Knowledge and Action: Toward a Non-Representational Theory of Knowledge*. Albany: State University of New York Press.

Frosh, P. (2016) 'The Mouse, the Screen and the Holocaust Witness: Interface Aesthetics and Moral Response', *New Media and Society* 20(1): 351–368.
Fuchs, C. (2017) *Social Media: A Critical Introduction*. London: Sage.
Gadamer, H.G. (1975) *Truth and Method*. London: Sheed and Ward.
Gadamer, H.G. (2006) 'Classical and Philosophical Hermeneutics', *Theory, Culture and Society* 23(1): 29–56.
Gartner, C. (2013) 'Cognition, Knowing and Learning in the Flesh: Six Views on Embodied Knowing in Organization Studies', *Scandinavian Journal of Management* 29: 338–352.
Gaviria, P.R. and C. Bluemelhuber (2010) 'Consumers' Transformations in a Liquid Society: Introducing the Concepts of Autobiographical-Concern and Desire-Assemblage', *Journal of Consumer Behaviour* 9(2): 126–138.
Geanellos, R. (2000) 'Exploring Ricoeur's Hermeneutic Theory of Interpretation as a Method of Analysing Research Texts', *Nursing Inquiry* 7: 112–119.
Geise, S. and C. Baden (2015) 'Putting the Image Back into the Frame: Modeling the Linkage between Visual Communication and Frame-Processing Theory', *Communication Theory* 25: 46–69.
Geniusas, S. (2015) 'Between Phenomenology and Hermeneutics: Paul Ricoeur's Philosophy of Imagination', *Human Studies* 38: 223–241.
Gherardi, S. (2015) 'How the Turn to Practice May Contribute to Working Life Studies', *Nordic Journal of Working Life Studies* 5(3a): 13–25.
Gibson, J.J. (1986) *The Ecological Approach to Visual Perception*. Hillsdale, NJ: Lawrence Erlbaum Associates.
Giddens, A. (1979) *Central Problems in Social Theory: Action, Structure and Contradiction in Social Analysis*. Berkeley and Los Angeles: University of California Press.
Giddens, A. (1981a) 'Hermeneutics and Social Theory', *Contemporary Sociology* 10(6): 771–772.
Giddens, A. (1981b) *A Contemporary Critique of Historical Materialism Volume One Power, Property and the State*. Berkeley and Los Angeles: University of California Press.
Giddens, A. (1982) *Profiles and Critiques in Social Theory*. London: Macmillan.
Giddens, A. (1984) *The Constitution of Society: Outline of the Theory of Structuration*. Cambridge: Polity Press.
Giddens, A. (1991a) 'Structuration Theory: Past, Present and Future', in C.G.A. Bryant and D. Jary (eds.) *Giddens Theory of Structuration: A Critical Appreciation*, pp. 201–221. London: Routledge.
Giddens, A. (1991b) *Modernity and Self-Identity: Self and Society in Late Modern Age*. Stanford, CA: Stanford University Press.
Giddens, A. (1993) *New Rules of Sociological Method A Positive Critique of Interpretative Sociologies*. Second Edition. Cambridge, UK and US: Polity-Blackwell.
Giesler, M. and C.J. Thompson (2016) 'Process Theorization in Cultural Consumer Research', *Journal of Consumer Research* 43: 497–508.
Gimbel, E.W. (2016) 'Interpretation and Objectivity: A Gadamerian Reevaluation of Max Weber's Social Science', *Political Research Quarterly* 69(1): 72–82.
Ginev, D. (2016) *Hermeneutic Realism Reality within Scientific Inquiry*. Basel, Switzerland: Springer.
Giorgi, A. (2011) 'IPA and Science: A Response to Jonathan Smith', *Journal of Phenomenological Psychology* 42: 195–216.
Given, L.M. (2017) 'It's a New Year . . . So Let's Stop the Paradigm Wars (Editorial)', *International Journal of Qualitative Methods* 16(1): 1–2.

Glasscoe, C. and J.A. Smith (2010) 'Unravelling Complexities Involved in Parenting a Child with Cystic Fibrosis: An Interpretative Phenomenological Analysis', *Clinical Child Psychology and Psychiatry* 16(2): 279–298.
Goh, E.C.L. and K. Göransson (2011) 'Doing Ethnographic Research in Chinese Families: Reflections on Methodological Concerns from Two Asian Cities', *International Journal of Qualitative Methods* 10(3): 265–281.
Golsworthy, R. and A. Coyle (2001) 'Practitioners' Accounts of Religious and Spiritual Dimensions in Bereavement Therapy', *Counselling Psychology Quarterly* 14(3): 183–202.
Gonzalez-Polledo, E. and J. Tarr (2016) 'The Thing About Pain: The Remaking of Illness Narratives in Chronic Pain Expressions on Social Media', *New Media and Society* 18(8): 1455–1472.
Gough, B. and A. Madill (2012) 'Subjectivity in Psychological Science: From Problem to Prospect', *Psychological Methods* 17(3): 374–384.
Gough, B. and J.A. Deatrick (2015) 'Qualitative Health Psychology Research: Diversity, Power, and Impact', *Health Psychology* 34(4): 289–292.
Gough, B. and A. Lyons (2016) 'The Future of Qualitative Research in Psychology: Accentuating the Positive', *Integrative Psychological and Behavioral Science* 50(2): 234–243.
Granot, E., T.G. Brashear and P.C. Motta (2012) 'A Structural Guide to In-Depth Interviewing in Business and Industrial Marketing Research', *Journal of Business and Industrial Marketing* 27(7): 547–553.
Grondin, J. (2002) 'Gadamer's Basic Understanding of Understanding', in R.J. Dostal (ed.) *The Cambridge Companion to Gadamer*, pp. 36–51. Cambridge: Cambridge University Press.
Grondin, J. (2015) 'Ricoeur: The Long Way of Hermeneutics', in J. Malpas and H.-H. Gander (eds.) *The Routledge Companion to Hermeneutics*, pp. 149–159. London and New York: Routledge.
Grossberg, L. (1984) 'Strategies of Marxist Cultural Interpretation', *Critical Studies in Mass Communication* 1: 392–421.
Grossberg, L. and C.G. Christians (1978) 'Hermeneutics and the Study of Communication', paper presented at the Annual Meeting of the Association for Education in Journalism, Seattle, Washington.
Guignon, C.B. (1993) 'Introduction', in C.B. Guignon (ed.) *The Cambridge Companion to Heidegger*. Cambridge: Cambridge University Press.
Gurstein, M. (2011) 'Open Data: Empowering the Empowered or Effective Data Use for Everyone?', *First Monday* 16(2): 1–8.
Hadjioannou, C. (2017) 'What Can We Do with Heidegger in the Twenty-First Century?', *The Journal of the British Society for Phenomenology* 48: 1–10.
Halkier, B. and I. Jensen (2011) 'Methodological Challenges in Using Practice Theory in Consumption Research: Examples from a Study on Handling Nutritional Contestations of Food Consumption', *Journal of Consumer Culture* 11(1): 101–123.
Hallinan, B. and T. Striphas (2016) 'Recommended for You: The Netflix Prize and the Production of Algorithmic Culture', *New Media and Society* 18(1): 117–137.
Halpin, H. and A. Monnin (2016) 'The Decentralization of Knowledge: How Carnap and Heidegger Influenced the Web', *First Monday* 21(12) <http://firstmonday.org/ojs/index.php/fm/article/view/7109/5655>.
Hamilton, J.F. and R. Bodle (2017) 'Introduction Critical Traditions', in J.F. Hamilton, R. Bodle and E. Korin (eds.) *Explorations in Critical Studies of Advertising*, pp. 1–10. London and New York: Routledge.
Hamzah, A. and Md A. Md Syed (2013) 'Imagining Modernity in Contemporary Malaysia: Non-Western Soap Opera and the Negative Urban Morality', in

L. Fitzsimmons and J.A. Lent (eds.) *Popular Culture in Asia: Memory, City, Celebrity*, pp. 142–164. London and New York: Palgrave Macmillan.

Hancock, J.E. (1995) 'The Interpretive Turn: Radical Hermeneutics and the Work of Architecture', *History/Theory/Criticism*: 183–188. 83rd ACSA Annual Meeting. Washington: Association of Collegiate Schools of Architecture.

Hand, M. and M. Gorea (2018) 'Digital Traces and Personal Analytics: iTime, Self Tracking, and the Temporalities of Practice', *International Journal of Communication* 12: 666–682.

Hans, J.S. (1980) 'Hermeneutics, Play, Deconstruction', *Philosophy Today* 24: 299–317.

Harre, R. (1993) *Social Being*. Second Edition. Oxford: Blackwell.

Harvey, L. and M.D. Myers (1995) 'Scholarship and Practice: The Contribution of Ethnographic Research Methods to Bridging the Gap', *Information Technology and People* 8(3): 13–27.

Haslett, B.B. (2012) *Communicating and Organizing in Context: The Theory of Structurational Interaction*. London and New York: Routledge.

Hatch, M.J. and J. Rubin (2006) 'The Hermeneutics of Branding', *Journal of Brand Management* 14: 40–59.

Hawkins, B., A. Pye and F. Correia (2017) 'Boundary Objects, Power and Learning: The Matter of Developing Sustainable Practice in Organisations', *Management Learning* 48(3): 292–310.

Hedges, P. (2016) 'Comparative Theology and Hermeneutics: A Gadamerian Approach to Interreligious Interpretation', *Religions* 7(7): 1–20.

Heidegger, M. (1962) *Being and Time*. New York: Harper and Row.

Heidegger, M. (2001) *Phenomenological Interpretations of Aristotle: Initiation into Phenomenological Research*. Bloomington: Indiana University Press.

Hein, W., S. O'Donohoe and A. Ryan (2011) 'Mobile Phones as an Extension of the Participant Observer's Self: Reflections on the Emergent Role of an Emergent Technology', *Qualitative Market Research: An International Journal* 14(3): 258–273.

Hepp, A. (2010) 'Researching "Mediatized Worlds": Non-Media-Centric Media and Communication Research as a Challenge', in N. Carpentier, I.T. Trivundza, P. Pruulmann-Vengerfeldt, E. Sundin, T. Olsson, R. Kilborn, H. Nieminen and B. Cammaerts (eds.) *Media and Communication Studies: Interventions and Intersections*, pp. 37–48. Estonia: Tartu University.

Hepp, A. (2013) 'The Communicative Figurations of Mediatized Worlds: Mediatization Research in Times of the "Mediation of Everything"', *European Journal of Communication* 28(6): 615–629.

Hepp, A. (2016) 'Pioneer Communities: Collective Actors in Deep Mediatization', *Media, Culture and Society* 38(6): 918–933.

Hepp, A., A. Breiter and U. Hasebrink (2018) 'Rethinking Transforming Communications: An Introduction', in A. Hepp, A. Breiter and U. Hasebrink (eds.) *Communicative Figurations: Transforming Communications in Times of Deep Mediatization*, pp. 3–14. London and New York: Palgrave Macmillan.

Hepp, A. and U. Hasebrink (2018) 'Researching Transforming Communications in Times of Deep Mediatization: A Figurational Approach', in A. Hepp, A. Breiter and U. Hasebrink (eds.) *Communicative Figurations: Transforming Communications in Times of Deep Mediatization*, pp. 15–48. London and New York: Palgrave Macmillan.

Hermes, J. (1993) 'Media, Meaning and Everyday Life', *Cultural Studies* 7(3): 493–505.

Hirst, M. (2017) 'Towards a Political Economy of Fake News', *The Political Economy of Communication* 5(2): 82–94.

Hoijer, B. (2000) 'Audiences' Expectations and Interpretations of Different Television Genres: A Socio-Cognitive approach', in I. Hagen and J. Wasko (eds.) *Consuming Audiences? Production and Reception in Media Research*, pp. 189–207. Cresskill, NJ: Hampton Press.

Holbrook, M.B. and J. O'Shaughnessy (1988) 'On the Scientific Status of Consumer Research and the Need for an Interpretive Approach to Studying Consumption Behaviour', *Journal of Consumer Research* 15: 398–402.

Holloway, I. and L. Todres (2003) 'The Status of Method: Flexibility, Consistency and Coherence', *Qualitative Research* 3(3): 345–357.

Holub, R.C. (1984) *Reception Theory*. London: Methuen.

Hood, R. (2016) 'Combining Phenomenological and Critical Methodologies in Qualitative Research', *Qualitative Social Work* 15(2): 160–174.

Houston, S. and C. Mullan-Jensen (2012) 'Towards Depth and Width in Qualitative Social Work: Aligning Interpretative Phenomenological Analysis with the Theory of Social Domains', *Qualitative Social Work* 11(3): 266–281.

Howes, H., D. Benton and S. Edwards (2005) 'Women's Experience of Brain Injury: An Interpretative Phenomenological Analysis', *Psychology and Health* 20(1): 129–142.

Hui, A. (2013) 'Moving with Practices: The Discontinuous, Rhythmic and Material Mobilities of Leisure', *Social and Cultural Geography* 14(8): 888–908.

Hui, A., T. Schatzki and E. Shove (eds.) (2017) *The Nexus of Practices: Connections, Constellations, Practitioners*. London and New York: Routledge.

Huizinga, J. (1970) *Homo Ludens: A Study of the Play Element in Culture*. London: Temple Smith. [Published previously, London: Routledge and Kegan Paul, 1949 and Boston: Beacon Press, 1955].

Hume, D. (1748) *Philosophical Essays Concerning Human Understanding*. London: Millar.

Hunt, M.R. (2010) '"Active Waiting": Habits and the Practice of Conducting Qualitative Research', *International Journal of Qualitative Methods* 9(1): 69–76.

Ilias, K., J.H.J. Liaw, K. Cornish, M.S.-A. Park and K.J. Golden (2016) 'Wellbeing of Mothers of Children with "A-U-T-I-S-M" in Malaysia: An Interpretative Phenomenological Analysis Study', *Journal of Intellectual and Developmental Disability* 42(1): 74–89.

Iser, W. (1974) *The Implied Reader*. Baltimore: Johns Hopkins University Press.

Ivens, B. and K.S. Valta (2012) 'Customer Brand Personality Perception: A Taxonomic Analysis', *Journal of Marketing Management* 28(9–10): 1062–1093.

Izberk-Bilgin, E. (2012) 'Infidel Brands: Unveiling Alternative Meanings of Global Brands at the Nexus of Globalization, Consumer Culture, and Islamism', *Journal of Consumer Culture* 39(December): 663–687.

Jansson, A. (2002) 'The Mediatization of Consumption towards an Analytical Framework of Image Culture', *Journal of Consumer Culture* 2(1): 5–31.

Jarman, M., J.A. Smith and S. Walsh (1997) 'The Psychological Battle for Control: A Qualitative Study of Health-Care Professionals' Understandings of the Treatment of Anorexia Nervosa', *Journal of Community & Applied Social Psychology* 7: 137–152.

Jarrahi, M.H. and L. Thomson (2017) 'The Interplay between Information Practices and Information Context: The Case of Mobile Knowledge Workers', *Journal of the Association for Information Science and Technology* 68(5): 1073–1089.

Jauss, H.R. (1982a) *Aesthetic Experience and Literary Hermeneutics*. Minneapolis: University of Minnesota Press.

Jauss, H.R. (1982b) *Towards an Aesthetic of Reception*. Brighton: Harvester Press.

Jensen, K.B. (1986) *Making Sense of the News: Towards a Theory and an Empirical Model of Reception for the Study of Mass Communication*. Aarhus: Aarhus University Press.

Jensen, K.B. (2002) 'The Humanities in Media and Communication Research', in K.B. Jensen (ed.) *A Handbook of Media and Communication Research Qualitative and Quantitative Methodologies*, pp. 15–39. London and New York: Routledge.

Jensen, K.B. (2005) 'Interactivity in the Wild: An Empirical Study of "Interactivity" as Understood in Organizational Practices', *Nordicom Review* 26(1): 3–30.

Jensen, K.B. (2013) 'How to Do Things with Data: Meta-Data, Meta-Media and Meta-Communication', *First Monday* 18(10): 1–14.

Jensen, K.B. and R. Helles (2017) 'Speaking into the System: Social Media and Many-to-One Communication', *European Journal of Communication* 32(1): 16–25.

Jin, H. (2011) 'British Cultural Studies, Active Audiences and the Status of Cultural Theory: An Interview with David Morley', *Theory, Culture and Society* 28(4): 124–144.

Joas, H. (1987) 'Giddens Theory of Structuration: Introductory Remarks on a Sociological Transformation of the Philosophy of Praxis', *International Sociology* 2(1): 13–26.

Johnson, R., D. Chambers, P. Raghuram and E. Tincknell (2004) *The Practice of Cultural Studies*. London: Sage.

Johnstone, M.L. (2012) 'The Servicescape: The Social Dimensions of Place', *Journal of Marketing Management* 28(11–12): 1399–1418.

Jonas, M., B. Littig and A. Wroblewski (2017) 'Introduction', in M. Jonas, B. Littig and A. Wroblewski (eds.) *Methodological Reflections on Practice Oriented Theories*, pp. xv–xxi. New York: Springer.

Jones, G. (1989) 'Phenomenology and Theology: A Note on Bultmann and Heidegger', *Modern Theology* 5(2): 161–179.

Kanai, A. (2016) 'Sociality and Classification: Reading Gender, Race, and Class in a Humorous Meme', *Social Media + Society* October–December: 1–12.

Keane, J. (1982) 'Communication, Ideology and the Problem of "Voluntary Servitude"', *Media, Culture and Society* 4: 161–170.

Kearney, R. (1991) 'Between Tradition and Utopia the Hermeneutical Problem of Myth', in D. Wood (ed.) *On Paul Ricoeur Narrative and Interpretation*, pp. 55–73. London and New York: Routledge.

Kearney, R. (2015) 'The Wager of Carnal Hermeneutics', in R. Kearney and B. Treanor (eds.) *Carnal Hermeneutics*, pp. 15–56. New York: Fordham University Press.

Keller, M. and B. Halkier (2014) 'Positioning Consumption: A Practice Theoretical Approach to Contested Consumption and Media Discourse', *Marketing Theory* 14(1): 35–51.

Kelly, M., J. Devries-Erich, E. Helmich, T. Dornan and N. King (2017) 'Embodied Reflexivity in Qualitative Analysis: A Role for Selfies', *Forum: Qualitative Social Research* 18(2): Art. 12.

Kerssens, N. (2017) 'When Search Engines Stopped Being Human: Menu Interfaces and the Rise of the Ideological Nature of Algorithmic Search', *Internet Histories* 1(3): 219–237.

Kilpinen, E. (2009) 'The Habitual Conception of Action and Social Theory', *Semiotica* 173(1/4): 99–128.

Kinsella, E.A. (2006) 'Hermeneutics and Critical Hermeneutics: Exploring Possibilities within the Art of Interpretation', *Forum: Qualitative Social Research* 7(3): Art 19.

Kitchin, R. (2014) 'Big Data, New Epistemologies and Paradigm Shifts', *Big Data and Society* 1(1): 1–12.
Kitchin, R. and M. Dodge (2011) *Code/Space: Software and Everyday Life*. Cambridge, US: MIT Press.
Klein, J., M. Walter and U. Schimank (2018) 'Researching Individuals' Media Repertoires: Challenges of Qualitative Interviews on Cross-Media Practices', in A. Hepp, A. Breiter and U. Hasebrink (eds.) *Communicative Figurations: Transforming Communications in Times of Deep Mediatization*, pp. 363–386. London and New York: Palgrave Macmillan.
Knotts, M.W. (2014) 'Readers, Texts and the Fusion of Horizons: Theology and Gadamer's Hermeneutics', *Theologica* 4(2): 233–246.
Koca-Atabey, M. (2017) 'Re-Visiting the Role of Disability Coordinators: The Changing Needs of Disabled Students and Current Support Strategies from a UK University', *European Journal of Special Needs Education* 32(1): 137–145.
Koch, T. (1995) 'Interpretive Approaches in Nursing Research: The Influence of Husserl and Heidegger', *Journal of Advanced Nursing* 21: 827–836.
Koster, A. (2017) 'Personal History, Beyond Narrative: An Embodied Perspective', *Journal of Phenomenological Psychology* 48(2): 163–187.
Kozinets, R.V., J.F. Sherry Jr., D. Storm, A. Duhachek, K. Nuttavuthisit and B. Deberry-Spence (2004) 'Ludic Agency and Retail Spectacle', *Journal of Consumer Research* 31(December): 658–672.
Krajina, Z. (2014) *Negotiating the Mediated City: Everyday Encounters with Public Screens*. London and New York: Routledge.
Krajina, Z., S. Moores and D. Morley (2014) 'Non-Media-Centric Media Studies: A Cross-Generational Conversation', *European Journal of Cultural Studies* 17(6): 682–700.
Kramsch, C. (2013) *The Multilingual Subject*. Oxford: Oxford University Press.
Kress, G. (2003) *Literacy in the New Media Age*. London and New York: Routledge.
Kress, G. (2012) 'Genre as Social Process', in B. Cope and M. Kalantzis (eds.) *The Powers of Literacy: A Genre Approach to Teaching Writing*, pp. 22–37. London and New York: Routledge.
Kücklich, J. (2004) 'Play and Playability as Key Concepts in New Media Studies', Research Report. Stem Centre, Dublin City University, Dublin.
Kuhn, T. (1962) *The Structure of Scientific Revolutions*. Chicago: University of Chicago Press.
Kuipers, G. (2018) 'Communicative Figurations: Towards a New Paradigm for the Media Age?', in A. Hepp, A. Breiter and U. Hasebrink (eds.) *Communicative Figurations: Transforming Communications in Times of Deep Mediatization*, pp. 425–436. London and New York: Palgrave Macmillan.
Kumar, A. (2017) 'Hermeneutics from the Margins: Provisional Notes', *Tropos: Journal of Hermeneutics and Philosophical Criticism* 10(1): 163–183.
Küpers, W. (2011) 'Dancing on the Līmen~~~Embodied and Creative Inter-Places as Thresholds of Be(com)ing: Phenomenological Perspectives on Liminality and Transitional Spaces in Organization and Leadership', *Tamara: Journal for Critical Organization Inquiry* 9(3–4): 45–59.
Kupers, W. (2015) *Phenomenology of the Embodied Organization: The Contribution of Merleau-Ponty for Organization Studies and Practice*. London and New York: Palgrave Macmillan.
Lahtinen, V.V. (2014) 'A Shared World: The Relationship between Pierre Bourdieu's Social Ontology and Martin Heidegger's Early Philosophy', Master's Thesis (unpublished), University of Helsinki, Finland.
Lai, A.-L., J. Dermody and S. Hanmer-Lloyd (2007) 'Exploring Cadaveric Organ Donation: A "Mortal Embodiment" Perspective', *Journal of Marketing Management* 23(5–6): 559–585.

Laitinen, A. (2002) 'Charles Taylor and Paul Ricoeur on Self-Interpretations and Narrative Identity', in R. Huttunen, H.L.T. Heikkinen and L. Syrjälä (eds.) *Narrative Research: Voices of Teachers and Philosophers*, pp. 57–71. Finland: University of Jyväskylä and SoPhi.

Langdridge, D. (2008) 'Phenomenology and Critical Social Psychology: Directions and Debates in Theory and Research', *Social and Personality Psychology Compass* 2: 1126–1142.

Larkin, M. and M.D. Griffiths (2004) 'Dangerous Sports and Recreational Drug-Use: Rationalizing and Contextualizing Risk', *Journal of Community and Applied Social Psychology* 14: 215–232.

Larkin, M., S. Watts and E. Clifton (2006) 'Giving Voice and Making Sense in Interpretative Phenomenological Analysis', *Qualitative Research in Psychology* 3: 102–120.

Larkin, M., V. Eatough and M. Osborn (2011) 'Interpretative Phenomenological Analysis and Embodied, Active, Situated Cognition', *Theory & Psychology* 21(3): 318–337.

Larkin, M. and A. Thompson (2012) 'Interpretative Phenomenological Analysis', in A. Thompson and D. Harper (eds.) *Qualitative Research Methods in Mental Health and Psychotherapy: A Guide for Students and Practitioners*, pp. 99–116. Boston and Oxford: Wiley.

Larsen, J. (2005) 'Families Seen Sightseeing: Performativity of Tourist Photography', *Space and Culture* 8(4): 416–434.

Laverty, S.M. (2003) 'Hermeneutic Phenomenology and Phenomenology: A Comparison of Historical and Methodological Considerations', *International Journal of Qualitative Methods* 2(3): 21–35.

Law, Y.-Y. and G. Crawford (2016) 'Play', in K.B. Jensen, R.T. Craig, J.D. Pooley and E.W. Rothenbuhler (eds.) *The International Encyclopedia of Communication Theory and Philosophy*, pp. 1–4. Boston and Oxford: Wiley.

Lee, S. (1999) 'Private Uses in Public Spaces: A Study of an Internet Cafe', *New Media and Society* 1(3): 331–350.

Lefebvre, H., C. Régulier and M. Zayani (1999) 'The Rhythmanalytical Project', *Rethinking Marxism: A Journal of Economics, Culture and Society* 11(1): 5–13.

LeMahieu, D.L. (2015) 'Being-Here: Heidegger in the 21st Century', *New Media and Society* 17(3): 470–475.

Leonardi, P.M. (2013) 'Theoretical Foundations for the Study of Sociomateriality', *Information and Organization* 23: 59–76.

Lewis, C. (1992) 'Making Sense of Common Sense: A Framework for Tracking Hegemony', *Critical Studies in Mass Communication* 9: 277–292.

Lie, R. (2000) 'Anthropology and Television Studies: An Overview of Disciplinarity and Interdisciplinarity', paper presented at the International Association for Media and Communication Research Conference, Singapore.

Lie, R. and J. Servaes (2000) 'Globalisation: Consumption and Identity: Towards Researching Nodal Points', in G. Wang, J. Servaes and A. Goonasekera (eds.) *The New Communications Landscape: Demystifying Media Globalisation*, pp. 307–332. London and New York: Routledge.

Lin, T.T.C., T.H. Yeo and Y.-H. Chiang (2016) 'Understanding Second Screen User's Motivations, User Patterns and Engagement in Singapore', paper presented at the International Association for Media and Communication Research Conference, University of Leicester, United Kingdom.

Linehan, C. and J. McCarthy (2000) 'Positioning in Practice: Understanding Participation in the Social World', *Journal for the Theory of Social Behaviour* 30(4): 435–453.

Lister, M., J. Dovey, S. Giddings, I. Grant and K. Kelly (2009) *New Media: A Critical Introduction*. London and New York: Routledge.

Livingstone, S. (2000) 'On the Cutting Edge, or Otherwise, of Media and Communication Research', *Nordicom Review* 21(2): 7–13.

Livingstone, S. (2004) 'The Challenge of Changing Audiences: Or, What Is the Audience Researcher to Do in the Age of the Internet?', *European Journal of Communication* 19(1): 75–86.

Livingstone, S. (2008) 'Engaging with Media: A Matter of Literacy?', *Communication, Culture and Critique* 1: 51–62.

Livingstone, S. (2009) 'On the Mediation of Everything: ICA Presidential Address 2008', *Journal of Communication* 59(1): 1–18.

Livingstone, S. (2012) 'Exciting Moments in Audience Research: Past, Present and Future', in H. Bilandzic, G. Patriarche and P.J. Traudt (eds.) *The Social Use of Media*, pp. 184–197. Bristol: Intellect.

Livingstone, S. (2015) 'Active Audiences? The Debate Progresses But Is Far from Resolved', *Communication Theory* 25: 439–446.

Livingstone, S. (2017) 'The Class: Living and Learning in the Digital Age', in S. Tosoni, N. Carpentier, M.F. Murru, R. Kilborn, L. Kramp, R. Kunelius, A. McNicholas, T. Olsson and P. Pruulmann-Vengerfeldt (eds.) *Present Scenarios of Media Production and Engagement*, pp. 55–66. Bremen: Edition Lumiere.

Livingstone, S. and Das, R. (2013) 'The End of Audiences? Theoretical Echoes of Reception amid the Uncertainties of Use', in J. Hartley, J. Burgess and A. Bruns (eds.) *A Companion to New Media Dynamics*, pp. 104–121. Oxford: Wiley-Blackwell.

Lowrey, T.M., C.C. Otnes and M.A. McGrath (2005) 'Shopping with Consumers: Reflections and Innovations', *Qualitative Market Research: An International Journal* 8(2): 176–188.

Ludik, D., F. Carrillat and M. Tadajewski (2015) 'Belk's (1988) "Possessions and the Extended Self" Revisited', *Journal of Historical Research in Marketing* 7(2): 184–207.

Lull, J. (1990) *Inside Family Viewing*. London and New York: Routledge.

Lunt, P. and S. Livingstone (2013) 'Media Studies' Fascination with the Concept of the Public Sphere: Critical Reflections and Emerging Debates', *Media, Culture and Society* 35(1): 87–96.

Lupton, D. (2013) *Introducing Digital Sociology*. Sydney: University of Sydney.

Lynch, M. (2001) 'Ethnomethodology and the Logic of Practice', in T.R. Schatzki, K.K. Cetina and E. Von Savigny (eds.) *The Practice Turn in Contemporary Theory*, pp. 140–157. London and New York: Routledge.

Maciel, A.F. and M. Wallendorf (2016) 'Taste Engineering: An Extended Consumer Model of Cultural Competence Constitution', *Journal of Consumer Research* DOI: http://dx.doi.org/10.1093/jcr/ucw054.

Macleod, R., D. Craufurd and K. Booth (2002) 'Patients' Perceptions of What Makes Genetic Counselling Effective: An Interpretative Phenomenological Analysis', *Journal of Health Psychology* 7(2): 145–156.

Maller, C.J. (2015) 'Understanding Health through Social Practices: Performance and Materiality in Everyday Life', *Sociology of Health and Illness* 37(1): 52–66.

Malpas, J. (2006) *Heidegger's Topology: Being, Place, World*. Cambridge, MA: MIT Press.

Mann, E. and C. Abraham (2006) 'The Role of Affect in UK Commuters' Travel Mode Choices: An Interpretative Phenomenological Analysis', *British Journal of Psychology* 97: 155–176.

Mao, L., A.M. Akram, D. Chovanec and M.L. Underwood (2016) 'Embracing the Spiral: Researcher Reflexivity in Diverse Critical Methodologies', *International Journal of Qualitative Methods* 15(1): 1–8.

Marchant, C. and S. O'Donohue (2014) '"Edging Out of the Nest: Emerging Adults" Use of Smartphones in Maintaining and Transforming Family Relationships', *Journal of Marketing Management* 30(15–16): 1554–1576.

Marotta, V. (2009) 'Intercultural Hermeneutics and the Cross-Cultural Subject', *Journal of Intercultural Studies* 30(3): 267–284.

Marres, N. and C. Gerlitz (2016) 'Interface Methods: Renegotiating Relations between Digital Social Research, STS and Sociology', *The Sociological Review* 64: 21–46.

Martin, J. and J. Sugarman (2001) 'Is the Self a Kind of Understanding?', *Journal for the Theory of Social Behaviour* 31(1): 103–114.

Martin, P.Y. (2003) '"Said and Done" versus "Saying and Doing": Gendering Practices, Practicing Gender at Work', *Gender and Society* 17(3): 342–366.

Mathieu, D. (2015) 'Audience Research Beyond the Hermeneutics of Suspicion', *International Journal of Media and Cultural Politics* 11(2): 251–258.

Mathieu, D., M.J. Brites, N. Chimirri and M. Saariketo (2016) 'In Dialogue with Related Fields of Inquiry: The Interdisciplinarity, Normativity and Contextuality of Audience Research', *Participations* 13(1): 462–475.

Mathieu, D. and T. Pavlickova (2017) 'Crossmedia *within* the *Facebook* Newsfeed: The Role of the Reader in Cross-Media Uses', *Convergence: The International Journal of Research into New Media Technologies* 23(4): 425–438.

McCaffrey, G., S. Raffin-Bouchal and N.J. Moules (2012) 'Hermeneutics as Research Approach: A Reappraisal', *International Journal of Qualitative Methods* 11(3): 214–229.

McCaffrey, G. and N.J. Moules (2016) 'Encountering the Great Problems in the Street: Enacting Hermeneutic Philosophy as Research in Practice Disciplines', *Journal of Applied Hermeneutics* (January 2): 1–7.

McConnell-Henry, T., Y. Chapman and K. Francis (2009) 'Husserl and Heidegger: Exploring the Disparity', *International Journal of Nursing Practice* 15: 7–15.

McCracken, G. (1986) 'Culture and Consumption: A Theoretical Account of the Structure and Movement of the Cultural Meaning of Consumer Goods', *Journal of Consumer Research* 13: 71–84.

McLeod, J. (2001) *Qualitative Research in Counselling and Psychotherapy*. London: Sage.

McWilliam, C.L. (2010) 'Phenomenology', in I. Bourgeault, R. Dingwall and R. De Vries (eds.) *Sage Handbook of Qualitative Methods in Health Research*, pp. 229–249. London: Sage.

Mei, T.S. (2009) *Heidegger, Work, and Being*. London: Continuum Publishing.

Melhuish, C. (2005) 'Towards a Phenomenology of the Concrete Megastructure: Space and Perception at the Brunswick Centre, London', *Journal of Material Culture* 10(1): 5–29.

Merleau-Ponty, M. (1962) *Phenomenology of Perception*. London and New York: Routledge.

Meyen, M., S. Pfaff-Rüdiger, K. Dudenhöffer and J. Huss (2010) 'The Internet in Everyday Life: A Typology of Internet Users', *Media, Culture and Society* 32(5): 873–882.

Mick, D.G. and C. Buhl (1992) 'A Meaning-Based Model of Advertising Experiences', *Journal of Consumer Research* 19(December): 317–338.

Midgley, N. (2006) 'Psychoanalysis and Qualitative Psychology: Complementary or Contradictory Paradigms?', *Qualitative Research in Psychology* 3(3): 213–231.

Miller, C.R. (1984) 'Genre as Social Action', *Quarterly Journal of Speech* 70: 151–167.

Miller, D. (2008) *The Comfort of Things*. Cambridge: Polity Press.
Miller, V. (2011) *Understanding Digital Culture*. London: Sage.
Moen, T. (2006) 'Reflections on the Narrative Research Approach', *International Journal of Qualitative Methods* 5(4): 56–69.
Moores, S. (1988) 'The Box on the Dresser: Memories of Early Radio and Everyday Life', *Media, Culture and Society* 10(1): 23–40.
Moores, S. (1990) 'Texts, Readers and Contexts of Reading: Developments in the Study of Media Audiences', *Media, Culture and Society* 12(1): 9–29.
Moores, S. (2000) *Media and Everyday Life in Modern Society*. Edinburgh: Edinburgh University Press.
Moores, S. (2009) 'That Familiarity with the World Born of Habit: A Phenomenological Approach to the Study of Media Uses in Daily Living', *Interactions: Studies in Communication and Culture* 1(3): 301–312.
Moores, S. (2012) *Media, Place and Mobility*. London and New York: Palgrave Macmillan.
Moores, S. (2013) 'We Find our Way about: Everyday Media Use and "Inhabitant Knowledge"', *Mobilities* 10(1): 17–35.
Moores, S. (2017) 'Arguments for a Non-Media-Centric, Non-Representational Approach to Media and Place', in P.C. Adams, J. Cupples, K. Glynn, A. Jansson and S. Moores *Communications/Media/Geographies*. London and New York: Routledge.
Moores, S. (2018) *Digital Orientations: Non-Media-Centric Media Studies and Non-Representational Theories of Practice*. New York: Peter Lang.
Moran, D. (2000) *Introduction to Phenomenology*. London and New York: Routledge.
Moran, D. (2011) 'Edmund Husserl's Phenomenology of Habituality and Habitus', *Journal of the British Society for Phenomenology* 42(1): 53–77.
Morley, D. (1986) *Family Television: Cultural Power and Domestic Leisure*. London: Comedia.
Morley, D. (1992) *Television, Audiences and Cultural Studies*. London and New York: Routledge.
Morley, D. (1996) 'Populism, Revisionism and the "New" Audience Research', in J. Curran, D. Morley and V. Walkerdine (eds.) *Cultural Studies and Communications*, pp. 279–293. London: Arnold.
Morley, D. (2000) *Home Territories: Media, Mobility and Identity*. London and New York: Routledge.
Morley, D. (2009) 'For a Materialist Non-Media-Centric Media Studies', *Television and New Media* 10(1): 114–116.
Morris, M. (2005) 'Interpretability and Social Power, or, Why Postmodern Advertising Works', *Media, Culture and Society* 27(5): 697–718.
Mortari, L. (2015) 'Reflectivity in Research Practice: An Overview of Different Perspectives', *International Journal of Qualitative Methods* December: 1–9.
Mulhall, S. (2005) *Heidegger and Being and Time*. London and New York: Routledge.
Murphy, S. (2015) 'Exploring Embodiment through the Senses: A Case in High-Risk Leisure', paper presented at the Academy of Marketing Conference, University of Limerick, Ireland.
Murru, M.F. (2016) 'Listening, Temporalities and Epistemology: A Hermeneutical Perspective on Mediated Civic Engagement', *Participations* 13(1): 392–401.
Murtola, A.-M. (2010) 'Commodification of Utopia: The Lotus Eaters Revisited', *Culture and Organization* 16(1): 37–54.
Mustafa, S.E. and A. Hamzah (2011) 'Online Social Networking: A New Virtual Playground', *International Proceedings of Economics Development and Research* 5(2): 314–318.

Mutch, A. (2013) 'Sociomateriality: Taking the Wrong Turning?', *Information and Organization* 23: 28–40.
Nagel, M. (1998) 'Play in Culture and the Jargon of Primordiality: A Critique of Homo Ludens', in M. Duncan, G. Chick and A. Aycock (eds.) *Diversions and Divergences in Fields of Play*, pp. 19–29. Greenwich, CT: Ablex.
Neill, E. (2014) 'Michael Oakeshott and Hans-Georg Gadamer on Practices, Social Science and Modernity', *History of European Ideas* 40(3): 406–436.
Nelson, E.S. (2001) 'Questioning Practice: Heidegger, Historicity, and the Hermeneutics of Facticity', *Philosophy Today* 44: 150–159.
Nenon, T.J. (2016) 'Horizonality', in N. Keane and C. Lawn (eds.) *The Blackwell Companion to Hermeneutics*, pp. 248–252. Malden and Oxford: Wiley.
Nicolini, D. (2009) 'Zooming In and Out: Studying Practices by Switching Theoretical Lenses and Trailing Connections', *Organization Studies* 30(12): 1391–1418.
Nicolini, D. (2011) 'Practice as the Site of Knowing: Insights from the Field of Telemedicine', *Organization Science* 22(3): 602–620.
Nicolini, D. (2012) *Practice Theory, Work, and Organization: An Introduction*. Oxford: Oxford University Press.
Nicolini, D., S. Gherardi and D. Yanow (2003) 'Introduction: Toward a Practice-Based View of Knowing and Learning in Organizations', in D. Nicolini, S. Gherardi and D. Yanow (eds.) *Knowing in Organizations: A Practice-Based Approach*, pp. 3–31. New York: Sharpe.
Nicolini, D., J. Mengis and J. Swan (2012) 'Understanding the Role of Objects in Cross-Disciplinary Collaboration', *Organization Science* 23: 612–629.
Nolan, M. (2013) 'Masculinity Lost: A Systematic Review of Qualitative Research on Men with Spinal Cord Injury', *Spinal Cord*: 1–8.
Norlyk, A. and I. Harder (2010) 'What Makes a Phenomenological Study Phenomenological? An Analysis of Peer-Reviewed Empirical Nursing Studies', *Qualitative Health Research* 20(3): 420–431.
O'Connor, T. (2016) 'Play', in N. Keane and C. Lawn (eds.) *The Blackwell Companion to Hermeneutics*, pp. 265–269. Malden and Oxford: Wiley.
Olivier, A. (2017) 'Understanding Place', in B.B. Janz (ed.) *Place, Space and Hermeneutics*, pp. 9–22. Cham, Switzerland: Springer.
Orlikowski, W.J. (2000) 'Using Technology and Constituting Structures: A Practice Lens for Studying Technology in Organizations', *Organization Science* 11(4): 404–428.
Orlikowski, W.J. (2009) 'The Sociomateriality of Organizational Life: Considering Technology in Management Research', *Cambridge Journal of Economics* 34: 125–141.
Osborn, M. and J.A. Smith (1998) 'The Personal Experience of Chronic Benign Lower Back Pain: An Interpretative Phenomenological Analysis', *British Journal of Health Psychology* 3: 65–83.
O'Shaughnessy, J. (2013) *Consumer Behaviour: Perspectives, Findings and Explanations*. London and New York: Palgrave Macmillan.
Palmer, M., M. Larkin, R.O. De Visser and G. Fadden (2010) 'Developing an Interpretative Phenomenological Approach to Focus Group Data', *Qualitative Research in Psychology* 7(2): 99–121.
Pantzar, M. and M. Ruckenstein (2015) 'The Heart of Everyday Analytics: Emotional, Material and Practical Extensions in Self-Tracking Market', *Consumption Markets and Culture* 18(1): 92–109.
Papacharissi, Z. (2015) 'The Unbearable Lightness of Information and the Impossible Gravitas of Knowledge: Big Data and the Makings of a Digital Orality', *Media, Culture and Society* 37(7): 1095–1100.
Parkes, G. (1992) 'Thoughts on the Way: Being and Time via Lao-Chuang', in G. Parkes (ed.) *Heidegger and Asian Thought*, pp. 105–144. Hawaii: University of Hawaii Press.

Patterson, M.E. and D.R. Williams (2002) *Collecting and Analyzing Qualitative Data: Hermeneutic Principles, Methods, and Case Examples*. Champaign, IL: Sagamore Publishing.

Pavlickova, T. (2012) 'At the Crossroads of Hermeneutic Philosophy and Reception Studies: Understanding Patterns of Cross-Media Consumption', in H. Bilandzic, G. Patriarche and P.J. Traudt (eds.) *The Social Use of Media*, pp. 24–34. Bristol: Intellect.

Pavlickova, T. (2013) 'Bringing the Author Back into the Audience Research: A Hermeneutical Perspective on the Audience's Understanding of the Author', *The Communication Review* 16(1–2): 31–39.

Pavlickova, T. and J. Kleut (2016) 'Produsage as Experience and Interpretation', *Participations* 13(1): 349–359.

Peacock, S.E. (2014) 'How Web Tracking Changes User Agency in the Age of Big Data: The Used User', *Big Data and Society* July–December: 1–11.

Peñaloza, L. (1998) 'Just Doing It: A Visual Ethnographic Study of Spectacular Consumption Behavior at Nike Town', *Consumption, Markets and Culture* 2(4): 337–400.

Penman, C. and M. Omar (2011) 'Figuring Home: The Role of Commodities in the Transnational Experience', *Language and Intercultural Communication* 11(4): 338–350.

Penny, E., E. Newton and M. Larkin (2009) 'Whispering on the Water: British Pakistani Families' Experiences of Support from an Early Intervention Service for First-Episode Psychosis', *Journal of Cross-Cultural Psychology* 40(6): 969–987.

Peters, C. and S. Allan (2016) 'Everyday Imagery: Users' Reflections on Smartphone Cameras and Communication', *Convergence: The International Journal of Research into New Media Technologies* First Published 25 November 2016.

Peters, J.D. (1994) 'The Gaps of which Communication Is Made', *Critical Studies in Mass Communication* 11(2): 117–140.

Phelan, S. (2016) 'Reinvigorating Ideology Critique: Between Trust and Suspicion', *Media, Culture and Society* 38(2): 274–283.

Philipse, H. (2009) 'Overcoming Epistemology', in M. Rosen and B. Leiter (eds.) *The Oxford Handbook of Continental Philosophy*, pp. 1–44. Oxford: Oxford University Press.

Phipps, M. and J.L. Ozanne (2017) 'Routines Disrupted: Reestablishing Security through Practice Alignment', *Journal of Consumer Research* 44(2): 361–380.

Pickering, A. (2001) 'Practice and Posthumanism Social Theory and a History of Agency', in T.R. Schatzki, K.K. Cetina and E. Von Savigny (eds.) *The Practice Turn in Contemporary Theory*, pp. 172–183. London and New York: Routledge.

Pickering, M. (1999) 'History as Horizon Gadamer, Tradition and Critique', *Rethinking History* 3(2): 177–195.

Picone, I. (2017) 'Conceptualizing Media Users across Media: The Case for "Media User/Use" as Analytical Concepts', *Convergence: The International Journal of Research into New Media Technologies* 1–13.

Piercey, R. (2016) 'Paul Ricoeur', in N. Keane and C. Lawn (eds.) *The Blackwell Companion to Hermeneutics*, pp. 412–416. Malden and Oxford: Wiley.

Pink, S. and K.L. Mackley (2013) 'Saturated and Situated: Expanding the Meaning of Media in the Routines of Everyday Life', *Media, Culture and Society* 35(6): 677–691.

Polkinghorne, D.E. (1994) 'A Path of Understanding for Psychology', *Journal of Theoretical and Philosophical Psychology* 14(2): 128–145.

Polkinghorne, D.E. (2000) 'Psychological Inquiry and the Pragmatic and Hermeneutic Traditions', *Theory and Psychology* 10(4): 453–479.

Polt, R. (1999) *Heidegger: An Introduction*. New York: Cornell University Press.

Pongsakornrungsilp, S. and J.E. Schroeder (2011) 'Understanding Value Co-Creation in a Co-Consuming Brand Community', *Marketing Theory* 11(3): 303–324.

Postill, J. (2010) 'Introduction: Theorising Media and Practice', in B. Brauchler and J. Postill (eds.) *Theorising Media and Practice*, pp. 1–34. New York: Berghahn Books.

Powell, A.B. (2015) 'Open Culture and Innovation: Integrating Knowledge across Boundaries', *Media, Culture and Society* 37(3): 376–393.

Prasad, A. (2002) 'The Contest over Meaning: Hermeneutics as an Interpretive Methodology for Understanding Texts', *Organizational Research Methods* 5(1): 12–33.

Preston, J., C. Ballinger and H. Gallagher (2014) 'Understanding the Lived Experience of People with Multiple Sclerosis and Dysexecutive Syndrome', *British Journal of Occupational Therapy* 77(10): 484–490.

Price, L.L. (2013) 'Family Stuff: Materiality and Identity', in A.A. Ruvio and R.W. Belk (eds.) *The Routledge Companion to Identity and Consumption*, pp. 302–312. London and New York: Routledge.

Priest, P.J. (1995) *Public Intimacies: Talk Show Participants and Tell-All TV*. Cresskill, NJ: Hampton Press.

Purvis, M.K. and M.A. Purvis (2012) 'Institutional Expertise in the Service-Dominant Logic: Knowing How and Knowing What', *Journal of Marketing Management* 28(13–14): 1626–1641.

Rabinow, P. and N. Rose (2003) 'Foucault Today', in P. Rabinow and N. Rose (eds.) *The Essential Foucault: Selections from the Essential Works of Foucault, 1954–1984*, pp. 7–35. New York: New Press.

Rácz, J., Z. Kaló, S. Kassai, M. Kiss and J.N. Pintér (2017) 'The Experience of Voice Hearing and the Role of Self-Help Group: An Interpretative Phenomenological Analysis', *International Journal of Social Psychiatry* 1–7.

Radovan, M. (2001) 'Information Technology and the Character of Contemporary Life', *Information, Communication and Society* 4(2): 230–246.

Raff, J.-H. and G. Melles (2010) 'Everyday Practice as Design', *Journal of Writing in Creative Practice* 3(2): 149–159.

Ratner, C. (2000) 'Agency and Culture', *Journal for the Theory of Social Behaviour* 30(4): 413–434.

Ray, T. (2012) 'To De-Westernize, Yes, But with a Critical Edge: A Response to Gunaratne and Others', *Media, Culture and Society* 34(2): 238–249.

Reckwitz, A. (2002a) 'Toward a Theory of Social Practices: A Development in Culturalist Theorizing', *European Journal of Social Theory* 5(2): 243–263.

Reckwitz, A. (2002b) 'The Status of the "Material" in Theories of Culture: From "Social Structure" to "Artefacts"', *Journal for the Theory of Social Behaviour* 32(2): 195–217.

Reckwitz, A. (2012) 'Affective Spaces: A Praxeological Outlook', *Rethinking History* 16(2): 241–258.

Redhead, M. (2002) *Charles Taylor: Thinking and Living Deep Diversity*. London and New York: Rowman and Littlefield.

Reed, I. (2008) 'Justifying Sociological Knowledge: From Realism to Interpretation', *Sociological Theory* 26(2): 101–129.

Reed, I. (2010) 'Epistemology Contextualized: Social-Scientific Knowledge in a Postpositivist Era', *Sociological Theory* 28(1): 20–39.

Reid, K., P. Flowers and M. Larkin (2005) 'Exploring Lived Experience', *The Psychologist* 18(1): 20–23.

Ricoeur, P. (1973) 'The Hermeneutical Function of Distanciation', *Philosophy Today* 17(2): 129–141.

Ricoeur, P. (1974) *The Conflict of Interpretations Essays in Hermeneutics* (ed. D. Ihde). Evanston: Northwestern University Press.

Ricoeur, P. (1975) 'Philosophical Hermeneutics and Theological Hermeneutics', *Studies in Religion: Sciences Religieuses* 6(1): 14–33.

Ricoeur, P. (1976) *Interpretation Theory: Discourse and the Surplus of Meaning.* Fort Worth: Texas Christian University Press.

Ricoeur, P. (1981a) 'The Hermeneutical Function of Distanciation', in J.B. Thompson (ed.) *Paul Ricoeur: Hermeneutics and the Human Sciences*, pp. 131–144. Cambridge: Cambridge University Press.

Ricoeur, P. (1981b) 'The Model of the Text: Meaningful Action Considered as a Text', in J.B. Thompson (ed.) *Paul Ricoeur: Hermeneutics and the Human Sciences*, pp. 197–221. Cambridge: Cambridge University Press.

Ricoeur, P. (1981c) 'A Response by Paul Ricoeur', in J.B. Thompson (ed.) *Paul Ricoeur: Hermeneutics and the Human Sciences*, pp. 32–40. Cambridge: Cambridge University Press.

Ricoeur, P. (1983) *Time and Narrative*, Vol. 1 (Trans. K. McLaughlin and D. Pellauer). Chicago: University of Chicago Press.

Ricoeur, P. (1985) *Time and Narrative*, Vol. 2 (Trans. K. McLaughlin and D. Pellauer). Chicago: University of Chicago Press.

Ricoeur, P. (1988) *Time and Narrative*, Vol. 3 (Trans. K. Blarney and D. Pellauer). Chicago: University of Chicago Press.

Ricoeur, P. (1991a) 'Phenomenology and Hermeneutics', in *From Text to Action Essays in Hermeneutics, II* (Trans. K. Blamey and J.B. Thompson), pp. 25–52. Evanston, IL: Northwestern University Press.

Ricoeur, P. (1991b) 'Hermeneutics and the Critique of Ideology', in *From Text to Action Essays in Hermeneutics, II* (Trans. K. Blamey and J.B. Thompson), pp. 270–307. Evanston, IL: Northwestern University Press.

Ringma, C. and C. Brown (1991) 'Hermeneutics and the Social Sciences: An Evaluation of the Function of Hermeneutics in a Consumer Disability Study', *The Journal of Sociology and Social Welfare* 18(3): 57–73.

Roberge, J. (2011) 'What Is Critical Hermeneutics?', *Thesis Eleven* 106(1): 5–22.

Robinson, S. and R. Kerr (2015) 'Reflexive Conversations: Constructing Hermeneutic Designs for Qualitative Management Research', *British Journal of Management* 26: 777–790.

Rodriguez, L. and J.A. Smith (2014) '"Finding Your Own Place": An Interpretative Phenomenological Analysis of Young Men's Experience of Early Recovery from Addiction', *International Journal of Mental Health and Addiction* 12(4): 477–490.

Rofil, L.E.F., A. Hamzah and Md A. Md Syed (2015) 'The Practice of Traditional Healthcare among Malay Women of Javanese Descent in Malaysia: *Jamu*, Cultural Identity and Sense of Belonging', *New Zealand Journal of Asian Studies* 17(2): 61–74.

Rogers, R. (2018) 'Otherwise Engaged: Social Media from Vanity Metrics to Critical Analytics', *International Journal of Communication* 12: 450–472.

Roig, A., G.S. Cornelio, E. Ardèvol, P. Alsina and R. Pagès (2009) 'Videogame as Media Practice: An Exploration of the Intersections between Play and Audiovisual Culture', *Convergence: The International Journal of Research into New Media Technologies* 15(1): 89–103.

Rolfe, G. (2015) 'Foundations for a Human Science of Nursing: Gadamer, Laing, and the Hermeneutics of Caring', *Nursing Philosophy* 16: 141–152.

Rouse, J. (2001) 'Two Concepts of Practices', in T.R. Schatzki, K.K. Cetina and E. Von Savigny (eds.) *The Practice Turn in Contemporary Theory*, pp. 198–208. London and New York: Routledge.

Rouse, J. (2006) 'Practice Theory', in S. Turner and M. Risjord (eds.) *Handbook of the Philosophy of Science, Volume 15: Philosophy of Anthropology and Sociology*, pp. 499–540. London: Elsevier.

Rouse, J. (2007) 'Social Practices and Normativity', *Philosophy of the Social Sciences* 37(1): 46–56.

Roy, A. and W.J. Starosta (2001) 'Hans-Georg Gadamer, Language and Intercultural Communication', *Language and Intercultural Communication* 1(1): 6–20.

Roy, A. and B. Oludaja (2009) 'Hans-Georg Gadamer's *Praxis*: Implications for Connection and Action in Communication Studies', *Communication, Culture and Critique* 2: 255–273.

Russell, L.D. and A.S. Babrow (2011) 'Risk in the Making: Narrative, Problematic Integration, and the Social Construction of Risk', *Communication Theory* 21: 239–260.

Ryle, G. (1949) *The Concept of Mind*. Chicago: University of Chicago Press.

Scannell, P. (2004) 'What Reality Has Misfortune?', *Media, Culture and Society* 26(4): 573–584.

Schäfer, H. (2017) 'Relationality and Heterogeneity: Transitive Methodology in Practice Theory and Actor-Network Theory', in M. Jonas et al. (eds.) *Methodological Reflections on Practice Oriented Theories*, pp. 35–46. New York: Springer.

Schatzki, T.R. (1996) *Social Practices: A Wittgensteinian Approach to Human Activity and the Social*. New York: Cambridge University Press.

Schatzki, T.R. (1997) 'Practices and Actions: A Wittgensteinian Critique of Bourdieu and Giddens', *Philosophy of the Social Sciences* 27(3): 283–308.

Schatzki, T.R. (2000) 'Wittgenstein and the Social Context of an Individual Life', *History of the Human Sciences* 13(1): 93–107.

Schatzki, T.R. (2001a) 'Introduction: Practice Theory', in T.R. Schatzki, K.K. Cetina and E. Von Savigny (eds.) *The Practice Turn in Contemporary Theory*, pp. 10–23. London and New York: Routledge.

Schatzki, T.R. (2001b) 'Practice Minded Orders', in T.R. Schatzki, K.K. Cetina and E. Von Savigny (eds.) *The Practice Turn in Contemporary Theory*, pp. 50–63. London and New York: Routledge.

Schatzki, T.R. (2002) *The Site of the Social: A Philosophical Account of the Constitution of Social Life and Change*. Pennsylvania: Pennsylvania State University Press.

Schatzki, T.R. (2003a) 'A New Societist Social Ontology', *Philosophy of the Social Sciences* 33(2): 174–202.

Schatzki, T.R. (2003b) 'Living Out of the Past: Dilthey and Heidegger on Life and History', *Inquiry* 46(3): 301–323.

Schatzki, T.R. (2005) 'Peripheral Vision: The Sites of Organizations', *Organization Studies* 26(3): 465–484.

Schatzki, T.R. (2006) 'Peripheral Vision on Organizations as They Happen', *Organization Studies* 27(12): 1863–1873.

Schatzki, T.R. (2009) 'Timespace and the Organization of Social Life', in E. Shove, F. Trentmann and R. Wilk (eds.) *Time, Consumption and Everyday Life Practice, Materiality and Culture*, pp. 35–48. New York and Oxford: Berg.

Schatzki, T.R. (2010) *The TimeSpace of Human Activity on Performance, Society, and History as Indeterminate Teleological Events*. New York: Lexington.

Schatzki, T.R. (2012) 'A Primer on Practices: Theory and Research', in J. Higgs, R. Barnett, S. Billett, M. Hutchings and F. Trede (eds.) *Practice-Based Education Perspectives and Strategies*, pp. 13–26. Rotterdam: Sense Publishers.

Schatzki, T.R. (2014) 'Working Paper 5: Larger Scales', in *Demanding Ideas: Where Theories of Practice Might Go Next*, pp. 10–12. Lancaster: Lancaster University DEMAND Centre.

Schatzki, T.R. (2015) 'Space of Practices and of Large Social Phenomena', *Espaces Temps.net* <www.espacestemps.net/articles/spaces-of-practices-and-of-large-social-phenomena/>.

Schatzki, T.R. (2016) 'Practice Theory as Flat Ontology', in G. Spaargaren, D. Weenink and M. Lamers (eds.) *Practice Theory and Research: Exploring the Dynamics of Social Life*, pp. 28–42. London and New York: Routledge.

Schau, H.J., A.M. Muñiz Jr. and E.J. Arnould (2009) 'How Brand Community Practices Create Value', *Journal of Marketing* 73(September): 30–51.

Schivinski, B. and D. Dabrowski (2015) 'The Impact of Brand Communication on Brand Equity through Facebook', *Journal of Research in Interactive Marketing* 9(1): 31–53.

Schlitte, A. (2017) 'Narrative and Place', in B.B. Janz (ed.) *Place, Space and Hermeneutics*, pp. 35–48. Cham, Switzerland: Springer.

Schmidt, D.J. (2016) 'Hermeneutics and Ethical Life: On the Return to Factical Life', in N. Keane and C. Lawn (eds.) *The Blackwell Companion to Hermeneutics*, pp. 65–71. Malden and Oxford: Wiley.

Schmidt, S.J. (2010) 'Literary Studies from Hermeneutics to Media Culture Studies', *CLCWeb: Comparative Literature and Culture* 12(1) <http://dx.doi.org/10.7771/1481-4374.1569>.

Schön, D.A. (1983) *The Reflective Practitioner*. New York: Basic Books.

Schroder, K. (1988) 'Cultural Quality: Search for a Phantom?', paper presented at the International Television Studies Conference, British Film Institute, London.

Schroder, K. (1989) 'The Playful Audience: The Continuity of the Popular Cultural Tradition in America', in M. Skovmand (ed.) *Media Fictions*, pp. 7–20. Aarhus, Denmark: Aarhus University Press.

Schroeder, J.E. (2009) 'The Cultural Codes of Branding', *Marketing Theory* 9(1): 123–126.

Schröer, N. (2009) 'Hermeneutic Sociology of Knowledge for Intercultural Understanding', *Forum: Qualitative Social Research* 10(1): Art. 40.

Schuster, M. (2013) 'Hermeneutics as Embodied Existence', *International Journal of Qualitative Methods* 12: 195–206.

Scott, L.M. (1994a) 'Images in Advertising: The Need for a Theory of Visual Rhetoric', *Journal of Consumer Research* 21(September): 252–273.

Scott, L.M. (1994b) 'The Bridge from Text to Mind: Adapting Reader-Response Theory to Consumer Research', *Journal of Consumer Research* 21(December): 461–480.

Scott, R., J. Cayla and B. Cova (2017) 'Selling Pain to the Saturated Self', *Journal of Consumer Research* 44(February): 22–43.

Scott, S.V. and W.J. Orlikowski (2013) 'Sociomateriality: Taking the Wrong Turning? A Response to Mutch', *Information and Organization* 23: 77–80.

Seamon, D. (1979) *A Geography of the Lifeworld*. London: Croom Helm.

Seamon, D. (2000) 'A Way of Seeing People and Place: Phenomenology in Environment-Behavior Research', in S. Wapner, J. Demick, T. Yamamoto and H Minami (eds.) *Theoretical Perspectives in Environment-Behavior Research*, pp. 157–178. New York: Plenum.

Seamon, D. (2007) 'A Lived Hermetic of People and Place: Phenomenology and Space Syntax', Proceedings, Sixth International Space Syntax Symposium, İstanbul.

Seamon, D. (2013) 'Lived Bodies, Place and Phenomenology: Implications for Human Rights and Environmental Justice', *Journal of Human Rights and the Environment* 4(2): 143–166.

Seamon, D. (2018) 'Place as Organized Complexity: Understanding and Making Places Holistically' (forthcoming?). Kansas: Kansas State University Centre for Humans and Nature.

Seamon, D. and H.K. Gill (2016) 'Qualitative Approaches to Environment-Behavior Research: Understanding Environmental and Place Experiences,

Meanings, and Actions', in R. Gifford (ed.) *Research Methods for Environmental Psychology*, pp. 115–135. Malden and Oxford: Wiley.

Sefton-Green, J. (2016) 'Childhood and the Pursuit of Meaning in Today's Connected World', *Parenting for a Digital Future* <http://blogs.lse.ac.uk/parenting4digitalfuture/2016/08/24/childhood-and-the-pursuit-of-meaning-in-todays-connected-world/>.

Sefton-Green, J. (2017) 'What Is "Play" and "Playfulness" and What Does It Mean to Join Either Term Together with Learning?', *Parenting for a Digital Future* <http://blogs.lse.ac.uk/parenting4digitalfuture/2017/03/07/what-is-play-and-playfulness-and-what-does-it-mean-to-join-either-term-together-with-learning/>.

Senior, V., J.A. Smith, S. Michie and T.M. Marteau (2002) 'Making Sense of Risk: An Interpretative Phenomenological Analysis of Vulnerability to Heart Disease', *Journal of Health Psychology* 7(2): 157–168.

Seregina, A. and H.A. Weijo (2017) 'Play at Any Cost: How Cosplayers Produce and Sustain Their Ludic Communal Consumption Experiences', *Journal of Consumer Research* 44(1): 139–159.

Shalin, D.N. (2007) 'Signing in the Flesh: Notes on Pragmatist Hermeneutics', *Sociological Theory* 25(3): 193–224.

Shaw, J.A. and R.T. DeForge (2014) 'Qualitative Inquiry and the Debate between Hermeneutics and Critical Theory', *Qualitative Health Research* 24(11): 1567–1580.

Shaw, R.L. (2010) 'Embedding Reflexivity within Experiential Qualitative Psychology', *Qualitative Research in Psychology* 7(3): 233–243.

Shaw, R.L., K. West, B. Hagger and C.A. Holland (2016) 'Living Well to the End: A Phenomenological Analysis of Life in Extra Care Housing', *International Journal of Qualitative Studies on Health and Well-Being* 11: 1–12.

Sheehan, T. (2014) 'What, after All, Was Heidegger about?', *Continental Philosophy Review* 47(3): 249–274.

Sheller, M. (n.d.) 'Mobility', in *Sociopedia*. Madrid: International Sociological Association.

Sherry, J.F., Jr., R.V. Kozinets, D. Storm, A. Duhachek, K. Nuttavuthisit and B. Deberry-Spence (2001) 'Being in the Zone: Staging Retail Theater at ESPN Zone Chicago', *Journal of Contemporary Ethnography* 30(4): 465–510.

Shinebourne, P. (2011) 'The Theoretical Underpinnings of Interpretative Phenomenological Analysis (IPA)', *Existential Analysis* 22(1): 16–31.

Shotter, J. (2015) 'Undisciplining Social Science: Wittgenstein and the Art of Creating *Situated* Practices of Social Inquiry', *Journal for the Theory of Social Behaviour* 46(1): 60–83.

Shove, E. (2014a) 'Putting Practice into Policy: Reconfiguring Questions of Consumption and Climate Change', *Contemporary Social Science: Journal of the Academy of Social Sciences* 9(4): 415–429.

Shove, E. (2014b) 'Working Paper 10: Demanding Ideas: Where Theories of Practice Might Go Next', Lancaster University DEMAND Centre, Lancaster, pp. 29–35.

Shove, E. and M. Pantzar (2005) 'Consumers, Producers and Practices Understanding the Invention and Reinvention of Nordic Walking', *Journal of Consumer Culture* 5(1): 43–64.

Shove, E., M. Pantzar and M. Watson (2012) *The Dynamics of Social Practice: Everyday Life and How it Changes*. London: Sage.

Sia, B.C. (2012) 'Expressing Identity in Crossing to the New Year: A Case Study of the Malaysian Chinese Reunion Dinner', Thesis Submitted in Fulfillment of the Requirements for the Degree of Doctor of Philosophy of Cardiff University.

Siegel, G. (2002) 'Double Vision: Large-Screen Video Display and Live Sports Spectacle', *Television and New Media* 3(1): 49–73.
Sikh, B.S. and D. Spence (2016) 'Methodology, Meditation, and Mindfulness: Toward a Mindfulness Hermeneutic', *International Journal of Qualitative Methods* January–December: 1–8.
Silverstone, R. (1999) *Why Study the Media?* London: Sage.
Sitz, L. (2008) 'Beyond Semiotics and Hermeneutics. Discourse Analysis as a Way to Interpret Consumers' Discourses and Experiences', *Qualitative Market Research: An International Journal* 11(2): 177–191.
Smith, B. (2016) 'Narrative Analysis', in E. Lyons and A. Coyle (eds.) *Analysing Qualitative Data in Psychology*, pp. 202–221. London: Sage.
Smith, J.A. (1994) 'Reconstructing Selves: An Analysis of Discrepancies between Women's Contemporaneous and Retrospective Accounts of the Transition to Motherhood', *British Journal of Psychology* 85: 371–392.
Smith, J.A. (1995) 'Semi-Structured Interviewing and Qualitative Analysis', in J.A. Smith, R. Harre and L. Van Langenhove (eds.) *Rethinking Methods in Psychology*, pp. 9–26. London: Sage.
Smith, J.A. (1996) 'Beyond the Divide between Cognition and Discourse: Using Interpretative Phenomenological Analysis in Health Psychology', *Psychology and Health* 11(2): 261–271.
Smith, J.A. (1999) 'Towards a Relational Self: Social Engagement during Pregnancy and Psychological Preparation for Motherhood', *British Journal of Social Psychology* 38: 409–426.
Smith, J.A. (2004) 'Reflecting on the Development of Interpretative Phenomenological Analysis and Its Contribution to Qualitative Research in Psychology', *Qualitative Research in Psychology* 1(1): 39–54.
Smith, J.A. (2007) 'Hermeneutics, Human Sciences and Health: Linking Theory and Practice', *International Journal of Qualitative Studies on Health and Well-Being* 2: 3–11.
Smith, J.A. (2010) 'Interpretative Phenomenological Analysis: A Reply to Amedeo Giorgi', *Existential Analysis* 21(2): 186–192.
Smith, J.A. (2011a) 'Evaluating the Contribution of Interpretative Phenomenological Analysis: A Reply to the Commentaries and Further Development of Criteria', *Health Psychology Review* 5(1): 55–61.
Smith, J.A. (2011b) 'Evaluating the Contribution of Interpretative Phenomenological Analysis', *Health Psychology Review* 5(1): 9–27.
Smith, J.A., R. Harre and L. Van Langenhove (1995) 'Idiography and the Case Study', in J.A. Smith, R. Harre and L. Van Langenhove (eds.) *Rethinking Psychology*, pp. 59–69. London: Sage.
Smith, J.A., M. Jarman and M. Osborn (1999) 'Doing Interpretative Phenomenological Analysis', in M. Murray and K. Chamberlain (eds.) *Qualitative Health Psychology*, pp. 218–240. London: Sage.
Smith, J.A., S. Michie, M. Stephenson and O. Quarrell (2002) 'Risk Perception and Decision-Making Processes in Candidates for Genetic Testing for Huntington's Disease: An Interpretative Phenomenological Analysis', *Journal of Health Psychology* 7(2): 131–144.
Smith, J.A. and M. Osborn (2007) 'Pain as an Assault on the Self: An Interpretative Phenomenological Analysis of the Psychological Impact of Chronic Benign Low Back Pain', *Psychology and Health* 22(5): 517–534.
Smith, J.A. and M. Osborn (2008) 'Interpretative Phenomenological Analysis', in J.A. Smith (ed.) *Qualitative Psychology: A Practical Guide to Research Methods*, pp. 51–80. London: Sage.
Smith, J.A., P. Flowers and M. Larkin (2009) *Interpretative Phenomenological Analysis: Theory, Method and Research*. London: Sage.

Smith, J.A. and J.E. Rhodes (2015) 'Being Depleted and Being Shaken: An Interpretative Phenomenological Analysis of the Experiential Features of a First Episode of Depression', *Psychology and Psychotherapy: Theory, Research and Practice* 88: 197–209.
Smith, N.H. (2002) *Charles Taylor: Meaning, Morals and Modernity*. Cambridge: Polity Press.
Smith, N.H. (2004) 'Taylor and the Hermeneutic Tradition', in R. Abbey (ed.) *Charles Taylor*, pp. 29–51. Cambridge: Cambridge University Press.
Snelgrove, S. and C. Liossi (2009) 'An Interpretative Phenomenological Analysis of Living with Chronic Low Back Pain', *British Journal of Health Psychology* 14: 735–749.
Sobchack, V. (2004) *Carnal Thoughts: Embodiment and Moving Image Culture*. Berkeley and Los Angeles: University of California Press.
Spackman, J.S. and S.C. Yanchar (2013) 'Embodied Cognition, Representationalism, and Mechanism: A Review and Analysis', *Journal for the Theory of Social Behaviour* 44(1): 46–79.
Spiers, J. and J.A. Smith (2012) 'Using Autobiographical Poetry as Data to Investigate the Experience of Living with End-Stage Renal Disease: An Interpretative Phenomenological Analysis', *Creative Approaches to Research* 5(2): 119–137.
Spiers, J., J.A. Smith, E. Poliquin, J. Anderson and R. Horne (2016) 'The Experience of Antiretroviral Treatment for Black West African Women Who Are HIV Positive and Living in London: An Interpretative Phenomenological Analysis', *Aids and Behaviour* 20(9): 2151–2163.
Spinosa, C. (2001) 'Derridian Dispersion and Heideggerian Articulation General Tendencies in the Practices That Govern Intelligibility', in T.R. Schatzki, K.K. Cetina and E. Von Savigny (eds.) *The Practice Turn in Contemporary Theory*, pp. 209–222. London and New York: Routledge.
Star, S.L. (2010) 'This Is Not a Boundary Object: Reflections on the Origin of a Concept', *Science, Technology and Human Values* 35(5): 601–617.
Stark, L. and K. Crawford (2015) 'The Conservatism of Emoji: Work, Affect, and Communication', *Social Media + Society* July–December: 1–11.
Starks, H. and S.B. Trinidad (2007) 'Choose Your Method: A Comparison of Phenomenology, Discourse Analysis, and Grounded Theory', *Qualitative Health Research* 17(10): 1372–1380.
Stephansen, H.C. and N. Couldry (2014) 'Understanding Micro-Processes of Community Building and Mutual Learning on Twitter: A "Small Data" Approach', *Information, Communication and Society* 17(10): 1212–1227.
Stern, B.B. (1989) 'Literary Criticism and Consumer Research: Overview and Illustrative Analysis', *Journal of Consumer Research* 16(December): 322–334.
Stern, B.B., C.A. Russell and D.W. Russell (2005) 'Vulnerable Women on Screen and at Home: Soap Opera Consumption', *Journal of Macromarketing* 25(2): 222–225.
Storm-Mathisen, A. (2016) 'Grasping Children's Media Practices: Theoretical and Methodological Challenges', *Journal of Children and Media* 10(1): 81–89.
Sturgess, J.N. (2016) 'Drawing from Heidegger: *Dasein* and the Question of Communication', *Empedocles: European Journal for the Philosophy of Communication* 7(1): 23–37.
Susen, S. (2014) 'Reflections on Ideology: Lessons from Pierre Bourdieu and Luc Boltanski', *Thesis Eleven* 124(1): 90–113.
Sutton-Smith, B. (1997) *The Ambiguity of Play*. Cambridge, MA: Harvard University Press.
Svahn, F., O. Henfridsson and Y. Youngjin (2009) 'A Threesome Dance of Agency: Mangling the Sociomateriality of Technological Regimes in Digital

Innovation', paper presented at the International Conference on Information Systems, Phoenix, Arizona.

Svenaeus, F. (2011) 'Illness as Unhomelike Being-in-the-World: Heidegger and the Phenomenology of Medicine', *Medicine, Health Care and Philosophy* 14: 333–343.

Swidler, A. (2001) 'What Anchors Cultural Practices', in T.R. Schatzki, K.K. Cetina and E. Von Savigny (eds.) *The Practice Turn in Contemporary Theory*, pp. 83–101. London and New York: Routledge.

Syed, Md A. Md and C. Runnel (2014) 'Malay Women, Non-Western Soap Operas and Watching Competencies', *Journal of Consumer Culture* 14(3): 304–323.

Tadajewski, M. (2018) 'Critical Reflections on the Marketing Concept and Consumer Sovereignty', in M. Tadajewski, M. Higgins, J. Denegri-Knott and R. Varman (eds.) *The Companion to Critical Marketing Studies*, pp. 1–36. London and New York: Routledge.

Tadajewski, M., J. Chelekis, B. DeBerry-Spence, B. Figueiredo, O. Kravets, K. Nuttavuthisit, L. Peñaloza and J. Moisander (2014) 'The Discourses of Marketing and Development: Towards "Critical Transformative Marketing Research"', *Journal of Marketing Management* 30(17–18): 1728–1771.

Takayama, L. (2011) 'Toward Making Robots Invisible-in-Use. An Exploration into Invisible-in-Use Tools and Agents', in K. Dautenhahn and J. Saunders (eds.) *New Frontiers in Human-Robot Interaction*, pp. 111–132. Amsterdam: John Benjamin Publishing.

Tan, H., A. Wilson and I. Olver (2009) 'Ricoeur's Theory of Interpretation: An Instrument for Data Interpretation in Hermeneutic Phenomenology', *International Journal of Qualitative Methods* 8(4): 1–15.

Taylor, C. (1971) 'Interpretation and the Sciences of Man', *The Review of Metaphysics* 25(1): 3–51.

Taylor, C. (1985) *Philosophical Papers: Volume 2 Philosophy and the Human Sciences*. Cambridge: Cambridge University Press.

Taylor, C. (1989) *Sources of the Self*. Cambridge: Cambridge University Press.

Taylor, C. (1993) 'Engaged Agency and Background in Heidegger', in C.B. Guignon (ed.) *The Cambridge Companion to Heidegger*, pp. 317–336. Cambridge: Cambridge University Press.

Taylor, C. (1995a) 'Comparison, History, Truth', in C. Taylor, *Philosophical Arguments*, pp. 146–164. Cambridge: Harvard University Press.

Taylor, C. (1995b) 'To Follow a Rule', in C. Taylor, *Philosophical Arguments*, pp. 165–180. Cambridge: Harvard University Press.

Taylor, C. (2002) 'Gadamer on the Human Sciences', in R.J. Dostal (ed.) *The Cambridge Companion to Gadamer*, pp. 126–142. Cambridge: Cambridge University Press.

Taylor, C. (2004) *Modern Social Imaginaries*. Durham, NC: Duke University Press.

Tharakan, K. (2014) 'Repositioning Interpretative Social Science after Postmodernism: Understanding, Interpretation and Self', in R.C. Pradhan (ed.) *The Challenges of Postmodernism*, pp. 217–236. Shimla: Indian Institute of Advanced Study.

Thévenot, L. (2001) 'Pragmatic Regimes Governing the Engagement with the World', in T.R. Schatzki, K.K. Cetina and E. Von Savigny (eds.) *The Practice Turn in Contemporary Theory*, pp. 64–82. London and New York: Routledge.

Thompson, C.J. (1991) 'May the Circle Be Unbroken: A Hermeneutic Consideration of How Interpretive Approaches to Consumer Research Are Understood by Consumer Researchers', in R.H. Holman and M.R. Solomon (eds.) *Advances in Consumer Research*, Vol. 18, pp. 63–69. Provo, UT: Association for Consumer Research.

Thompson, C.J. (1996) 'Caring Consumers: Gendered Consumption Meanings and the Juggling Lifestyle', *Journal of Consumer Research* 22(4): 388–407.
Thompson, C.J. (1997) 'Interpreting Consumers: A Hermeneutical Framework for Deriving Marketing Insights from the Texts of Consumers' Consumption Stories', *Journal of Marketing Research* 34(4): 438–455.
Thompson, C.J. (1998) 'A Hermeneutic Approach to Social Marketing', in M. Rothschild and A.R. Andreasen (1998) 'Special Session Summary: Considering Social Marketing from the Perspective of Several Consumer Research Paradigms', in J.W. Alba and J.W. Hutchinson (eds.) *Advances in Consumer Research*, Vol. 25, pp. 295–298. Provo, UT: Association for Consumer Research.
Thompson, C.J., H.R. Pollio and W.B. Locander (1994) 'The Spoken and the Unspoken: A Hermeneutic Approach to Understanding the Cultural Viewpoints That Underlie Consumers' Expressed Meanings', *Journal of Consumer Research* 21(3): 432–453.
Thompson, C.J. and E.C. Hirschman (1995) 'Understanding the Socialized Body: A Poststructuralist Analysis of Consumers' Self-Conceptions, Body Images and Self-Care Practices', *Journal of Consumer Research* 22(2): 139–153.
Thompson, C.J. and D.L. Haytko (1997) 'Speaking of Fashion: Consumers' Uses of Fashion Discourses and the Appropriation of Countervailing Cultural Meanings', *Journal of Consumer Research* 24(2): 15–42.
Thompson, C.J. and E.C. Hirschman (1998) 'An Existential Analysis of the Embodied Self in Postmodern Consumer Culture', *Consumption, Markets and Culture* 2(4): 337–465.
Thompson, C.J. and T. Ustuner (2015) 'Women Skating on the Edge: Marketplace Performances as Ideological Edgework', *Journal of Consumer Research* 42(2): 235–265.
Thompson, J.B. (1981a) *Critical Hermeneutics: A Study in the Thought of Paul Ricoeur and Jürgen Habermas*. Cambridge: Cambridge University Press.
Thompson, J.B. (1981b) 'Editor's Introduction', in J.B. Thompson (ed.) *Paul Ricoeur: Hermeneutics and the Human Sciences*, pp. 1–26. Cambridge: Cambridge University Press.
Thompson, J.B. (1986) 'Language, Ideology and the Media: A Response to Martin Montgomery', *Media, Culture and Society* 8(1): 65–79.
Thrift, N. (2008) *Non-Representational Theory Space/Politics/Affect*. London and New York: Routledge.
Timotijevic, L. and G.M. Breakwell (2000) 'Migration and Threat to Identity', *Journal of Community and Applied Social Psychology* 10: 355–372.
Tiong, M.H.B. (2013) 'A Reception Study of Media Marketing Motorcycles', A dissertation submitted in fulfillment of the requirements for the degree of Master of Science (Marketing). Faculty of Economics and Business, University Malaysia Sarawak.
Todorov, T. (1990) *Genres in Discourse*. Cambridge: Cambridge University Press.
Todres, L., K. Galvin and K. Dahlberg (2007) 'Lifeworld-Led Healthcare: Revisiting a Humanising Philosophy That Integrates Emerging Trends', *Medicine, Health Care and Philosophy* 10: 53–63.
Tomkins, L. and V. Eatough (2013) 'Meanings and Manifestations of Care: A Celebration of Hermeneutic Multiplicity in Heidegger', *The Humanistic Psychologist* 41: 4–24.
Tomlinson, J. (1999) *Globalisation and Culture*. Cambridge: Polity Press.
Törrönen, J. (2013) 'Situational, Cultural and Societal Identities: Analysing Subject Positions as Classifications, Participant Roles, Viewpoints and Interactive Positions', *Journal for the Theory of Social Behaviour* 44(1): 80–98.
Tosoni, S. (2015) 'Beyond Space and Place: The Challenge of Urban Space to Urban Media Studies', in L. Kramp, N. Carpentier, A. Hepp, I. Tomanić

Trivundža, H. Nieminen, R. Kunelius, T. Olsson, E. Sundin and R. Kilborn (eds.) *Journalism, Representation and the Public Sphere.* Bremen: Edition Lumiere.

Tosoni, S. and M. Ciancia (2017) 'Vidding and Its Media Territories: A Practice-Centred Approach to User-Generated Content Production', in S. Tosoni, N. Carpentier, M.F. Murru, R. Kilborn, L. Kramp, R. Kunelius, A. McNicholas, T. Olsson and P. Pruulmann-Vengerfeldt (eds.) *Present Scenarios of Media Production and Engagement*, pp. 39–54. Bremen: Edition Lumiere.

Trede, F., J. Higgs and R. Rothwell (2009) 'Critical Transformative Dialogues: A Research Method Beyond the Fusions of Horizons', *Forum: Qualitative Social Research* 10(1): Art. 6.

Tresch, J. (2001) 'On Going Native Thomas Kuhn and Anthropological Method', *Philosophy of the Social Sciences* 31(3): 302–322.

Tuomela, R. (2004) *The Philosophy of Social Practices: A Collective Acceptance View.* Cambridge: Cambridge University Press.

Turley, D. and S. O'Donohoe (2012) 'The Sadness of Lives and the Comfort of Things: Goods as Evocative Objects in Bereavement', *Journal of Marketing Management* 28(11–12): 1331–1353.

Turner, De S. (2003) 'Horizons Revealed: From Methodology to Method', *International Journal of Qualitative Methods* 2(1): 1–17.

Turner, S. (1994) *The Social Theory of Practices, Tradition, Tacit Knowledge and Presuppositions.* Cambridge: Polity Press.

Turner, S. (2001) 'Throwing Out the Tacit Rule Book Learning and Practices', in T.R. Schatzki, K.K. Cetina and E. Von Savigny (eds.) *The Practice Turn in Contemporary Theory*, pp. 129–139. London and New York: Routledge.

Turner, V. (1967) *The Forest of Symbols.* Ithaca: Cornell University Press.

Urry, J. (2006) 'Travelling Times', *European Journal of Communication* 21(3): 357–372.

Vandenberghe, F. (2007) 'Avatars of the Collective: A Realist Theory of Collective Subjectivities', *Sociological Theory* 25(4): 295–324.

Vandermause, R.K. and S.E. Fleming (2011) 'Philosophical Hermeneutic Interviewing', *International Journal of Qualitative Methods* 10(4): 367–377.

Vandevelde, P. (2016) 'Karl-Otto Apel', in N. Keane and C. Lawn (eds.) *The Blackwell Companion to Hermeneutics*, pp. 435–439. Malden and Oxford: Wiley.

Van Dijck, J. (2013) *The Culture of Connectivity: A Critical History of Social Media.* Oxford: Oxford University Press.

Vangeli, E. and R. West (2012) 'Transition Towards a "Non-Smoker" Identity Following Smoking Cessation: An Interpretative Phenomenological Analysis', *British Journal of Health Psychology* 17: 171–184.

Van Manen, M. (2007) 'Phenomenology of Practice', *Phenomenology & Practice* 1(1): 11–30.

Van Marrewijka, A. and M. Broosa (2012) 'Retail Stores as Brands: Performances, Theatre and Space', *Consumption, Markets and Culture* 15(4): 374–391.

Venema, H. (2000) 'Paul Ricoeur on Refigurative Reading and Narrative Identity', *Symposium* 4(2) 237–248.

Venter, L. and D.P. Van Vuuren (2000) 'Out-of-Home Television Viewing: A Cross-Cultural Comparative Study', paper presented at the International Association for Media and Communication Research Conference, Singapore.

Vessey, D. (2009) 'Gadamer and the Fusion of Horizons', *International Journal of Philosophical Studies* 17(4): 531–542.

Vilhauer, M. (2009) 'Beyond the "Fusion of Horizons" Gadamer's Notion of Understanding as "Play"', *Philosophy Today* Winter: 359–364.

Vilhauer, M. (2015) 'Verbal and Nonverbal Forms of Play: Words and Bodies in the Process of Understanding', paper presented at the North American Society for Philosophical Hermeneutics Annual Conference, Philadelphia.
Vince, R. and S. Warren (2012) 'Participatory Visual Methods', in G. Symon and C. Cassell (eds.) *Qualitative Organizational Research: Core Methods and Current Challenges*, pp. 275–295. London: Sage.
Waisbord, S. and C. Mellado (2014) 'De-Westernizing Communication Studies: A Reassessment', *Communication Theory* 24: 361–372.
Wajcman, J. (2008) 'Life in the Fast Lane? Towards a Sociology of Technology and Time', *British Journal of Sociology* 59(1): 59–77.
Wajcman, J. and P.K. Jones (2012) 'Border Communication: Media Sociology and STS', *Media, Culture and Society* 34(6): 673–690.
Wallace, M.I. (2000) 'From Phenomenology to Scripture? Paul Ricoeur's Hermeneutical Philosophy of Religion', *Modern Theology* 16(3): 301–313.
Wallenborn, G. and H. Wilhite (2014) 'Rethinking Embodied Knowledge and Household Consumption', *Energy Research & Social Science* 1: 56–64.
Wang, G. (2014) 'Culture, Paradigm, and Communication Theory: A Matter of Boundary or Commensurability?', *Communication Theory* 24: 373–393.
Warde, A. (2005) 'Consumption and Theories of Practice', *Journal of Consumer Culture* 5(2): 131–153.
Warde, A. (2014) 'After Taste: Culture, Consumption and Theories of Practice', *Journal of Consumer Culture* 14(3): 279–303.
Warfield, K. (2016) 'Making the Cut: An Agential Realist Examination of Selfies and Touch', *Social Media and Society* April–June: 1–10.
Warnke, G. (2002) 'Hermeneutics, Ethics, and Politics', in R.J. Dostal (ed.) *The Cambridge Companion to Gadamer*, pp. 79–101. Cambridge: Cambridge University Press.
Warren, J. (2005) 'Towards an Ethical-Hermeneutics', *European Journal of Psychotherapy and Counselling* 7(1–2): 17–28.
Warren, S. (2002) '"Show Me How It Feels to Work Here": Using Photography to Research Organizational Aesthetics', *Ephemera: Critical Dialogues on Organization* 2(3): 224–245.
Watson, M. (2014) 'Working Paper 6: Demanding Ideas: Where Theories of Practice Might Go Next', Lancaster University DEMAND Centre, Lancaster, pp. 13–16.
Watson, M. and E. Shove (2008) 'Product, Competence, Project and Practice DIY and the Dynamics of Craft Consumption', *Journal of Consumer Culture* 8(1): 69–89.
Weick, K.E. (1995) *Sense Making in Organizations*. London: Sage.
Weissmann, E. (2013) 'Scheduling as Feminist Issue UK's Channel Four and US Female-Centred Sitcoms', in H. Thornham and E. Weissmann (eds.) *Renewing Feminisms Radical Narratives, Fantasies and Futures in Media Studies*, pp. 140–154. London and New York: I.B. Tauris.
Wenger, E., R. McDermott and W.M. Snyder (2002) *Cultivating Communities of Practice*. Boston, MA: Harvard Business School Press.
Wetherell, M. (2012) *Affect and Emotion: A New Social Science Understanding*. London: Sage.
Wheeler, M. (2005) *Reconstructing the Cognitive World: The Next Step*. Cambridge, MA: MIT Press.
Wheeler, M. (2011) 'Martin Heidegger', *Stanford Encyclopedia of Philosophy* <plato.stanford.edu>.
Wilcock, A.A. (2006) *An Occupational Perspective of Health*. Thorofare, NJ: Slack.

Wilken, R. and G. Goggin (2012) 'Mobilizing Place: Conceptual Currents and Controversies', in R. Wilken and G. Goggin (eds.) *Mobile Technology and Place*. London and New York: Routledge.

Willems, T. (2018) 'Seeing and Sensing the Railways: A Phenomenological View on Practice-Based Learning', *Management Learning* 49(1): 23–29.

Willig, C. (2001) *Introducing Qualitative Research in Psychology Adventures in Theory and Method*. Buckingham: Open University Press.

Willig, C. (2007) 'Reflections on the Use of a Phenomenological Method', *Qualitative Research in Psychology* 4(3): 209–225.

Willig, C. (2017) 'Interpretation in Qualitative Research', in C. Willig and W. Stainton-Rogers (eds.) *The Sage Handbook of Qualitative Research in Psychology*, pp. 276–290. London: Sage.

Wilson, R.E. (2015) 'Positioning within a Cultural Context: Using Ricoeur's Preunderstandings as a Heuristic for Narrative Data Analysis in Exploring Identity, Structure, and Agency', *International Journal of Qualitative Studies in Education* 28(8): 887–905.

Wilson, S. (2016) 'In the Living Room: Second Screens and TV Audiences', *Television and New Media* 17(2): 174–191.

Wilson, T. (1990) 'TV-am and the Politics of Caring', *Media, Culture and Society* 12(1): 125–137.

Wilson, T. (1993) *Watching Television: Hermeneutics, Reception and Popular Culture*. Cambridge, UK: Polity-Blackwell.

Wilson, T. (2004) *The Playful Audience: From Talk Show Viewers to Internet Users*. Cresskill, NJ: Hampton Press New Media and Policy Studies.

Wilson, T. (2009) *Understanding Media Users: From Theory to Practice*. Oxford: Blackwell.

Wilson, T. (2011) *Global Advertising, Attitudes and Audiences*. London and New York: Routledge.

Wilson, T. (2012) 'What Can Phenomenology Offer the Consumer?', *Qualitative Market Research: An International Journal* 15(3): 230–241.

Wilson, T. (2015) *Media Consumption in Malaysia: A Hermeneutics of Human Behaviour*. London and New York: Routledge.

Wittgenstein, L. (1991) *Philosophical Investigations*. Third Edition. Boston and Oxford: Wiley-Blackwell.

Yanow, D. and H. Tsoukas (2009) 'What Is Reflection-in-Action? A Phenomenological Account', *Journal of Management Studies* 46(8): 1339–1364.

Yardley, L. (2002) 'Introducing Material-Discursive Approaches to Health and Illness', in L. Yardley (ed.) *Material Discourses of Health and Illness*, pp. 1–24. London and New York: Routledge.

Zaborowski, R. and F. Dhaenens (2016) 'Old Topics, Old Approaches? "Reception" in Television Studies and Music Studies', *Participations* 13(1): 446–461.

Zhok, A. (2009) 'Towards a Theory of Social Practices', *Journal of the Philosophy of History* 3: 187–210.

Index

Printed in the United States
by Baker & Taylor Publisher Services